Instructor's Manual to Accompany

FOOD and BEVERAGE COST CONTROL

Fifth Edition

Lea R. Dopson   David K. Hayes

WILEY

JOHN WILEY & SONS, INC.

For general information on our other products and services or for technical support, please contact our Customer Care Department within the United States at (800) 762-2974, outside the United States at (317) 572-3993 or fax (317) 572-4002.

Wiley also publishes its books in a variety of electronic formats. Some content that appears in print may not be available in electronic books. For more information about Wiley products, visit our web site at www.wiley.com.

This material may be reproduced for testing and instructional purposes by instructors using the text, *Food and Beverage Cost Control, Fifth Edition* by Lea R. Dopson and David K. Hayes (ISBN: 978-0-470-25138-6).

Library of Congress Cataloging-in-Publication Data:

ISBN: 978-0-470-25738-8

Printed in the United States of America

10   9   8   7   6   5   4   3   2   1

Contents

To the Instructor   v

Chapter 1   Managing Revenue and Expense   1

Chapter 2   Determining Sales Forecasts   21

Chapter 3   Managing the Cost of Food   39

Chapter 4   Managing the Cost of Beverages   73

Chapter 5   Managing the Food and Beverage Production Process   95

Chapter 6   Managing Food and Beverage Pricing   123

Chapter 7   Managing the Cost of Labor   144

Chapter 8   Controlling Other Expenses   175

Chapter 9   Analyzing Results Using the Income Statement   194

Chapter 10   Planning for Profit   215

Chapter 11   Maintaining and Improving the Revenue Control System   244

Chapter 12   Global Dimensions of Cost Control   265

To the Instructor

All foodservice managers, regardless of the type of operation they are involved in, must understand and manage the costs associated with operating their business. ***Food and Beverage Cost Control, Fifth Edition*** focuses on helping students with the study of cost management to understand its logic and its systems.

The authors find the challenge of cost management to be creative, exciting, and fun! To be successful, talented foodservice managers must know where they want to take their operations and then apply their training and expertise to get there. In that regard, a professional hospitality manager is much like an airline pilot. Both utilize highly specialized skills and equipment. Both depend on other team members to reach their goals. Both must master a highly specialized area of study.

This ***Instructor's Manual*** is organized according to the 12 chapters in the text. Each chapter provides the following instructor's aids:

- Learning outcomes
- Lecture outline
- Answers to Consider The Cost cases
- Answers to Apply What You Have Learned cases
- Answers to Test Your Skills exercises
- Exam questions

The learning outcomes and lecture outlines are intended to help instructors organize their classes efficiently and effectively. The answers to ***Consider The Cost*** cases and ***Apply What You Have Learned*** cases are provided to give the instructor possible answers that may be generated by students. Since these cases are meant to provide a basis for discussion of the material, students may answer these cases in a variety of ways. Reviewing students' answers to the ***Test Your Skills*** exercises with the guidelines presented in this manual will help reinforce the key concepts in the chapters. The actual spreadsheets with answers for ***Test Your Skills*** exercises can also be found on the Wiley Instructor Companion website (for Food and Beverage Cost Control) at www.wiley.com/college/dopson. Also, the exam questions are broken down into multiple choice and true false. New questions for the ***Fifth Edition*** are found at the end of each of these sections. The test banks can be used both for reviewing the material in class and for testing the students' grasp of cost control concepts and techniques.

Special thanks go to Raktida Siri and Jackie Matte who assisted us with the instructor's manual. We hope that this exposure to the study of cost management creates in your students the same enjoyment that we have experienced in our careers. If so, the skills and tools they learn will ensure that their hospitality careers will really take off, allowing them to go wherever they want to go and as high as they want to go!

Lea R. Dopson
David K. Hayes

Chapter 1

Managing Revenue and Expense

Learning Outcomes

At the conclusion of this chapter, you will be able to:

- Apply the basic formula used to determine profit.
- Express both expenses and profit as a percentage of revenue.
- Compare actual operating results with budgeted operating results.

Lecture Outline

1. Professional Foodservice Manager

- A professional foodservice manager is unique because all the functions of product sales, from item conceptualization to product delivery are in the hands of the same individual.
- Because foodservice operators are in the service sector of business, many aspects of management are more difficult for them than for their manufacturing or retailing management counterparts.
- A foodservice manager is one of the few types of managers who actually has contact with the ultimate consumer. The foodservice operator must serve as a food factory supervisor, and a cost control manager.
- Excellence in operation is measured in terms of producing and delivering quality products in a way that assures an appropriate operating profit for the owners.

2. Profit: The Reward for Service

- If management focuses on controlling costs more than on servicing guests, problems will certainly surface.
- Management's primary responsibility is to deliver a quality product or service to the guest, at a price mutually agreeable to both parties. You do not want to get yourself in the mind-set of reducing costs to the point where it is thought that "low" costs are good, and "high" costs are bad.
- When management attempts to reduce costs, with no regard for the impact on the balance between managing costs and guest satisfaction, the business will surely suffer. Efforts to reduce costs that result in unsafe conditions for guests or employees are never wise.

- The question is whether costs are too high or too low, given management's view of the value it hopes to deliver to the guest and the goals of the foodservice operation's owners.
- The difference between what you have paid for the goods you sell and the price at which you sell them does not represent your actual profit.
- **Revenue** is the amount of dollars you take in.
- **Expenses** are the costs of the items required to operate the business.
- **Profit** is the amount of dollars that remain after all expenses have been paid.

> ### Revenue – Expenses = Profit

- For the purposes of this book, the authors will use the following terms interchangeably: revenue and sales; expenses and costs.
- All foodservice operations, including non-profit institutions, need revenue in excess of expenses if they are to thrive.
- Profit is the result of solid planning, sound management, and careful decision-making.

> ### Revenue – Desired Profit = Ideal Expense

- **Ideal Expense** is defined as management's view of the correct or appropriate amount of expense necessary to generate a given quantity of revenue.
- **Desired profit** is defined as the profit that the owner wants to achieve on that predicted quantity of revenue. Profit is the reward for providing service.
- Revenue varies with both the number of guests frequenting your business and the amount of money spent by each guest.
- You can increase revenue by increasing the number of guests you serve, by increasing the amount each guest spends, or by a combination of both approaches.
- Environmental sustainability is a term used to describe a variety of earth-friendly practices and policies designed to meet the needs of the present population without compromising the ability of future generations to meet their own needs.
- The positive benefits that accrue when businesses incorporate green activities are significant and they are increasing.
- There are four major foodservice expense categories that you must learn to control.
  a. **Food costs** are the costs associated with actually producing the menu items. In most cases, food costs will make up the largest or second largest expense category you must learn to manage.
  b. **Beverage costs** are those related to the sale of alcoholic beverages. Costs of a non-alcoholic nature are considered an expense in the Food Costs category. Alcoholic beverages accounted for in the Beverage Costs category include beer, wine, and liquor. It may also include the costs of ingredients necessary to produce these drinks, such as cherries, lemons, olives, limes, mixers like carbonated beverages and juices, and other items commonly used in the production and service of alcoholic beverages.

c. **Labor costs** include the cost of all employees necessary to run the business, including taxes. In most operations, labor costs are second only to food costs in total dollars spent. Some operators find it helpful to include the cost of management in this category. Others prefer to place the cost of managers in the Other Expense category.

d. **Other expenses** include all expenses that are not food, beverage or labor.

3. Getting Started

- Good managers learn to understand, control, and manage their expenses. Numbers can be difficult to interpret due to inflation. Therefore, the industry uses percentage calculations.
- Percentages are the most common standard used for evaluating costs in the foodservice industry. As a manager in the foodservice industry you will be evaluated primarily on your ability to compute, analyze, and control these percent figures.
- **Percent** (%) means "out of each hundred."
- There are three (3) ways to write a percent:

Common Form
In its common form, the "%" sign is used to express the percentage, as in 10%.
Fraction Form
In fraction form, the percent is expressed as the part, or a portion of 100, as in 10/100.
Decimal Form
The decimal form uses the decimal point (.) to express the percent relationship, as in 0.10.

- To determine what percent one number is of another number, divide the number that is the part by the number that is the whole.

$$\frac{\text{Part}}{\text{Whole}} = \text{Percent}$$

- If we want to know what percentage of our revenue went to pay for our expenses, we would compute it as follows:

$$\frac{\text{Expense}}{\text{Revenue}} = \text{Expense \%}$$

- As long as expense is smaller than revenue, some profit will be generated. You can computer profit % using the following formula:

$$\frac{\text{Profit}}{\text{Revenue}} = \text{Profit \%}$$

- Modified profit formula:

Revenue - (Food and Beverage Cost + Labor Cost + Other Expenses) = Profit

- Put in another format, the equation looks as follows:

Revenue (100%)
-    Food and Beverage Cost %
-    Labor Cost %
-    Other Expense %
=   Profit %

4. Understanding the Income (Profit and Loss) Statement

- An accounting tool that details revenue, expenses and profit, for a given period of time, is called the **income statement**, commonly referred to as a **profit and loss statement (P&L).** It lists revenue, food and beverage cost, labor cost, other expense, and profit.
- The P&L is important because it indicates the efficiency and profitability of an operation.
- The primary purpose of preparing a P&L is to identify revenue, expenses, and profits for a specific time period.
- Common percentages used in a P&L statement:

1. $\dfrac{\text{Food and Beverage Cost}}{\text{Revenue}}$ = Food and Beverage Cost %

2. $\dfrac{\text{Labor Cost}}{\text{Revenue}}$ = Labor Cost %

3. $\dfrac{\text{Other Expense}}{\text{Revenue}}$ = Other Expense %

4. $\dfrac{\text{Total Expense}}{\text{Revenue}}$ = Total Expense %

5. $\dfrac{\text{Profit}}{\text{Revenue}}$ = Profit %

- The Uniform System of Accounts is used to report financial results in most foodservice units. This system was created to ensure uniform reporting of financial results.

5. Understanding the Budget

- A **budget** is simply an estimate of projected revenue, expense, and profit.
- The budget is known as the **plan**, referring to the fact that the budget details the operation's estimated, or planned for, revenue and expense for a given period of time.
- All effective managers, whether in the commercial (for profit) or nonprofit sector, use budgets.
- **Performance to budget** is the percentage of the budget actually used.
- The **28-day-period approach** to budgeting divides a year into 13 equal periods of 28 days each. This helps the manager compare performance from one period to the next without having to compensate for "extra" days in any one period.
- Percentages are used to compare actual expense with the budgeted amount, using the formula

$$\frac{\text{Actual}}{\text{Budget}} = \% \text{ of Budget}$$

- If our budget was accurate, and we are within reasonable limits of our budget, we are said to be "in-line" or "in compliance" with our budget. Use the concept of "significant" variation to determine whether a cost control problem exists.
- A significant variation is any variation in expected costs that management feels is an area of concern.
- If significant variations with planned results occur, management must:

    1.   Identify the problem
    2.   Determine the cause
    3.   Take corrective action

6. Technology Tools

- Most hospitality managers would agree that an accurate and timely income statement (P&L statement) is an invaluable aid to their management efforts. There are a variety of software programs on the market that can be used to develop this statement for you.
- Variations include programs that compare your actual results to budgeted figures or forecasts, to prior-month performance, or to prior-year performance. In addition, P&Ls can be produced for any time period, including months, quarters, or years. Most income statement programs will have a budgeting feature and the ability to maintain historical sales and cost records.
- As you examine (in this chapter and others) the cost control technology tools available to you, keep in mind that not all information should be accessible to all parties, and that security of your cost and customer information can be just as critical as accuracy.

- Don't forget that to effectively manage your overall operation you will need to communicate with employees, guests, and vendors. Thus, the software you will need includes office products for word processing, spreadsheet building, faxes, and e-mail.

Consider The Cost

"I'm feeling pretty good about our cost management efforts," said Rachel. "Our labor cost is higher than our food cost."

"I'm pleased with our efforts too," said Julie. "Our food cost is higher than our labor cost."

"That's great, Julie," said Joseph. "I just calculated our monthly costs, and our food and labor expenses are just about equal. Sounds like we are all doing well!"

Rachel, Julie, and Joseph had all attended hospitality school together. Each had taken a job in the same large city so they often got together over coffee to talk about their businesses and their jobs. One manages Chez Paul's, a fine dining French-style restaurant known for impeccable service. Another manages Fuby's, a family-style cafeteria known for its tasty, home-style cooking, and one had taken a job with Gardinos, a national restaurant chain that offers mid-priced Italian foods in a beautiful Tuscan-style décor.

1. Which foodservice operation do you think Rachel manages? Why?

2. Which foodservice operation do you think Julie manages? Why?

3. Which foodservice operation do you think Joseph manages? Why?

Answers:

This case is designed to make students think about the fact that the type of food served and the style of service offered to guests will affect their costs of food and labor. In this case:

1. It is most likely that Rachel works at Chez Paul's. The high levels of personal service provided to fine-dining customers typically results in higher than average per-guest labor costs.

2. It is likely that Julie works at Fuby's. Cafeterias are self-service, and thus, the cost of labor, relative to the cost of food, would most likely be lower than for the average food service operation.

3. Joseph likely works at a Gardino's, a "typical" restaurant, where labor (and food) costs are likely to be somewhat in the "middle" compared to the operations of his friends.

For discussion purposes, students may be asked to identify other factors that would affect the food and labor costs of these friends. Student responses may include such items as complexity of menu, available equipment, price structure (for example, "All-You-Care-To-Eat" operations), and even types of clients served.

Apply What You Have Learned

Jennifer Caratini has recently accepted the job as the Foodservice Director for Techmar Industries, a corporation with 1000 employees. As Foodservice Director, Jennifer's role is to operate a company cafeteria, serving 800 to 900 meals per day, as well as an Executive Dining room, serving 100 to 200 meals per day. All of the meals are provided "free of charge" to the employees of Techmar. One of Jennifer's first jobs is to prepare a budget for next year's operations.

1. In addition to food products and foodservice employees, what are other expenses Techmar will incur by providing free meals to its employees?

   Answer: Other expenses Techmar will incur by providing free meals to its employee include utilities, linen, china, glassware, kitchen knives, and pot and pans.

2. Since employees do not pay for their food directly, what will Jennifer use as the "revenue" portion of her budget? How do you think this number should be determined?

   Answer: To prepare the "revenue" portion of her budget for next year's operations, Jennifer should first calculate an allowed expense for each meal served. Then, she should project total number of meals served and multiply the projection by the allowed expense. She should also make sure to include any projected surpluses in addition to allowed expenses.

3. In addition to her know-how as a foodservice manager, what skills will Jennifer need as she interacts with the executives at Techmar who must approve her budget?

   Answer: In addition to her know-how as a foodservice manager, Jennifer needs to demonstrate that she can analyze, manage, and control costs incurred while providing free meals to employees. She also needs to know how to present her budget using budget projections, pie charts, and the like so that the executives will clearly understand and approve her budget.

Test Your Skills

1. At the conclusion of her first month of operating Val's Donut Shop, Val computed the following revenue and expense figures:

Week	Revenue	Expense	Profit / Loss
1	$ 894.50	$ 761.80	$ 132.70
2	1,147.60	522.46	625.14
3	1,261.80	879.14	382.66
4	1,345.11	1,486.20	(141.09)
Month	$ 4,649.01	$ 3,649.60	$ 999.41
To Receive $1,200.00 Profit for the Month			
Month	$ 4,649.01	$ 3,449.01	$ 1,200.00

Prepare both weekly and monthly profit formulas so that Val has a good idea about her current profit situation. Also, given her sales for the month, tell her how much her expenses should have been to realize the $1,200.00 profit she had hoped for.

Answer: To realize the $1,200.00 profit she should have had $ 3,449.01 expenses for the month.

2. Su Chan manages a Chinese restaurant called The Bungalow. Her P&L for the month of March is as follows.

The Bungalow's March P&L

Revenue	$ 100,000.00	100.0%
F&B Expense	34,000.00	34.0%
Labor Expense	40,000.00	40.0%
Other Expense	21,000.00	21.0%
Total Expense	95,000.00	95.0%
Profit	$ 5,000.00	5.0%

Su has a meeting with the owner of the Bungalow next week, so she decided to create a pie chart showing the percentage of her costs to her total sales (see the following diagram).

8

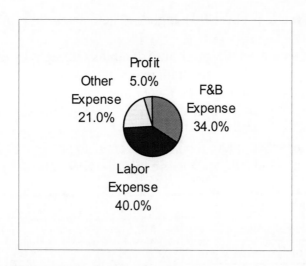

At the meeting with the owner, Su is asked to change the information on the pie chart to reflect next month's projections. The owner suggests that April revenues and costs should be as follows:

April revenues = $120,000, food and beverage expense = $44,000, labor and other expenses remain constant.

Revenue	$ 120,000.00	100.0%
F&B Expense	44,000.00	36.7%
Labor Expense	40,000.00	33.3%
Other Expense	21,000.00	17.5%
Total Expenses	105,000.00	87.5%
Profit	$ 15,000.00	12.5%

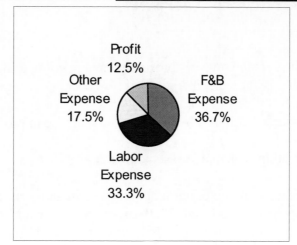

Using these numbers, is the owner's profit percentage going to be higher or lower than that in March? By how much?

Answer: The owner's profit will be higher. The increase in profit will be 7.5%.

After looking at the owner's projections, she thinks it might be too difficult (and not so good for her guests) if she cannot increase labor cost along with sales. She proposes a compromise and tells the owner that if he will agree to increased labor costs, she will try to decrease other expenses. So, Su proposes the following:

April revenues = $120,000, food and beverage expense = $44,000, labor expense = $50,000, and other expense = $19,000.

Revenue	$ 120,000.00	100.0%
F&B Expense	44,000.00	36.7%
Labor Expense	50,000.00	41.7%
Other Expense	19,000.00	15.8%
Total Expenses	113,000.00	94.2%
Profit	$ 7,000.00	5.8%

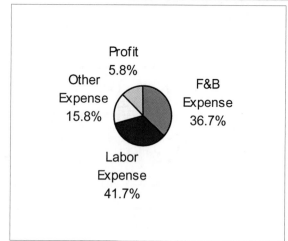

Using these numbers, is the owner's profit percentage going to be higher or lower than that in March? By how much?

Answer: The owner's profit will be higher. The increase in profit will be 0.8%.

Which set of projections has more reasonable goals?

Answer: Assuming that much of her labor expense includes management on salaries, reducing labor expense from 40% to 33.3% may not be feasible; therefore, the first set of projections may not be realistic. By using the second set of projections, Su can increase her profits while providing a higher quality of service by increasing labor costs slightly.

3. The dining room at the Roadrock Inn is extremely popular. Terry Ray, the food and beverage director, is pleased to see that his revenue is higher than last year. Of course, expenses are higher also. Express Terry's expenses and profit as a percentage of total revenue, both this year and last year (fill in all empty blanks).

	This Year	%	Last Year	%
Revenue	$ 965,971.00	100.0	$ 875,421.00	100.0
F&B Expense	367,069.00	38.0	350,168.00	40.0
Labor Expense	338,090.00	35.0	315,151.00	36.0
Other Expense	144,896.00	15.0	140,068.00	16.0
Total Expense	850,055.00	88.0	805,387.00	92.0
Profit	$ 115,916.00	12.0	$ 70,034.00	8.0

How is Terry doing in managing his expenses when comparing this year to last year?

Answer: Terry is able to decrease his total expense by 4% this year compared to last year.

How do changes in revenue affect his performance?

Answer: Terry had an increase in revenues and a subsequent increase in expenses. However, he was able to control his expenses and actually decrease them as a percentage of sales. Therefore, Terry experienced an increase in profit for this year.

4. Pamela Cantu operates a school foodservice department in a small, rural community. She feeds approximately 1,000 students per day in three different locations. She receives an average of $1.20 in revenues per meal. Her budget, set at the beginning of the school year by the superintendent, is developed in such a way so that a small amount is to be reserved for future equipment purchases and dining room renovation. These funds are available, however, only if Pamela meets her budget. She hopes to use this year's reserve to buy a $5,000 refrigerated salad bar for the high school. Since it is the mid-point of her school year, help her determine her "performance to budget" (fill in all empty blanks).

Item	Budget	Actual	% of Budget
Meals Served	300,000	149,800	49.9
Revenue	$360,000	$179,760	49.9
Food Expense	170,000	84,961	50.0
Labor Expense	125,000	63,752	51.0
Other Expense	60,000	31,460	52.4
Total Expenses	355,000	180,173	50.8
Reserve	5,000	-413	-8.3

11

Assuming the year is 50% completed and Pamela continues doing what she is doing, is she likely to meet the reserve requirement and thus be able to purchase the salad bar by the end of the year? If not, what changes should she make over the next 6 months to ensure that she will have the $5,000 in reserve?

Answer: No, if Pamela continues to do what she is doing she will not meet the reserve required to purchase the salad bar by the end of the year since she already has a -$413 balance in the account. Pamela should decrease labor expense and other expense since she has already spent over 50% of her budget on these items.

5. Sam Guild operates a dining room reserved for doctors in a large hospital in the Northeast. Sam's boss has given Sam a target of a 33% food cost but has indicated that the target may be adjusted. Currently, the doctors' meals sell for $15.00. Sam knows he currently can spend $4.95 for the food required to produce each meal. Fill out the chart below to help Sam find out how much he will be able to spend on each meal at various food cost % levels if his boss adjusts his target.

Meal Selling Price	Food Cost %	Amount that Can Be Spent for Food
$15.00	20%	$3.00
$15.00	25%	$3.75
$15.00	30%	$4.50
$15.00	33%	$4.95
$15.00	35%	$5.25
$15.00	40%	$6.00

How will the doctors' meals likely be affected if the target cost percentage is reduced? If it is increased?

Answer: If the target cost percentage is reduced, the quality and/or portion size of the meals may be reduced. If the target cost percentage is increased, the quality and/or portion size of the meals may be increased.

6. Dawne Juan is the Food and Beverage Director for a mid-size hotel in a beach destination area. The General Manager of the hotel has given Dawne a target of 10% profit for this year. Dawne's staff is predominately her beach buddies. Although she is good at controlling most of her costs, she has a hard time telling her friends to go home when business slows down and she needs to reduce her staff. If she doesn't make her profit goal, her general manager will likely reprimand her, and she could possibly lose her job. Express Dawne's expenses and profit as a percentage of total revenue, both this year and last year, to determine if she met her profit goal (fill in all empty blanks).

	This Year	%	Last Year	%
Revenue	$1,448,956	100%	$1,094,276	100%
F&B Expense	463,666	32%	382,997	35%
Labor Expense	652,030	45%	437,710	40%
Other Expense	217,343	15%	186,027	17%
Total Expense	1,333,039	92%	1,006,734	92%
Profit	115,917	8%	87,542	8%

Was Dawne effective at controlling her expenses? Did she meet the profit goal set by the General Manager? If not, what could Dawne do in the future to help her make her target profit?

Answer: Dawne was effective at controlling her food and beverage expense and her other expense. However, she did not control her labor expense well. She did not meet the profit goal set by the General Manager. She should work on being more of a manager and less of a "buddy" to her employees. She needs to be able to send her employees home when business is slow, or she may risk losing her job in the future.

7. Lee Ray operates the Champs Steak and Seafood restaurant. Last month, Lee budgeted $3,500 for food, in the specific categories listed below. It was a busy month, but Lee thought he did a good job managing his costs. Imagine his surprise when, at the end of the month, when Lee calculated his actual expenses and entered in them in the chart below, he found he was way over budget! Calculate Lee's % of Budget in each category listed on the chart, as well as the total.

	Budget	Actual	% of Budget
Meats and Poultry	$ 1500	$ 1600	106.7
Seafood	1200	1500	125.0
Fruits and Vegetables	350	370	105.7
Dairy Products	200	210	105.0
Groceries	250	270	108.0
Total	3,500	3,950	112.9

By how much money was Lee over his total budget? In which categories did Lee's costs vary more than 10% from the amount he had originally budgeted? Lee said it was a busy month. Would the number of customers he served affect his actual costs? What would you recommend he do next to further analyze the reasons for his restaurant's budget performance last month?

Answer: Lee was over his total budget by $450. Lee's costs vary more than 10% from budget in the seafood category and the total. The higher number of customers should cause his actual costs to be higher than budgeted. He should compare the increases in customers with the amount he should spend in each category to maintain his product and service quality. Based on this, his budget may be too low for the increased number of guests.

8. Some foodservice professionals feel the best way to improve profits is to reduce costs. Others feel increasing revenue is the best way to increase profits. Name three specific steps a manager can take to reduce current costs. Name three specific steps a manager can take to increase revenues. Which approach do you feel would be best for the type of operation you want to manage?

   Answer:

   Controlling costs is important. So is improving revenue levels. Student answers will vary; however, typical cost reduction steps likely to be identified include:

   1. Reducing product (portion) sizes
   2. Reducing the quality of product ingredients used
   3. Reducing staffing/service levels
   4. Reducing operating hours

   Typical revenue enhancement activities designed to attract more guests include:

   1. Increasing product (portion) sizes
   2. Increasing the quality of product ingredients
   3. Increasing staffing/service levels
   4. Increasing operating hours

   Notice that these two sets of actions affect guests differently. In many cases, the ability to vary selling price (an ability which varies by industry segment) is a critical factor in determining which of the alternative steps would be considered the "best" thing to do.

Exam Questions

Multiple Choice
Choose the letter of the best answer to the questions listed below.

1. When significant variations with your planned results occur, as a foodservice manager you must:
   a. Determine the cause, identify the problem, and take corrective action
   b. Take corrective action, determine the cause, and identify the problem
   c. Identify the problem, take corrective action, and determine the cause
   d. Identify the problem, determine the cause, and take corrective action
   Correct answer is d   (See: Understanding the Budget)

14

2. How is the term "expenses" defined in the textbook?
   a. The number of guests you serve
   b. The sales dollars generated by the business
   c. The dollars that remain after all the expenses have been paid
   d. The cost of the items required to operate the business
   Correct answer is d   (See: Profit: The Reward for Service)

3. Select the answer that best completes the following statement: Revenue - Desired
   Profit = _____.
   a. Ideal Expense
   b. Food Cost
   c. Other Expense
   d. None of the above
   Correct answer is a   (See: Profit: The Reward for Service)

4. Identify which of the following is not a major foodservice expense category.
   a. Food costs
   b. Beverage costs
   c. Labor costs
   d. Other expenses
   e. Room costs
   Correct answer is e   (See: Expenses)

5. According to the textbook which of the following costs are not considered part of
   food costs?
   a. Produce
   b. Coffee
   c. Paper wrappers for burgers
   d. Linen
   Correct answer is d   (See: Expenses)

Questions 6, 7, 8, and 9 are based on the following information:
A simplified annual P & L statement for The Tampopo Noodle House is shown below:

Description	Dollars	Percentages
Revenues	$800,000	
Food & Beverage Costs	$300,000	
Labor Costs	350,000	
Other Costs	50,000	
Total Expense		
Profit		

6. What was the profit expressed as a percentage for The Tampopo Noodle House?
   a. 6.25%
   b. 12.50%
   c. 37.50%
   d. Cannot be determined
   Correct answer is b (See: Understanding the Profit and Loss Statement)

7. If the desired profit for this level of annual revenues was 15.00%, what was the ideal expense?
   a. $100,000
   b. $120,000
   c. $680,000
   d. Cannot be determined
   Correct answer is c (See: Understanding the Profit and Loss Statement)

8. If the budget for food and beverage costs was $280,000, what was the budgeted food and beverage cost percentage and what was the actual percent of budget?
   a. The budgeted food and beverage cost percentage was 35.00% and the actual percent of budget was approximately 107.1%.
   b. The budgeted food and beverage cost percentage was 37.50 % and the actual percent of budget was approximately 100.0%.
   c. The budgeted food and beverage cost percentage was 50% and the actual percent of budget was approximately 7.1%.
   d. Cannot be determined
   Correct answer is a   (See: Understanding the Budget)

9. If the budget for Labor Costs was $375,000, what was the performance to budget?
   a. 107.1%
   b. 93.3%
   c. 128%
   d. 46.9%
   Correct answer is b (See: Understanding the Budget)

10. Which if the following tasks are not part of a retail manager's responsibility?
    a. Distribute to end-user
    b. Secure raw materials
    c. Market to the end user
    d. Reconcile problems with the end user
    Correct answer is b (See: Professional Foodservice Manager)

11. Which of the following best defines revenue?
    a. The dollars that remain after all the expenses have been paid
    b. The cost of the items required to operate your business
    c. The term used to indicate the dollars you take in
    d. The profit that the owner desires to achieve on a predicted quantity of revenue
    Correct answer is c (See: Profit: The Reward for Service)

12. In what category do nonalcoholic beverages belong?
    a. Beverage costs
    b. Other expenses
    c. Food costs
    d. Soft drink costs
    Correct answer is c   (See: Expenses)

13. What is the equation for profit?
    a. Revenue + expenses
    b. Expenses – food and beverage cost – labor cost
    c. Revenue – expenses
    d. Revenue – desired profit
    Correct answer is c   (See: Profit: The Reward for Service)

14. What is the formula to calculate total expense %?
    a. Labor cost / revenue
    b. Total expense / revenue
    c. Total expense / profit
    d. Total expense / other expense
    Correct answer is b   (See: Understanding the Profit and Loss Statement)

15. Sam Hunky is a foodservice manager. Last month his Food Expense equaled $30,000, his Labor Expense equaled $26,000, and his Other Expenses equaled $12,000. His Revenue equaled $83,000. What is his total expense percentage?
    a. 67.5%
    b. 122%
    c. 81.9%
    d. None of the above
    Correct answer is c (See: Understanding the Profit and Loss Statement)

16. To increase revenue dollars you can _____.
    a. Increase the number of guests you serve
    b. Increase the amount each guest spends
    c. Both a and b
    d. None of the above
    Correct answer is c   (See: Revenue)

17. A _____ is simply a forecast or estimate of projected revenue, expense and profit.
    a. Budget
    b. Expenses
    c. Performance to budget
    d. Variation
    Correct answer is a   (See: Understanding the Budget)

18. What is the formula for food cost %?
    a. Food cost / food sales
    b. Profit / revenue
    c. Total expense / revenue
    d. Labor expense / revenue
    Correct answer is a   (See: Understanding the Profit and Loss Statement)

19. Profit is the result of:
    a. Solid planning
    b. Sound management
    c. Decision making
    d. All of the above
    Correct answer is d   (See: Profit: The Reward for Service)

20. The money left over after a "Non-Profit" organization pays its bills is called:
    a. Profit
    b. Emergency money
    c. Savings
    d. Cash reserve
    Correct answer is d   (See: Profit: The Reward For Service)

21. Many foodservice operations are changing from "one month" budget to periods to periods of _____ in order to make each period equal to the next.
    a. 30 days
    b. 3 weeks
    c. 28 days
    d. 92 days
    Correct answer is c   (See: Understanding the Budget)

22. What statement is an accounting tool that details revenues, expenses, and profits for a given time period?
    a. Balance Sheet
    b. Income Statement
    c. Statement of Cash Flows
    d. All of the Above
    Correct answer is b   (See: Understanding the Profit and Loss Statement)

23. Jordan Lee is a foodservice manager. Last month his Food Expense equaled $30,000, his Labor Expense equaled $26,000, and his Other Expenses equaled $15,000. His Revenue equaled $95,000. What is his profit percentage?
    a. 25.3%
    b. 252%
    c. 3.95%
    d. None of the above
    Correct answer is a (See: Understanding the Profit and Loss Statement)

True/False
Choose the letter of the best answer to the questions listed below.

24. When considering costs, foodservice managers just need to remember that low costs are good and high costs are bad.
    a. True
    b. False
    Correct answer is b   (See: Profit: The Reward for Service)

25. Non-profit institutions are only interested in generating enough revenue to cover their costs.
    a. True
    b. False
    Correct answer is b   (See: Profit: The Reward For Service)

26. Ideal expense is defined as management's view of the correct or appropriate amount of expense necessary to generate a given quantity of sales.
    a. True
    b. False
    Correct answer is a   (See: Profit: The Reward for Service)

27. Revenue varies with both the number of guests frequenting the business and the amount of money spent by each guest.
    a. True
    b. False
    Correct answer is a   (See: Revenue)

28. The four major expense categories that must be controlled by management are: food costs, labor costs, beverage costs, and other expenses.
    a. True
    b. False
    Correct answer is a   (See: Expenses)

29. The three ways to write a percent are: common, fraction, and decimal.
    a. True
    b. False
    Correct answer is a   (See: Percent Review)

30. A budget is simply a record of previous sales, expenses, and generated net income.
    a. True
    b. False
    Correct answer is b   (See: Understanding the Budget)

31. If a budget was accurate, and the foodservice operator is within reasonable limits of the budget he or she is said to be "in line" with the budget.
    a. True
    b. False
    Correct answer is a   (See: Understanding the Budget)

32. The sign of a good foodservice manager is that his or her actual costs are significantly lower than what was budgeted.
    a. True
    b. False
    Correct answer is b   (See: Profit: The Reward For Service)

33. The budget shows the actual revenue, expense, and profit of an operation.
    a. True
    b. False
    Correct answer is b   (See: Understanding the Budget)

34. Security of your cost and customer information can be just as critical as accuracy, and not all information should be accessible to all parties.
    a. True
    b. False
    Correct answer is a   (See: Technology Tools)

35. To manage an operation efficiently, the manager should be able to communicate with guests, employees and vendors using software products for word processing, spreadsheet building, faxes, and e-mail.
    a. True
    b. False
    Correct answer is a   (See: Technology Tools)

36. "Environmental awareness" is a term used to describe a variety of earth-friendly practices and policies designed to meet the needs of the present population without compromising the ability of future generations to meet their own needs.
    a. True
    b. False
    Correct answer is b   (See: Green and Growing)

37. "Clean" is the term used to describe those foodservice operations that incorporate environmentally-conscious activities into the design, construction and operation of their businesses.
    a. True
    b. False
    Correct answer is b   (See: Green and Growing)

Chapter 2

Determining Sales Forecasts

Learning Outcomes

At the conclusion of this chapter, you will be able to:

- Develop a procedure to record current sales.
- Compute percentage increases or decreases in sales over time.
- Develop a procedure to predict future sales.

Lecture Outline

1. Importance of Forecasting Sales

- The first question operating managers must ask themselves is very simple: "How many guests will I serve today?" - "This week?" - "This year?" The answer to questions such as these are critical, since these guests will provide the revenue from which the operator will pay basic operating expenses and create a profit.
- In an ongoing operation, it is often true that future sales estimates, or projected sales, will be heavily based upon your sales history since what has happened in the past in your operation is usually the best predictor of what will happen in the future.
- A **sales forecast** predicts the number of guests you will serve and the revenues they will generate in a given future time period.
- You can determine your actual sales for a current time period by using a computerized system called a **point of sales (POS) system** that has been designed to provide specific sales information.
- Remember that a distinction is made in the hospitality industry between sales (revenue), and **sales volume**, which is the number of units sold.
- Sales may be a blend of cash and non-cash.
- With accurate sales records, a sales history can be developed for each foodservice outlet you operate and better decisions will be reached with regard to planning for each unit's operation.

2. Sales History

- **Sales history** is the systematic recording of all sales achieved during a pre-determined time period. Sales histories can be created to record revenue, guests served, or both.

- **Sales to date** is the cumulative total of sales reported in the unit.
- An **average or mean** is defined as the value arrived at by adding the quantities in a series and dividing the sum of the quantities by the number of items in the series.
- The two major types of averages you are likely to encounter as a foodservice manager are as follows:
  - **Fixed average** is an average in which you determine a specific time period, for example, the first fourteen days of a given month, and then you compute the mean or average amount of sales or guest activity for that period.
  - **Rolling average** is the average amount of sales or volume over a changing time period. Essentially, where a fixed average is computed using a specific or constant set of data, the rolling average is computed using data that will change.
  - The use of the rolling average, while more complex and time consuming than that of a fixed average, can be extremely useful in recording data to help you make effective predictions about the sales levels you can expect in the future.
- **Guest count** is the term used in the hospitality industry to indicate the number of people you have served, and is recorded on a regular basis.
- When managers record both revenue *and* guest counts, information needed to compute **average sales per guest**, a term also known as **check average**, is provided.

$$\frac{\text{Total Sales}}{\text{Number of Guests Served}} = \text{Average Sales per Guest}$$

- Most POS systems report the amount of revenue you have generated in a selected time period, the number of guests you have served, and the average sales per guest. Of course, the same data could be compiled manually.
- A **weighted average** is an average that weights the number of guests with how much they spend in a given time period.
- The weighted average sales per guest for 2 days is as follows:

$$\frac{\text{Day 1 Sales} + \text{Day 2 Sales}}{\text{Day 1 Guests} + \text{Day 2 Guests}} = \frac{\text{Two Day}}{\text{Average Sales per Guest}}$$

3. Maintaining Sales Histories

- Sales history may consist of revenue; number of guests served, and average sales per guest. You may want to use even more detailed information, such as the number of a particular menu item served, the number of guests served in a specific meal or time period, or the method of meal delivery (for example, drive-through vs. counter sales).

- In most cases, your sales histories should be kept for a period of at least two years.

- **Sales variances** are changes from previously experienced sales levels. (See figure 2.9)
- The variance is determined by subtracting sales last year from sales this year.

> **Sales This Year – Sales Last Year = Variance**

- **Percentage variance** indicates the percentage change in sales from one time period to the next.

$$\frac{\textbf{Sales This Year – Sales Last Year}}{\textbf{Sales Last Year}} = \textbf{Percentage Variance}$$

or

$$\frac{\textbf{Variance}}{\textbf{Sales Last Year}} = \textbf{Percentage Variance}$$

or

$$\frac{\textbf{Sales This Year}}{\textbf{Sales Last Year}} - 1 = \textbf{Percentage Variance}$$

4. Predicting Future Sales

- Depending on the type of facility you manage, you may be interested in predicting, or forecasting, future revenues, guest counts, or average sales per guest levels.
- Revenue forecast is calculated using the following formula:

> **Sales Last Year + (Sales Last Year x % Increase Estimate) = Revenue Forecast**

or

> **Sales Last Year x (1 + % Increase Estimate) = Revenue Forecast**

- Use the revenue increases you have experienced in the past to predict increases you may experience in the future.
- Using the same techniques employed in estimating increases in sales, the non-cash operator or any manager interested in guest counts can estimate increases or decreases in the number of guests served.
- The guest count forecast is determined by multiplying guest count last year by the % increase estimate, and then adding the guest count last year.

> **Guest Count Last Year + (Guest Count Last Year x % Increase Estimate)
> = Guest Count Forecast**

or

> **Guest Count Last Year x (1.00 + % Increase Estimate) = Guest Count Forecast**

- Average sales per guest (check average) is simply the average amount of money each guest spends during a visit.
- Using data taken from the sales history, the following formula is employed:

> **Last Year's Average Sales per Guest**
> **+ Estimated Increase in Sales per Guest**
> **= Sales per Guest Forecast**

- An average sales per guest forecast is obtained by dividing the revenue forecast by the guest count forecast.

$$\frac{\text{Revenue Forecast}}{\text{Guest Count Forecast}} = \text{Average Sales per Guest Forecast}$$

- It is important to note that sales histories, regardless of how well they have been developed and maintained, are not sufficient, used alone, to accurately predict future sales.
- Your knowledge of potential price changes, new competitors, facility renovations, and improved selling programs are just a few of the many factors that you must consider when predicting future sales.
- Guest counts can be increased by undertaking green initiatives. It is important to market the products and services directly to the rapidly growing market segment of educated, savvy customers who care about the food they eat and their impact on the world around them.
- Implementing sustainable practices that focus on conservation as well as utilizing organic, seasonal, and locally grown products can help build customer and employee loyalty, as well as boost profits.

5. Technology Tools

- The importance of accurate sales histories for use in forecasting future sales is unquestionable. Your POS system can be invaluable in this effort. Many systems today can be utilized to do the following:

    1. Track sales by guest count
    2. Track sales by date
    3. Monitor cash vs. credit sales
    4. Maintain products sold histories
    5. Maintain check average data
    6. Compare actual sales to prior-period sales
    7. Maintain rolling sales averages
    8. Forecast future sales in increments
    9. Maintain actual sales to forecasted sales variance reports
    10. Maintain reservations systems

- For those operations that rely on reservations to control bookings, software of this type is available to instantly identify repeat guests, giving the operator a display screen that can include such information as frequency of visit, purchase preferences, and total dollars spent in the operation.
- Reservations software makes it possible for operators to reward repeat guests by developing their own "frequent dining" programs, similar to a hotel or airlines' frequent-traveler programs.
- Customer complaints can be tracked and, if desired, coupons to compensate guests for difficulties can be printed and distributed.
- Reservations-related programs such as these can store information on reservation demand, predict optimal reservation patterns, identify frequent no-show guests, and even allow guests to make their own reservations via on-line Internet connections.

Consider The Cost

"A 60-minute wait! You've got to be kidding!" said the guest.

"I'm sorry sir," replied Romy. "We'll seat your party as quickly as possible."

Romy was the dining room host at the Al-Amir restaurant. The Al-Amir featured Middle Eastern and North African Cuisine. Guests loved the Al-Amir's Baba Gannouj, Tabouleh, and Kibbeh. As a result, the restaurant often was very busy. When that happened, the waiting lists for tables got long and customers sometimes got upset.

"Listen," replied the guest, "I understand when places are busy. It can take a while to serve everyone. But look, nearly half your dining room is empty. The tables just need to be cleared and reset."

"Yes sir," replied Romy. "But the workers we do have are clearing tables as fast as they can."

"Then you need more dining room help. We'll just come back another time," said the guest, as he left the restaurant along with his female dining companion, their two small children in hand.

"I'm really very sorry, sir," said Romy to the guest's back as he watched him leave. Romy thought to himself, "This happens way too often!"

Assume the Al-Amir does not have an effective sales forecast system in place.
1. What will be the likely long-term impact on the revenue-generating ability of the restaurant by understaffing its dining room?
2. What would be the long-term impact on the Al-Amir's staff?
3. Sometimes even the best sales forecasts are inaccurate. What steps can managers take to ease the difficulties encountered when their sales forecasts prove to be incorrect?

Answers:

This case is designed to make students think about the relationship between accurate revenue forecasts and the ability of an operation to provide its guests quality food and service.

1. When sales forecasting is poor and restaurants are not staffed to operate at their full capacities, the ability of the restaurant to maximize revenues is compromised. Even the restaurant's revenue generating capacity in slower times will be reduced as guests who were turned away during busy times seek out alternative places to eat. If those alternative facilities do a good job with guest service and products, the understaffed restaurant may simply never get a "second chance" to make a good impression on those customers. Also, when restaurants are severely understaffed, the quality of service for those diners who are seated usually suffers as staff does their best but, because they are short-handed, cannot offer the high levels of guest service originally intended.

2. Overworked staff will get frustrated because their customers get frustrated. Tip levels decline and, over the long run, so will employee morale. In the back-of-the house, poor guest count forecasting results in running out of menu items, as well as longer guest waits to actually get their food (and this after they have waited a long time to get their table)!

3. Answers will vary, but student suggestions should include maintaining lists of employees who can be called to help on short notice. As well, clean, comfortable and entertaining waiting areas for guests are vital. This is especially true in restaurants that cater to families. Tech-savvy operations will take waiting guests' cells phone numbers to call or text them when their tables are ready (thus allowing guests to use the own wait-time productively).

Apply What You Have Learned

Pauline Cooper is a registered dietitian (R.D.) and the Foodservice Director at Memorial Hospital. Increasingly, the hospital's marketing efforts have emphasized its skill in treating diabetic patients. As a result, the number of diabetic meals served by Pauline's staff has been increasing. As a professional member of hospital's management team, Pauline has been asked to report on how the hospital's diabetic treatment marketing efforts have affected her area.

1. How important is it that Pauline have historical records of the "type" of meals served by her staff, and not merely the number of meals served? Why?

    Answer: It is so important that Pauline have historical records of the type of meals served by her staff because she can use these to report on how the hospital's diabetic treatment marketing efforts have affected her area. She can make comparisons between types of meals served last year and this year. By using these comparisons, she can present the increasing number of diabetic meals served. In addition, she can use this data to develop future plans and budgets.

2. Assume that Pauline's "per meal" cost has been increasing because diabetic meals are more expensive to produce than regular meals. Could Pauline use sales histories to estimate the financial impact of serving additional diabetic meals in the future? How?

   Answer: Yes, she can use sales history to estimate financial impact of serving additional diabetic meals in the future. Knowing per meal cost last year and this year, she can compute per meal cost variance, total cost variance, as well as sales variance.

3. What are other reasons managers in a foodservice operation might keep detailed records of meal "types" (i.e. vegetarian, low-sodium, etc) served, as well as total number of meals served?

   Answer: Keeping detailed records of meal types served and total number of meals served would help managers to know exactly what types of meals are increasing or decreasing. Managers also can analyze overall operating performance by looking at sales history of total meals served.

Test Your Skills

1. Laurie Fitsin owns a small sandwich shop called Laurie's Lunch Box. She has developed a sales history of the first week of March using total sales and guests served. Help Laurie calculate her average sales per guest for each day of the week and calculate her totals.

LAURIE'S LUNCH BOX

Sales Period	Date	Sales	Guests Served	Average Sales Per Guest
Monday	3/1	$1,248.44	200	$6.24
Tuesday	3/2	1,686.25	360	4.68
Wednesday	3/3	1,700.00	350	4.86
Thursday	3/4	1,555.65	300	5.19
Friday	3/5	1,966.31	380	5.17
Saturday	3/6	2,134.65	400	5.34
Sunday	3/7	2,215.77	420	5.28
Total		$12,507.07	2,410	$5.19
Average Sales Per Guest (sum divided by 7):				$5.25

Laurie has decided that she could take a shortcut and calculate the average sales per guest for the week by adding Monday through Sunday's average sales per guest and dividing by seven. Would this shortcut make a difference in her total average sales

27

per guest for the week? If so, how much of a difference? Should she take this shortcut? Why or why not?

> **Answer**: The shortcut would make a difference of $0.06 ($5.25 - $5.19). She should not take this shortcut because she would be overstating the average sales per guest.

2. Peggy Richey operates Peggy's Pizza Place in Southern California. She has maintained a sales history for January through June, and she wants to compare this year's sales with last year's sales. Calculate her sales variances and percentage variances for the first 6 months of the year.

Peggy's Pizza Place

Month	Sales This Year	Sales Last Year	Variance	Percentage Variance
January	$ 37,702.73	$ 34,861.51	$ 2,841.22	8.15%
February	33,472.03	31,485.60	1,986.43	6.31%
March	36,492.98	33,707.79	2,785.19	8.26%
April	35,550.12	32,557.85	2,992.27	9.19%
May	36,890.12	37,852.42	(962.30)	(2.54)%
June	37,482.52	37,256.36	226.16	0.61%
Total	$ 217,590.50	$ 207,721.53	$ 9,868.97	4.75%

3. Peggy (from preceding exercise) wants to use the sales and variance information from her first six months of the year to forecast her revenues for the last six months of the year. She decides to use her six-month total percentage variance of 4.75% to predict her changes in sales. Help her calculate the projected sales increases and revenue forecasts for the last six months of the year.

Peggy's Pizza Place

Month	Sales Last Year	Predicted Change	Projected Sales Increase	Revenue Forecast
July	$36,587.91	4.75%	$1,737.93	$38,325.84
August	36,989.73	4.75%	1,757.01	38,746.74
September	40,896.32	4.75%	1,942.58	42,838.90
October	37,858.63	4.75%	1,798.28	39,656.91
November	37,122.45	4.75%	1,763.32	38,885.77
December	37,188.71	4.75%	1,766.46	38,955.17
Total	226,643.75	4.75%	$10,765.58	237,409.33

4. The Lopez brothers, Victor, Tony, and Soren, own the Lopez Cantina. Victor is in charge of marketing, and he is developing his sales forecast for next year. Because of his marketing efforts, he predicts a 5% increase in his monthly guest counts. Victor is not aware of any anticipated menu price increases and assumes, therefore, that his weighted check average will remain stable.

a. Using last year's sales and guest counts, estimate Victor's weighted check average (average sales per guest) for the year. (Spreadsheet hint: Use the

Month	Sales Last Year	Guest Count Last Year	Check Average
January	$ 45,216.00	4,800	$ 9.42
February	48,538.00	5,120	9.48
March	50,009.00	5,006	9.99
April	45,979.00	4,960	9.27
May	49,703.00	5,140	9.67
June	48,813.00	5,300	9.21
July	55,142.00	5,621	9.81
August	59,119.00	6,002	9.85
September	55,257.00	5,780	9.56
October	50,900.00	5,341	9.53
November	54,054.00	5,460	9.90
December	50,998.00	5,400	9.44
Total	$ 613,728.00	63,930	$ 9.60

Weighted Check Average

ROUND function to two decimal places on weighted check average, cell D18, because it will be used in another formula in part b.)

b. Using the weighted check average calculated in part a, determine Victor's projected sales assuming a 5% increase in guest counts. (Spreadsheet hint: Use the ROUND function to zero decimal places in the Guest Count Forecast column, cells C23:C34. Use the SUM function for the total, cell C35. Otherwise, your answers will not be correct.)

Month	Guest Count Last Year	Guest Count Forecast	Weighted Check Average	Projected Sales
January	4,800	5,040	$ 9.60	$48,384.00
February	5,120	5,376	9.60	51,609.60
March	5,006	5,256	9.60	50,457.60
April	4,960	5,208	9.60	49,996.80
May	5,140	5,397	9.60	51,811.20
June	5,300	5,565	9.60	53,424.00
July	5,621	5,902	9.60	56,659.20
August	6,002	6,302	9.60	60,499.20
September	5,780	6,069	9.60	58,262.40
October	5,341	5,608	9.60	53,836.80
November	5,460	5,733	9.60	55,036.80
December	5,400	5,670	9.60	54,432.00
Total	63,930	67,126	9.60	644,409.60

5. Donna Berger is a hotel Food and Beverage Director at a 500-room hotel. Donna knows that as the number of rooms sold in the hotel increases, the number of guests she serves for breakfast increases also. Based on historical records, Donna will serve breakfast to 55% of the hotel's registered guests. Help Donna more easily plan for the number of breakfasts she will serve by completing the following chart:

Number of Guests in Hotel	Historical % of Guests Eating Breakfast	Estimated Number of Guests To Be Served
100	55%	55
175	55%	96
225	55%	124
275	55%	151
325	55%	179
375	55%	206
425	55%	234
475	55%	261
500	55%	275

What information would Donna need to determine the historical percentage of guests who eat breakfast?

Answer: Donna would need to know the historical number of breakfast meals served divided by the total number of hotel guests during a predetermined comparison time period (i.e. week, month, year).

6. Amy Pelletier operates Hall's House, an upscale restaurant with a $30.00 check average in mid-town Manhattan. Her clientele consists of business persons and tourists visiting the city. Based on the historical sales records she keeps, next year Amy believes her business will achieve a food sales increase of 4% per month for each of the first six months of the year. She feels this increase will be the result of increases in guest counts (not check average).

At mid-year (July 1), Amy intends to increase her menu prices (and thus, her check average) by 2%. She feels that while these price increases could result in a slight, short-term reduction in her guest counts, the restaurant's guest counts will still increase 3% for the last six months of the year.

Taking into account her guest count growth estimates and mid-year price increases, Amy would like to estimate her predicted year-end food revenues. Prepare the revenue estimates for Hall's House. (Spreadsheet hint: Use the ROUND function to zero decimal places in the Guest Count Forecast columns, cells D5:D10 and D15:D20. Use the SUM function for the totals, cells D11 and D21. Otherwise, your answers will not be correct.)

Months January Through June

Month	Guest Count Last Year	Guest Count % Increase Estimate	Guest Count Forecast	Original Check Average	Revenue Forecast
January	6,270	4%	6,521	$30.00	$195,630.00
February	6,798	4%	7,070	$30.00	$212,100.00
March	6,336	4%	6,589	$30.00	$197,670.00
April	6,400	4%	6,656	$30.00	$199,680.00
May	6,930	4%	7,207	$30.00	$216,210.00
June	6,864	4%	7,139	$30.00	$214,170.00
6 month total	39,598	4%	41,182	$30.00	$1,235,460.00

Months July Through December

Month	Guest Count Last Year	Guest Count % Increase Estimate	Guest Count Forecast	New Check Average	Revenue Forecast
July	6,845	3%	7,050	$30.60	$215,730.00
August	6,430	3%	6,623	$30.60	$202,663.80
September	6,283	3%	6,471	$30.60	$198,012.60
October	6,402	3%	6,594	$30.60	$201,776.40
November	6,938	3%	7,146	$30.60	$218,667.60
December	7,128	3%	7,342	$30.60	$224,665.20
6 month total	40,026	3%	41,226	$30.60	$1,261,515.60

7. Raktida is the manager of a popular Italian Restaurant on Mott Street, and she is trying to predict guest counts for the first week of November so that she can estimate an accurate number of servers to schedule. Business is very good, but her sales history from last month indicates that fewer guests are served during the first few days of the week compared to last year, while more guests per day are served in the later part of the week. Raktida has entered the guest counts from last year and the estimated percentage change in guest counts for this year in the chart below. Because good service is so important to her, she wants to ensure that enough servers are scheduled to work each day. One server can provide excellent service to 50 guests. Help Raktida calculate how many servers to schedule each day by completing the following chart. Note: Raktida always rounds the number of servers required **up** to the next whole number to ensure the best service possible for her guests! (Spreadsheet hint: Use ROUNDUP to 0 decimal places in the Estimated Guest Count This Year and the Number of Servers Needed This Year columns.)

Raktida's Guest Forecast and Server Scheduling Worksheet for the first week of November

	Guest Count Last Year	Estimated Change This Year	Estimated Guest Count This Year	Number of Servers Needed This Year
Sunday	625	-5%	594	12
Monday	750	-5%	713	15
Tuesday	825	0	825	17
Wednesday	850	5%	893	18
Thursday	775	5%	814	17
Friday	1,250	10%	1,375	28
Saturday	1,400	10%	1,540	31

32

How would Raktida's server scheduling efforts this year be affected if last year she had recorded only her weekly (not daily) guest counts?

Answer: Without last year's daily guest counts, Raktida would not be able to accurately estimate different daily increases and decreases in guest counts this year.

8. Sales forecasts are important because knowing how many people you will serve is important. What are three specific problems that will occur when managers *underestimate* the number of guests they will serve on a given day? What are three specific difficulties that would likely result if managers *overestimate* the number they will serve?

Answer:
Inaccurate (or a complete absence of) revenue forecasts will have a variety of negative effects.

When managers underestimate the number of guests they will serve:
1. Guest waiting times for seating increases.
2. Service levels provided to seated guests decline.
3. Revenues are not maximized because seating capacities cannot be maintained at 100%.
4. Because service levels are poor, tipping levels decrease, reducing employee income and satisfaction.
5. Employee morale decreases as employees who are constantly "in the weeds" get burned out.

When managers overestimate the number of guests they will serve:
1. Too much food is purchased and product loss increases as these items are held in storage.
2. Too much food is prepared and product loss increases; especially if these items must be discarded at the end of the day.
3. Labor-related costs (relative to revenues) increase because workers cannot remain productive at all times (because they have too few guests to serve).
4. Because there are too many service staff relative to guests, total tips received by employees decrease, reducing employee income and satisfaction.
5. Employee morale decreases as employees who are constantly "standing around doing nothing" seek better managed restaurants where they can maximize their incomes and job satisfaction.

Exam Questions

Multiple Choice

Choose the letter of the best answer to the questions listed below.

1. Which of the following best defines the term "Rolling Average"?
   a. The average amount of sales or volume over a changing time period
   b. The average for a specific time period that is then applied to future time periods
   c. The average of the highest sales or volume and the lowest sales or volume that is computed once per year
   d. All of the above

   Correct answer is a (See: Sales History)

2. Which of the following are advantages of precise sales forecasts?
   a. Improved budging ability
   b. Better accuracy in purchasing the correct amount of food for immediate use
   c. Greater efficiency in scheduling needed workers
   d. Increased profit levels and stockholder value
   e. All of the above

   Correct answer is e (See: Importance of Forecasting Sales)

3. Which of the following formulas is correct?
   a. Percentage Variance = Sales Last Year – Sales This Year
   b. Percentage Variance = Sales Last Year + (Sales Last Year x %Increase Estimate)
   c. Average Sales per Guest = Total Sales/Number of Guests Served
   d. All of the above
   e. Only a. and b. above

   Correct answer is c (See: Recording Revenue, Guest Counts, or Both?)

4. What is the equation for percentage variance?
   a. (Sales This Year - Sales Last Year)/ Sales Last Year
   b. Variance/Sales Last Year
   c. (Sales This Year / Sales Last Year) – 1
   d. All of the above
   e. Only a. and b. above

   Correct answer is d (See: Maintaining Sales Histories)

5. How is the term sales history defined in the textbook?
   a. The systematic recording of all sales achieved during a predetermined time period
   b. The value arrived at by adding the quantities in a series and dividing the sum of the quantities by the number of items in the series
   c. The average that weights the number of guests with how much they spend in a given time period
   d. All of the above
   e. Only b. and c. above

   Correct answer is a (See: Sales History)

Questions 6, 7, and 8 are based on the following information:

Based on his education and work experience, Nimesh was recently hired as a Food & Beverage Supervisor by the Bombay Adventure Restaurant. One of his first tasks is to forecast the sales for the next six months based on the following information.

Month	Sales last year	Estimated % Increase in Sales	Estimated $ Increase in Sales	Total Revenue Forecast
January	$40,000	2.00%		
February	41,000	2.00		
March	39,000	3.00		
April	42,000	2.50		
May	46,000	4.00		
June	50,000	3.00		
Six-Month Total				

6. What is the total revenue forecast for the six-month period?
   a. $263,160
   b. $264,450
   c. $265,180
   d. $268,320
   e. None of the above
   Correct answer is c (See: Future Revenues)

7. What is the total estimated dollar increase in sales for the six-month period?
   a. $5,160
   b. $6,450
   c. $7,180
   d. $10,320
   e. None of the above
   Correct answer is c (See: Future Revenues)

8. What is the weighted average percentage increase in sales?
   a. 2.00%
   b. 2.75%
   c. 2.78%
   d. 4.00%
   e. None of the above
   Correct answer is c (See: Future Revenues)

9. Sales this year – Sales last year =_____
   a. Profit This Year
   b. Variance
   c. Sales History
   d. None of the above
   Correct answer is b (See: Sales Variances)

10. Revenue forecast = Sales last year * (_____)
    a. (1 + % increase estimate)
    b. (% increase estimate)
    c. (1 - % increase estimate)
    d. None of the above
    Correct answer is a (See: Predicting Future Sales)

11. Sales history helps you to:
    a. Predict expenses
    b. Manage employees
    c. Develop a budget
    d. All of the above
    e. Only a. and c. above
    Correct answer is e (See: Sales History)

12. Which best describes "fixed average"?
    a. The average of a specific time period
    b. The average amount of sales or volume over a changing time period
    c. The average of the sales and volume
    Correct answer is a (See: Fixed Average)

13. What is the formula for average sales per guest?
    a. Number of guests served / total sales
    b. Total sales / number of guests served
    c. Total sales * number of guests served
    d. None of the above
    Correct answer is b (See: Recording Revenue, Guest Counts, or Both?)

14. Which of the following is used to indicate the number of people you have served?
    a. Sales forecast
    b. Check average
    c. Guest counts
    d. Sales history
    Correct answer is c (See: Recording Revenue, Guest Counts, or Both?)

15. Weighted average is defined as:
    a. Average determined in a specific time period
    b. Average amount of sales or volume over a changing time period
    c. Average that weights the number of guests with how much they spend in a given time period
    d. None of the above
    Correct answer is c (See: Recording Revenue, Guest Counts, or Both?)

16. If revenue this year is $853,564 and revenue last year was $769,278 what is the *percentage variance*?
    a. 11% increase
    b. 10% decrease
    c. 90% increase
    d. 85% decrease
    Correct answer is a (See: Maintaining Sales Histories)

17. If revenue forecast is $147,274 and guest count forecast is 26,785, what is the average sales per guest forecast?
    a. 18%
    b. $4.50
    c. $5.50
    d. 21%
    e. None of the above
    Correct answer is c (See: Predicting Future Sales)

18. Many POS Systems can be utilized to do which of the following?
    a. Forecast future sales
    b. Maintain product sold histories
    c. Track sales by date
    d. All of the above
    Correct answer is d (See: Technology Tools)

19. If revenue forecast is $159,425 and guest count forecast is 42,000, what is the average sales per guest forecast?
    a. 15%
    b. $7.50
    c. $3.80
    d. 35%
    e. None of the above
    Correct answer is c (See: Predicting Future Sales)

True/False
Choose the letter of the best answer to the questions listed below.

20. Knowledge of past sales really is not important to a foodservice manager since so many different variables will affect how much business is done during a particular period of time.
    a. True
    b. False
    Correct answer is b (See: Computing Averages for Sales Histories)

21. In the restaurant industry, sales are generally recorded in terms of dollar sales and customers served.
    a. True
    b. False
    Correct answer is a (See: Recording Revenue, Guest Counts, or Both?)

22. A fixed average is an average in which a foodservice operator computes the average amount of sales or volume over a changing period of time.
    a. True
    b. False
    Correct answer is b (See: Computing Averages for Sales Histories)

23. A rolling average is the average amount of sales or volume over a changing time period.
    a. True
    b. False
    Correct answer is a (See: Computing Averages for Sales Histories)

24. In most cases, sales record histories should be kept for a period of at least two years.
    a. True
    b. False
    Correct answer is a (See: Maintaining Sales Histories)

25. Sales histories alone are sufficient to accurately predict future sales.
    a. True
    b. False
    Correct answer is b (See: Future Average Sales per Guest)

26. New competitors, facility renovations, and potential price changes should be considered when predicting future sales.
    a. True
    b. False
    Correct answer is a (See: Future Average Sales per Guest)

27. Reservation-related programs can store information on reservation patterns, identify frequent no show guests and even allow guests to make their own reservations online.
    a. True
    b. False
    Correct answer is a (See: Technology Tools)

28. Implementing sustainable practices that focus on conservation as well as utilizing organic, seasonal, and locally grown products can help build customer and employee loyalty, as well as boost profits.
    a. True
    b. False
    Correct answer is a (See: Green and Growing)

Chapter 3

Managing the Cost of Food

Learning Outcomes

At the conclusion of this chapter, you will be able to:

- Use sales histories and standardized recipes to determine the amount of food products to buy in anticipation of forecasted sales.
- Purchase, receive, and store food products in a cost-effective manner.
- Compute the cost of food sold and food cost percentage.

Lecture Outline

1. Menu Item Forecasting

- The menu determines the success of most foodservice operations. Part of this success comes from being able to answer the questions "How many people will I serve today?" and "What will they order?"
- Once you know the average number of people selecting a given menu item, and the total number of guests who made the selections, you can compute the **popularity index**, which is defined as the percentage of total guests choosing a given menu item from a list of alternatives.

> **Popularity Index =** $\dfrac{\text{Total Number of a Specific Menu Item Sold}}{\text{Total Number of All Menu Items Sold}}$

- The basic formula for individual menu item forecasting, based on an item's individual sales history, is as follows:

> **Number of Guests Expected** x **Item Popularity Index**
> **= Predicted Number of That Item to Be Sold**

- The **predicted number to be sold** is simply the quantity of a specific menu item likely to be sold given an estimate of the total number of guests expected.

- A variety of factors such as competition, weather, special events in your area, facility occupancy, your own promotions, your competitor's promotions, quality of service, and operational consistency come together to influence the number of guests you can expect to serve on any specific day.
- Remember that sales histories track only the general trends of an operation. They are not able to estimate precisely the number of guests who may arrive on any given day.
- Forecasting is crucial if you are to effectively manage your food expenses. Consistency in food production and guest service will greatly influence your overall success.

2. Standardized Recipes

- The **standardized recipe** controls both the quantity and quality of what the kitchen will produce. It details the procedures to be used in preparing and serving each of your menu items.
- Good standardized recipes contain the following information:

  1. Menu item name
  2. Total yield (number of servings)
  3. Portion size
  4. Ingredient list
  5. Preparation/method section
  6. Cooking time and temperature
  7. Special instructions, if necessary
  8. Recipe cost (optional)

- The following list contains arguments often used against standardized recipes:

  1. They take too long to use.
  2. My people don't need recipes; they know how we do things here.
  3. My chef refuses to reveal his or her secrets.
  4. They take too long to write up.
  5. We tried them but lost some, so we stopped using them.
  6. They are too hard to read, or many of my people cannot read English.

- Reasons for incorporating a system of standardized recipes include:

  1. Accurate purchasing is impossible without the existence and use of standardized recipes.
  2. Dietary concerns require some foodservice operators to know exactly the kinds of ingredients and the correct amount of nutrients in each serving of a menu item.
  3. Accuracy in menu laws requires that food service operators be able to tell guests about the type and amount of ingredients in their recipes.

4. Accurate recipe costing and menu pricing is impossible without standardized recipes.
5. Matching food used to cash sales is impossible to do without standardized recipes.
6. New employees can be better trained with standardized recipes.
7. The computerization of a foodservice operation is impossible unless the elements of standardized recipes are in place; thus, the advantages of advanced technological tools available to the operation are restricted or even eliminated.

- Standardized recipes are the cornerstones of any serious effort to produce consistent, high quality food products at an established cost. Any recipe can be standardized.
- When adjusting recipes for quantity (total yield), two general methods may be employed. They are:

1. Factor Method
2. Percentage Technique

- When using the factor method, you utilize the following formula to arrive at a recipe conversion factor:

$$\frac{\text{Yield Desired}}{\text{Current Yield}} = \text{Conversion Factor}$$

- The percentage method deals with recipe weight, rather than with a conversion factor. It is sometimes more accurate than using a conversion factor alone. The proper conversion of weights and measures is important in recipe expansion or reduction.
- The percentage method of recipe conversion is as follows:

Ingredient Weight / Total Recipe Weight = % of Total

Then

% of Total x Total Amount Required = New Recipe Amount

3. Inventory Control

- A desired inventory level is simply the answer to the question, "How much of each needed ingredient should I have on hand at any one time?"
- **Working stock** is the amount of an ingredient you anticipate using before purchasing that item again.
- **Safety stock** is the extra amount of that ingredient you decide to keep on hand to meet higher than anticipated demand.

- Inventory levels are determined by a variety of factors such as:
  1. Storage capacity
  2. Item perishability
  3. Vendor delivery schedule
  4. Potential savings from increased purchase size
  5. Operating calendar
  6. Relative importance of stock outages
  7. Value of inventory dollars to the operator

- Operators must be careful not to overload storage capacity. Increased inventory of items generally leads to greater spoilage and loss due to theft.
- **Shelf life** is the amount of time a food item retains its maximum freshness, flavor, and quality while in storage. The shelf life of food products varies greatly.
- The cost to the vendor for frequent deliveries will be reflected in the cost of the goods to the operator.
- Sometimes you will find that you can realize substantial savings by purchasing needed items in large quantities, and thus receive a lower price from your vendor. There are costs associated with extraordinarily large purchases. These may include: storage costs, spoilage, deterioration, insect or rodent infestation or theft. The operating calendar plays a large part in determining desired inventory levels.
- Some operators over-buy or "stockpile" inventory causing too many dollars to be tied up in non-interest-bearing food products. When this is done, managers incur **opportunity costs.** An opportunity cost is the cost of foregoing the next best alternative when making a decision.
- A state institution that is given its entire annual budget at the start of its **fiscal year** (a year that is 12 months long but may not follow the calendar year) may find it advantageous to use its purchasing power to acquire large amounts of inventory at the beginning of the year and at very low prices.
- A **purchase point**, as it relates to inventory levels, is simply that point in time when an item should be reordered. This point is typically designated by one of two methods:

  1. As needed (just in time)
  2. Par level

- When you elect to use the **as needed,** or **just in time** method of determining inventory levels, you are basically purchasing food based on your prediction of unit sales and the sum of the ingredients (from standardized recipes) necessary to produce those sales.
- Foodservice operators may set predetermined purchase points, called **par levels,** for some items. When determining par levels, you must establish both minimum and maximum amounts required.

- As a rule, highly perishable items should be ordered on an as-needed basis, while items with a longer shelf life can often have their inventory levels set using a par level system.

4. Purchasing

- Purchasing is essentially a matter of determining the following:

    1. What should be purchased?
    2. What is the best price to pay?
    3. How can a steady supply be assured?

- A **product specification (spec)** is simply a detailed description of an ingredient or menu item. A spec is a way for you to communicate in a very precise way with a vendor so that your operation receives the *exact* item requested every time.
- Each menu item or ingredient should have its own spec.
- A foodservice specification generally consists of the following information:

    1. Product name or specification number
    2. Pricing unit
    3. Standard or grade
    4. Weight range/size
    5. Processing and/or packaging
    6. Container size
    7. Intended use
    8. Other information such as product yield

- The exact product name is important when writing specs. When developing the product specification, you may find it helpful to assign a number to the item as well as its name. This can be useful when, for example, many forms of the same ingredient or menu item may be purchased.
- The product name must be specific enough to clearly and precisely identify the item you wish to buy.
- A pricing unit may be established in terms of pounds, quarts, gallons, cases, or any other commonly used unit.
- Many food items are sold with varying degrees of quality or desirability. Because that is true, the U.S. Department of Agriculture, Bureau of Fisheries, and the Food and Drug Administration have developed standards for many food items.
- Weight range or size is important when referring to meats, fish, poultry, and some vegetables. **Count,** in the hospitality industry, is a term that is used to designate size.

- Processing and/or packaging refer to the product's state when you buy it. Also, the labor cost of washing, trimming, and otherwise preparing fresh products, must be considered when comparing their price to that of a canned or frozen product.

- "Farm to Fork" refers to the path food follows from those who grow or raise it, to those who will prepare and serve it. Ideally, this path would be short, to maximize freshness, minimize health risks and be environmentally friendly. For that reason many foodservice operators prefer to seek out and buy locally grown foods whenever possible.

- In addition to their freshness, locally grown foods are good for the environment because their lessened storing, shipping and packaging requirements mean they require less energy to transport and generate less solid waste from excessive packing materials. Reduced transportation and packaging costs often translate into lower prices charged to foodservice operators.

- Container size refers to the can size, number of cans per case, or weight of the container in which the product is delivered. An operator should spec container size.

- Different types of the same item are often used in the same foodservice operation, but in a variety of ways. That is why managers should spec the intended use of each product.

- Additional information such as product yield may be included in a specification if it helps the vendor understand exactly what you have in mind when your order is placed. **Product yield** is simply the amount of product that you will have remaining after cooking, trimming, portioning, or cleaning.

- The **best price** is more accurately stated as the lowest price that meets the long-term goals of both the foodservice operation and its vendor.

- The vehicle used to engage in comparison-shopping among vendors is called the **bid sheet.**

- After you have received bids from your suppliers, you can compare those bids on a **Price comparison sheet.**

- Bid sheets and price comparison sheets may be used to determine the specific vendor who can supply the lowest price, but they do not give enough information to determine the best price.

- Even with the use of product specifications, vendor dependability, quality of vendor service, and accuracy in delivery can be determining factors when attempting to determine the "best price."

- Buying strictly from the price comparison sheet may result in orders too small to meet a supplier's **minimum order requirement**, that is, the smallest order that can be placed with a vendor who delivers. If the minimum order requirement cannot be met using the lowest prices, then the manager may have to choose the supplier with the next highest price to fill a complete order.

- Your food salesperson can be one of your most important allies in controlling costs. Suppliers have a variety of prices based on the customer to whom they are quoting them.

- It is simply in the best interest of a supplier to give a better price to a high volume customer.
- **Cherry Pickers** is the term used by the suppliers to describe the customer who gets bids from multiple vendors, then buys only those items each vendor has "on sale" or for the lowest price.
- Operators who are slow to pay will find that the vendor has decided to add the extra cost of carrying their account to the price the operator pays for his or her products.
- Vendors can be a great source of information related to new products, cooking techniques, trends, and alternative product usage.
- Using one or perhaps two primary vendors tends to bring the average delivery size up, and should result in lower per-item prices. On the other hand, giving one vendor all of the operation's business can be dangerous and costly if the items to be purchased vary widely in quality and price.
- Staples and non-perishables are best purchased in bulk from one vendor. Orders for meats, produce, and some bakery products are best split among several vendors, perhaps with a primary and secondary vendor in each category so that you have a second alternative should the need arise.
- **Ethics** have been defined as the choices of proper conduct made by an individual in his or her relationships with others.
- Ethics come into play in purchasing products because of the tendency for some suppliers to seek an unfair advantage over the competition by providing "personal" favors to the buyer.
- A **daily inventory sheet** will have the items listed in your storage areas, their unit of purchase, and their par values pre-printed on the sheet. In addition, the form will have the following columns: on-hand, special order, and order amount.
- The par value is listed so that you know how much inventory you *should* have in storage at any given time.
- The amount to be ordered is calculated as follows:

Par Value – On-Hand x **Special Order = Order Amount**

- Regardless of your communication method, it is critical that you prepare a written **purchase order**, or record of what you have decided to buy. The purchase order (PO) should be made out in triplicate (3 copies).
  The written Purchase Order form should contain space for the following information:

  Purchase Order Information
  1. Item Name
  2. Spec #, if appropriate
  3. Quantity Ordered
  4. Quoted Price Per Unit
  5. Extension Price
  6. Total Price of Order
  7. Vendor Information
  8. Purchase Order Number
  9. Date Ordered
  10. Delivery Date
  11. Name of person who placed order
  12. Name of person who received order
  13. Delivery Instructions
  14. Comments

- The advantages of a written Purchase Order are many and include the following:

  1. Written verification of quoted price
  2. Written verification of quantity ordered
  3. Written verification of the receipt of all goods ordered
  4. Written and special instructions to the receiving clerk, as needed
  5. Written verification of conformance to product specification
  6. Written authorization to prepare vendor invoice for payment

5. Receiving

- It is wise for you to establish the purchasing and receiving functions so that one individual places the order, while another individual is responsible for verifying delivery and acceptance of the product.
- **Auditors** are individuals responsible for reviewing and evaluating proper operational procedures. They can determine the potential for fraud or theft.
- If it is not possible to have more than one person involved in the buying process, the work of the purchasing agent/receiving clerk must be carefully monitored by management to prevent fraud.
- Proper receiving demands:

  1. Proper location
  2. Proper tools and equipment
  3. Proper delivery schedules
  4. Proper training

- The receiving area must be large enough to allow for checking products delivered against both the delivery invoice (the seller's record) and the PO (the buyer's record).
- Accessibility to equipment required to move products to their proper storage area and to dispose of excess packaging is important. Make sure the area stays free of trash and clutter, as these make it too easy to hide delivered food items.
- Remember that the delivery person is also a potential thief.
- The receiving area should be kept extremely clean, since you do not want to contaminate incoming food, or provide a carrying vehicle for pests. The area should be well lit and properly ventilated.
- Receiving clerks should have the following equipment: scales, wheeled equipment, box cutter, thermometer, calculator, and records area.
- Scales should be of two types; those accurate to the fraction of a pound, and those accurate to the fraction of an ounce.
- Some operators demand that deliveries be made only at certain times; these are called **acceptance hours**.
- **Refusal hours** are the times that operators will not accept deliveries.
- Receiving clerks should be trained to verify the following product characteristics: weight, quantity, quality, and price.
- Receiving clerks should be required to weigh all meat, fish, and poultry delivered, with the exception of unopened Cryovac (sealed) packages.
- When an item is ordered by weight, it should be verified by weight.
- The counting of boxes, cases, barrels, etc. should be routine. The counting of individual items in a box, such as lemons should be done periodically, but the value of counting on a regular basis is questionable.
- No area is of greater concern to the operator than that of the appropriate quality of product delivered. Checking for quality means checking the entire shipment for conformance to specifications.
- In cases when the vendor is out of the spec item, clerks must know whether it is management's preference to accept a product of higher quality, lower quality, or no product as a substitute.
- Clerks need to be trained in two areas regarding pricing: matching PO unit price to invoice unit price, and verifying price extensions and total.
- When the person responsible for purchasing food places an order, the confirmed quoted price should be recorded on the PO.
- When a discrepancy is discovered, management should be notified immediately. The ethical manager is not happy with either an over-charge or an under-charge situation.
- If management notification is not possible, both the driver and the receiving clerk should initial the "Comment" section of the PO, showing the difference in the two prices.
- **Shorting** is the term used in the industry to indicate that an ordered item has not been delivered as promised.

- A **credit memo** is simply a formal way of notifying the vendor that an item listed on the original invoice is missing, and thus the value of that item should be deducted from the invoice total.
- Some operators deal with suppliers in such a way that a contract price is established. A **contract price** is simply an agreement between buyer and seller to hold the price of a product constant over a defined period of time.
- **Extended price** is simply the unit price multiplied by the number of units delivered.
- Never assume extensions are correct because a computer did them!
- If a supplier consistently shorts your operation, that supplier is suspect both in terms of honesty and lack of concern for your operation's long-term success.
- Training your receiving clerk to assess and evaluate quality products is a continuous process.
- Some large operations use a receiving record when receiving food.
- A receiving record generally contains the following information: name of supplier, invoice number, item description, unit price, number of units delivered, total cost, storage area, and date of activity.
- Receiving reports can be helpful if it is important to record where items are to be delivered, or have been delivered.

Part 2

6. Storage

- Remember that storage costs money, in terms of the space for items, and the money that is tied up in inventory items.
- In most establishments, the storage process consists of four parts: placing products in storage, maintaining product quality and safety, maintaining product security, and determining inventory value.
- Most often, in foodservice, the high perishability dictates that the same person responsible for receiving the items is the person responsible for their storage.
- The two storage methods used are LIFO and FIFO.
- When using the **LIFO** (last in, first out) method, the store-room operator intends to use the most recently delivered product before he or she uses any part of that same product previously on hand.
- **FIFO** (first in, first out) means that the operator intends to rotate stock in such a way that product already on hand is sold prior to the sale of more recently delivered products.
- FIFO is the preferred storage technique for most perishable and non-perishable items. Failure to implement a FIFO system of storage management can result in excessive product loss due to spoilage, shrinkage, and deterioration of quality.
- Some foodservice managers require the storeroom clerk to mark or tag each delivered item with the date of delivery.

- Some operators prefer to go even further when labeling some products for storage. These operators date the item and then also indicate the day (or hour) in which the product should be pulled from storage, thawed, or even discarded.
- Products are generally placed in one of three major storage areas: dry storage, refrigerated storage, or frozen storage.
- Dry storage areas should generally be maintained at a temperature ranging between 65°F and 75°F (18°C and 24°C).
- Shelving must be sturdy, easy to clean, and at least 6 inches above the ground to allow for proper cleaning beneath the shelving and to ensure proper ventilation.
- Dry goods should never be stored directly on the floor. Labels should face out for easy identification.
- Refrigerator temperatures should generally be maintained between 32°F (0°C) and 36°F (2°C). Refrigerators actually work by removing heat from the contents, rather than "making" food cold.
- Refrigerators should have easily cleaned shelving units that are at least six inches off the floor and are slotted to allow for good air circulation.
- Freezer temperatures should be maintained between 0°F and –10°F (–18°C and –23°C). What is usually called a freezer, however, is more properly a "frozen food storage unit."
- Frozen food holding units must be regularly maintained, a process that includes cleaning inside and out, and constant temperature monitoring to detect possible improper operation.
- Regardless of the storage type, food and related products should be stored neatly in some logical order.
- Food product quality rarely improves with increased storage time.
- The primary method for ensuring the quality of stored products is through proper product rotation and high standards of storeroom sanitation.
- Storage areas are excellent breeding grounds for insects, some bacteria, and also rodents. To protect against these hazards, you should insist on a regular cleaning of all storage areas.
- Refrigerators and frozen-food holding units remove significant amounts of stored product moisture, causing shrinkage in meats and produce and **freezer burn.** Freezer burn refers to deterioration in product quality resulting from poorly wrapped or stored items kept at freezing temperatures.
- Both refrigerators and frozen food holding units should be kept six to ten inches from walls to allow for the free circulation of air around, and efficient operation of, the units.
- Drainage systems in refrigerators should be checked at least weekly.
- In larger storage areas, hallways should be kept clear and empty of storage materials or boxes.
- Some employee theft is impossible to detect. Even the most sophisticated, computerized control system is not able to determine if an employee or vendor's employee walked into the produce walk-in and ate one green grape.
- Make it difficult to remove significant amounts of food from storage without authorization.

- Most foodservice operators attempt to control access to the location of stored products.
- It is your responsibility to see to it that the storeroom clerk maintains good habits in securing product inventory.
- As a general rule, if storerooms are to be locked, only one individual should have access during any shift.
- It is not possible to know your actual food expense without an accurate inventory.
- **Issuing** is the process of placing of products into the production system.
- Valuing, or establishing a dollar value for your entire inventory is achieved by using the following inventory value formula:

> **Item Amount** x **Item Value** = **Item Inventory Value**

- Item amount may be determined by counting the item, as in the case of cans, or by weighing items, as in the case of meats.

- If inventory amounts are overstated, or **padded inventory**, costs will appear artificially low until the proper inventory values are determined.
- Either the LIFO or FIFO method determines item value.
- When the LIFO method is used, the item's value is said to be the price paid for the least recent (oldest) addition to item amount.
- If the FIFO method is used, the item value is said to be the price paid for the most recent (newest) product on hand.
- FIFO is the more common method for valuing foodservice inventory.
- Inventory value is determined using a form similar to the **inventory valuation sheet** shown in Figure 3.22. The inventory valuation sheet should be completed each time the inventory is counted. It can be manually prepared or produced as part of an inventory evaluation software program.
- It is recommended that one person takes the actual physical inventory, and a different person extends the value of that inventory.
- A **physical inventory**, one in which the food products are actually counted, must be taken to determine your actual food usage.

7. Determining Actual Food Expense

- **Cost of food sold** is the dollar amount of all food actually sold, thrown away, wasted or stolen. It is computed as follows:

> **Beginning Inventory**
> **PLUS**
> **Purchases**
> **= Goods Available for Sale**
> **LESS**
> **Ending Inventory**
> **= Cost of Food Consumed**
> **LESS**
> **Employee Meals**
> **= Cost of Food Sold**

- **Beginning inventory** is the dollar value of all food on hand at the beginning of the accounting period.
- **Purchases** are the sum cost of all food purchased during the accounting period.
- **Goods available for sale** is the sum of the beginning inventory and purchases.
- **Ending inventory** refers to the dollar value of all food on hand at the end of the accounting period.
- **Cost of food consumed** is the actual dollar value of all food used, or consumed, by the operation.
- **Employee meal** cost is actually a labor-related, *not* food-related cost. Free or reduced-cost employee meals are a benefit much in the same manner as medical insurance or paid vacation.
- It is important to note that ending inventory for one accounting period becomes the beginning inventory figure for the next period.
- Food or beverage products may be transferred from one food service unit to another. For example, it is likely that fruits, juices, vegetables, and similar items are taken from the kitchen for use in the bar, while wine, sherry, and similar items may be taken from the bar for use in the kitchen.
- Transfers out of the kitchen are subtracted from the cost of food sold and transfers in to the kitchen are added to the cost of food sold.
- A foodservice operation's cost of food consumed is affected by a variety of factors. One such factor relates to the "source reduction" decisions made by the operation's suppliers. Where recycling occurs within the foodservice operation and seeks to reuse materials, "source reduction" is utilized by suppliers to minimize the amount of resources initially required to package, store and ship the items they sell. The result of effective source reduction is a lessened impact on the environment and lower product costs.
- Food cost percentage is both the traditional way of looking at food expense and generally the method used by most operators when preparing the profit and loss statement.
- The formula used to compute actual food cost percentage is as follows:

$$\frac{\text{Cost of Food Sold}}{\text{Food Sales}} = \text{Food Cost \%}$$

- **Food Cost %** represents that portion of food sales that was spent on food expenses.
- The physical inventory may be taken as often as desired to estimate the daily cost of food sold.
- Figure 3.26 illustrates a six-column form, which you can use for a variety of purposes. One of them is to estimate food cost % on a daily or weekly basis.

Six Column Food Cost % Estimate

$$1. \quad \frac{\text{Purchases Today}}{\text{Sales Today}} = \text{Cost \% Today}$$

$$2. \quad \frac{\text{Purchases to Date}}{\text{Sales to Date}} = \text{Cost \% to Date}$$

8. Technology Tools

- This chapter focused on managing food-related costs by controlling the areas of purchasing, receiving, storage, and issuing. There are a variety of software programs that are available that can assist in these areas such as:

  1. Recipe Software can maintain and cost standardized recipes as well as maintain and supply dietary information by portion.
  2. Menu Programs can create and print physical menus and even produce purchase orders based on selected menus.
  3. Purchasing Software can compare bids and make purchase recommendations based on best cost/best value.
  4. Receiving Software can prepare a daily receiving report and maintain receiving histories.
  5. Storage/Inventory Assessment Programs can maintain product inventory values by food category and even compute LIFO or FIFO inventory values.
  6. Cost of Goods Sold Programs can compare forecasted to actual cost of goods sold as well as maintain employee meal records.

- Perhaps it is in the area of managing food products, from their purchase to usage, that you can most effectively utilize the rapidly advancing technological tools available today.

Consider The Cost

Part One:

Billy DeGates is the new President of Big B's coffee shops, a chain of 15 units that competes directly with Starbucks. At this year's first quarterly meeting with his unit managers, he is surprised to find that one of the reasons they are having difficulty tracking their purchasing costs and easily reporting them on a weekly basis is that not all of their office computers have Microsoft "Excel" software installed on them.

"It would cost $200 per computer to buy it," says one manger, "so we were never authorized to purchase it."

"It doesn't have to cost that much," said another manager. "I have a real 'techie' kind of employee at my store that made a copy of Excel for me and loaded it on my computer. He's a whiz, and it works great. It didn't cost me anything. I can just have him make discs for everyone, and you can all install it yourself. Why should we buy 15 copies of Excel when we don't need to?"

1. Assume you were Billy. Would you allow the pirated software program to be illegally installed on the manager's computers?

2. Assume, for this illustration, that the action suggested by the unit manager was not actually illegal, and that it would not be detected by Microsoft. Utilizing the six step questioning process introduced in this chapter would you personally, at some point in the questioning process, decide the purchasing action proposed was unethical? If so, which steps would apply?

Answers:

Most students would quickly recognize that vendor "kickbacks" in the form of cash payments are unethical. The question of accepting supplier "gifts" such as complimentary tickets to concerts, the theater, or sporting events can be less clear. If a foodservice operation has an ethical guidelines policy, issues such as these are often addressed. This case, however, was designed to illustrate to students that a variety of ethical issues can face foodservice managers. In this situation, Billy must address "purchasing" an item some of his managers very likely believe can be pirated and copied because: 1) the seller is so big, 2) the theft will likely go undetected, and 3) the savings are significant. This ethical dilemma is one faced almost daily by students with easy online access to music, videos, and games that can often be downloaded with no payment to their producers. They will be familiar with the issue and may have strong feelings about it. Instructors may wish to point out the current legal environment related to such downloads.

The second portion of the case asks students to address the ethical issue of software piracy if it were NOT illegal. Using the ethical behavior model introduced in this chapter, students will make their own ethical determinations. Instructors may wish to point out the potential long-term damage of unethical behavior, both to the individual committing the act and to those who are treated in an unethical manner.

Part Two:

"Come on Gloria, give me a break. I'm already behind because my truck broke down this morning, and I've got people all over town calling my boss to scream about their deliveries. It wasn't my fault I'm late. I'm just the driver," said Monte.

Monte made deliveries for Raider Produce and was talking to Gloria, the receiving clerk for the High-Five Restaurant. The delivery he was making was a big one, and it was two hours late.

"You know, Gloria," Monte continued, "You guys take longer to accept a delivery than any other restaurant on my route. Nobody else inspects and weighs like you do. And you hardly ever find any problems. Look, I know it's a big delivery, but just this once can't you just sign the invoice and let me get going? I want to see my son's ball game, and I won't make it if you take forever to inspect this load."

"I don't know Monte," replied Gloria, "we've got procedures to follow here, and I'm supposed to use them every time."

"Look, just sign the ticket. If you find a problem later, I'll take care of it. I promise you," said Monte, who seemed to be increasingly flustered.

1. What do you think Gloria will most likely do about Monte's request that she speed up?
2. Assume you were this restaurant's owner. If you were personally accepting the delivery, what would you say to Monte?

Answers:

This case explores one of several very common problems encountered by receiving clerks. While the reasons for it may vary, there is continual pressure on these employees to "just sign" the invoice without doing a thorough inspection of the products being delivered. It is important for students to recognize that the quality of the raw ingredients they buy will never improve after they are delivered. The quality upon delivery is the quality that will ultimately be served to guests. When shortcuts in inspection are taken, problems will inevitably occur for the reasons detailed in this chapter.

The case asks students what they believe Gloria will do in response to the pressure from Monte, and student answers to that question will surely vary. The follow-up question, however, asks students to imagine what the restaurant's owner would say in response to Monte's request. It would be good to emphasize that the owner of the restaurant would undoubtedly want to insist upon a thorough inspection of the delivery. Students should be asked what they would want their own employee to do if, in fact, it were their own money paying for the items delivered by Raider Produce.

Apply What You Have Learned

Tonya Johnson is the Regional Manager for Old Town Buffets. Each of the five units she supervises is in a different town. Produce for each unit is purchased locally by each buffet manager. One day, Tonya gets a call from Danny Trevino, one of the buffet managers reporting to her. Danny states that one of the local produce suppliers he uses has offered Danny the use of season tickets to the local university football games. Danny likes football and would like to accept them.

1. Would you allow Danny to accept the tickets? Why or why not?

   Answer: The manager should not allow Danny to accept the tickets from the supplier. When selling products, some suppliers tend to seek an unfair advantage over the competition by providing "personal" favors to the buyer. In this case, the supplier probably knows that Danny loves football, so the supplier offered him season tickets, expecting him, in exchange, to increase his business with the supplier. It is important that foodservice organizations have a formal set of ethical codes of conduct for their buyers.

2. Would you allow your managers to accept a gift of any kind (including holiday gifts) from a vendor?

   Answer: As far as ethics are concerned, a gift of any kind would be the property of the business, not the buyer. However, all suppliers' offerings should be carefully reviewed and comply with a formal set of ethical guidelines for buyers of the company.

3. Draft a "gifts" policy that you would implement in your region. Would you be subject to the same policy?

   Answer: The gifts policy would be as follows:

   1. When a supplier offers any employee any kinds of gifts, the employee must report the gift offer to the manager immediately.
   2. If an employee accepts a gift without management's approval, the employee is subject to penalties set by the company for unethical buying procedures.
   3. Each employee must conform to and strictly follow the rules for ethical guidelines for buying.

   All persons in the company would be subject to the same policy, including Tonya.

Test Your Skills

1. Saint John's Hospital foodservice director, Herman Zindu, has a problem. He has the following information about his operation for the month of April, but has forgotten how to compute cost of food sold for the month. Use Herman's figures to compute actual cost of food sold for his operation.

Inventory on March 31st	$22,184.50

April Purchases

Meats	$11,501.00
Dairy	6,300.00
Fruits and Vegetables	9,641.00
All Other Foods	*32,384.00*

Number of Employees Eating Daily	85
Cost per Employee for Employee Meals	$1.25
Inventory on April 30th	$23,942.06

Could Herman have computed this figure if he had not taken a physical inventory on April 30th? Why or why not?

Inventory March 31			$22,184.50
April Purchases:			
Meats		$11,501.00	
Dairy		6,300.00	
Fruits and Vegetables		9,641.00	
All Others Foods		32,384.00	
Total Purchases		59,826.00	
No. of Employees Eating Daily	85		
Cost per Employee Meal	$1.25		
Inventory on April 30th			$23,942.06
Beginning Inventory	$22,184.50		
Purchases	59,826.00		
Goods Available for Sale	82,010.50		
Ending Inventory	23,942.06		
Cost of Food Consumed	58,068.44		
Employee Meals (30 days)	3,187.50		
Cost of Food Sold	54,880.94		

Answer: Herman could not have accurately computed the cost of food sold if he had not taken a physical inventory on April 30th. His cost would have been overstated.

2. "Fast Eddie" Green operates a restaurant in the casino town of Taloona. He is checking over the work of his assistant manager who has been newly hired. One of the jobs of the assistant manager is to complete daily the six column food cost estimate. "Fast Eddie" finds that, while the data are there for the first ten days of the accounting period, the form has not been completed. Complete the form for "Fast Eddie" so that he can go home.

Six-Column Form

Date: __1/1-1/10__

Weekday	PURCHASES		SALES		COST %	
	Today	To Date	Today	To Date	Today	To Date
1/1	$1,645.80	$1,645.80	$3,842.50	$3,842.50	42.8	42.8
1/2	2,006.40	3,652.20	2,970.05	6,812.55	67.6	53.6
1/3	1,107.20	4,759.40	2,855.20	9,667.75	38.8	49.2
1/4	986.24	5,745.64	3,001.45	12,669.20	32.9	45.4
1/5	1,245.60	6,991.24	3,645.20	16,314.40	34.2	42.9
1/6	2,006.40	8,997.64	4,850.22	21,164.62	41.4	42.5
1/7	0.00	8,997.64	6,701.55	27,866.17	0.0	32.3
1/8	1,799.90	10,797.54	3,609.20	31,475.37	49.9	34.3
1/9	851.95	11,649.49	2,966.60	34,441.97	28.7	33.8
1/10	924.50	12,573.99	3,105.25	37,547.22	29.8	33.5
Total	12,573.99		37,547.22		33.5	

3. Billie Mendoza is the purchasing manager for a medium-sized suite hotel with a restaurant and a banquet hall. She needs to create the food purchase orders for tomorrow, and she wants to make sure that she is getting the best price for the best quality and service. At the beginning of this week, Billie received bids on produce items from Village Produce, City Produce, and Country Produce. She has listed these prices in the following price comparison sheet.

    a. Identify the best bid price and best company for each of Billie's produce items. (Spreadsheet hint: Use the MIN function in the **Best Bid $** column.)

Price Comparison Sheet

Item	Description	Unit	Village Produce	City Produce	Country Produce	Best Bid $	Best Company Quote	Last Price Paid
Avocados	48 ct.	Case	$61.80	$60.30	$59.46	$59.46	Country	$57.94
Cauliflower	12 ct.	Case	12.80	12.90	13.27	12.80	Village	13.26
Cucumbers	Medium	Case	11.10	11.52	10.91	10.91	Country	11.34
Grapes	Red Seedless	Lug	19.32	19.50	19.14	19.14	Country	18.72
Lettuce	Green Leaf, 24 ct.	Case	9.53	9.84	10.27	9.53	Village	10.02
Lettuce	Romaine, 24 ct.	Case	17.75	17.82	18.22	17.75	Village	18.10
Pears	D'Anjou	Case	20.82	20.58	20.64	20.58	City	20.62
Peppers	Green Bell, Med.	Case	8.30	8.38	9.28	8.30	Village	9.02
Pineapples	7 ct.	Case	10.50	10.38	10.68	10.38	City	10.08
Potatoes	B Reds	50# Bag	15.06	14.82	14.88	14.82	City	14.98
Potatoes	Peeled, Large	25# Bag	17.52	17.22	17.28	17.22	City	17.18
Squash	Yellow #2	30# Case	8.55	8.71	8.98	8.55	Village	9.10
Strawberries	Driscoll	Flat	18.29	18.06	17.10	17.10	Country	18.30

59

b. Now that Billie knows which vendors have the best prices, she decides to take the daily inventory to find out what she needs to order for tomorrow. Her par value, on-hand, and special order requirements are as follows. Help Billie determine the amount of each item she needs to order. (Spreadsheet hint: Use the ROUNDUP function in the **Order Amount** column.)

Item	Description	Unit	Par Value	On Hand	Special Order	Order Amount
Avocados	48 ct.	Case	6	2	3	7
Cauliflower	12 ct.	Case	5	1		4
Cucumbers	Medium	Case	3	0		3
Grapes	Red Seedless	Lug	4	1		3
Lettuce	Green Leaf, 24 ct.	Case	5	2	4	7
Lettuce	Romaine, 24 ct.	Case	3	0.5		3
Pears	D'Anjou	Case	3	1		2
Peppers	Green Bell, Med.	Case	7	2	5	10
Pineapples	7 ct.	Case	4	0		4
Potatoes	B Reds	50# Bag	3	0.5		3
Potatoes	Peeled, Large	25# Bag	4	1	4	7
Squash	Yellow #2	30# Case	5	2	2	5
Strawberries	Driscoll	Flat	3	1.5		2

c. Next, Billie needs to create the purchase orders for tomorrow. Help her create the correct purchase order for Village Produce based on her inventory needs (part b) and the bid prices for Village Produce located on the price comparison worksheet (part a).

		Purchase Order			
Supplier				**Purchase Order**	
Company Name:	Village Produce			P.O. Number	456
Street Address:	123 Somewhere			Order Date:	1/1
City, State, Zip:	Village, CA 12345			Delivery Date:	1/2
Phone Number:	555-5555			Phone Number:	555-5557
Fax Number:	555-5556			Fax Number:	555-5558
E-Mail:	Village@isp.org			E-mail:	Billie@isp.org
Contact:	Mr. Green			Buyer:	Ms. Mendoza
Item	**Description**	**Unit**	**Quantity**	**Unit Price $**	**Extension**
Cauliflower	12 ct.	Case	4	$12.80	$51.20
Lettuce	Green Leaf, 24 ct.	Case	7	9.53	66.71
Lettuce	Romaine, 24 ct.	Case	3	17.75	53.25
Peppers	Green Bell, Med.	Case	10	8.30	83.00
Squash	Yellow #2	30# Case	5	8.55	42.75
Total					296.91

4. Loralei operates the foodservice for a large elementary school. She buys produce from Shady Tree Produce Company. Wayne, Shady Tree's owner, makes many errors when he prepares invoices for his customers, but he is the only vendor who has the ability to deliver daily. Loralei needs daily delivery. Because she knows Wayne is careless with the invoices, Loralei checks each one carefully. For Monday, Loralei needs the items listed below.

Monday Order

Item	Unit price	Number of Cases Needed
Tomatoes	$18.50	3
Potatoes	$12.90	6
Carrots	$18.29	4

Using this information, complete her Purchase Order for Monday below.

Purchase Order

Supplier				Purchase Order	
Company Name:	Shady Tree			P.O. Number	123
Street Address:	123 Somewhere			Order Date:	1/1
City, State, Zip:	Village, TX 12345			Delivery Date:	1/2
Phone Number:	555-5555			Phone Number:	555-5557
Fax Number:	555-5556			Fax Number:	555-5558
E-Mail:	Shady@isp.org			E-Mail:	Lora@isp.org
Contact:	Wayne			Buyer:	Loralei
Item	**Description**	**Unit**	**Quantity**	**Unit Price $**	**Extension**
Tomatoes	4X5, Layered	Case	3	$18.50	$55.50
Potatoes	Peeled, Large	Case	6	12.90	$77.40
Carrots	Julienne, 5# bags	Case	4	18.29	$73.16
Total					$206.06

Upon delivery, Loralei checks her invoice from Wayne to see if he has, once again, made any errors.

Review the following invoice totals.

Shady Tree Produce Company Invoice for Monday Order

Item	Unit price	Number Delivered	Extended Price
Tomatoes	$18.50	3	$ 55.55
Potatoes	$19.20	6	$115.20
Carrots	$18.92	4	$ 75.68
Total Amount Due			$256.43

Does the invoice contain errors? If so, what are they? What is the total amount of "error" on the invoice, if any? How can Loralei detect such errors in the future?

Answer: Yes, the invoice contains errors. The price of potatoes was quoted as $12.90 but invoiced at $19.20, causing the extended price to be $115.20. Also, the price of the carrots was quoted as $18.29 but invoiced at $18.92, causing the extended price to be $75.68. Both errors were due to the transposition of numbers. Also, the extension of tomatoes should have been $55.50, but was invoiced at $55.55. These errors caused the invoice total to be stated incorrectly. The total amount of the error was $50.37.

Loralei should first point out the errors to the supplier, and request that the supplier pay more attention to the invoices in the future. Loralei then must train her receiving clerk to check all invoices against purchases orders for accuracy during the receiving process. Errors must then be reported immediately to the purchasing manager so that a credit memorandum can be processed, if necessary.

5. Barry Stiller is the assistant manager of the Pine Tree Grill. The Pine Tree is one food outlet located at the Great Bear Water Park and Resort. Each Sunday morning he is required to submit the dollar value of his inventory to his Food and Beverage Director. This data forms the basis for the F&B department's cost of food sold for the previous week. The Food and Beverage Director has given Barry a weekly food cost % goal of 28%. She has promised Barry a monthly bonus if he can stay at or under his food cost % goal. Complete Barry's Inventory Valuation Sheet below and calculate his food cost %.

Inventory Valuation Sheet

Unit Name: Pine Tree Grill   Inventory Date: Sunday 3/8
Counted By: Barry Stiller   Extended By: Barry Stiller

Item	Unit	Item Amount	Item Value	Inventory Value
Rib Eye Steaks (10 oz.)	units	44	$8.50	$374.00
Rib Eye Steaks (16 oz.)	units	34	$11.50	$391.00
New York Strip Steak	lb	28	$7.75	$217.00
Corned Beef	lb	22.5	$8.25	$185.63
Rib Roast	lb	60	$6.75	$405.00
Hamburger	lb	15	$2.75	$41.25
Chicken Breasts	lb	53	$2.50	$132.50
Sausage Links	pound	25.5	$2.40	$61.20
Bacon	case	3.5	$62.00	$217.00
Beef Base	jar	17	$8.00	$136.00
Tomatoes (4x5)	case	2	$25.00	$50.00
Bananas	case	3	$15.00	$45.00
Oranges	case	2.5	$30.00	$75.00
Lemons	case	2	$28.00	$56.00
Lettuce	case	3.5	$26.30	$92.05
Bread	unit	7	$2.50	$17.50
Rice	bags	4	$12.00	$48.00
Total				$2,544.13

Beginning Inventory 3/1	$2,735.70	
Purchases	$5,348.53	
Goods Available for Sale	$8,084.23	
Ending Inventory 3/8	$2,544.13	
Transfers Out	$470.40	
Transfers In	$336.60	
Cost of Food Consumed	$5,406.31	
Employee Meals	$740.00	
Cost of Food Sold	$4,666.31	

Sales	$17,538.46
Food Cost %	26.6%

Did Barry meet his food cost percentage goal for the week? Is he doing a good job at controlling his costs and managing his inventory? Is Barry likely to reach his monthly goal and receive his bonus?

Answer: Barry did meet his food cost percentage goal for the week. He is doing a good job at controlling his costs and managing his inventory. If he continues to perform well, he will likely receive his bonus.

6. Spike Dykes operates the student foodservice in a dormitory at Clairmont College. Spike is interested in calculating his "Food Cost Per Student Meal Served". Data about his costs and meals served for the Spring semester can be found in the table below, but some of it is missing. Help Spike complete the table, and then answer the questions he has about his operation.

	Jan	Feb	March	April	May	Total
Beginning Inventory	$22,500	$21,750	$26,500	$25,500	$16,000	$112,250
Purchases	$65,000	$64,750	$63,000	$64,500	$64,300	$321,550
Goods Available for Sale	$87,500	$86,500	$89,500	$90,000	$80,300	$433,800
Ending Inventory	$21,750	$26,500	$25,500	$16,000	$12,000	$101,750
Cost of Food Consumed	$65,750	$60,000	$64,000	$74,000	$68,300	$332,050
Employee Meals	$5,750	$5,500	$5,250	$5,000	$4,850	$26,350
Cost of Food Sold	$60,000	$54,500	$58,750	$69,000	$63,450	$305,700
Meals Served	20,750	20,100	21,500	21,250	19,000	102,600
Cost Per Meal	$2.89	$2.71	$2.73	$3.25	$3.34	$2.98

What was Spike's:

a. Cost of Food Sold in:
    February
    March
    May

Answers: February = $54,500; March = $58,750; May = $63,450

b. Cost Per Meal in:
    January
    February
    March
    April
    May

Answers:
January = $2.89; February = $2.71; March = $2.73; April = $3.25; May = $3.34

c. Total Cost of Employee Meals for the spring semester?   **Answer:** $26,350

d. Total Cost of Food Sold for the spring semester?   **Answer:** $305,700

e. Average Cost per Meal Served for the spring semester?   **Answer:** $2.98

7. Because drive through, take away, and delivery service constitutes increasingly large proportions of many foodservice operation's sales, more managers are considering adding paper and packaging costs to cost of food calculations. Assume you were managing a foodservice operation with significantly increasing "off-premise" food sales.

What would be some advantages of including "packaging" (containers, wrappings and the like) as a cost of food?

What could be some disadvantages of such an approach?

In addition, what could you do to ensure that you are following "green" practices with regard to packaging?

Answer: This question is designed to demonstrate that effective recordkeeping methods can sometimes change as a business's needs change. Those in favor of including paper/packaging costs would point to the real (and increasing) expenses incurred for these items. Of course, monitoring and managing these costs is important.

Those opposed would point out that dish washing costs (for dine-in customers) are not included in Cost of Food Sold calculations, thus an inconsistency would arise if packaging goods were included in food cost calculations. This is an excellent time to point out to students the importance of utilizing the Uniform System of Accounts (introduced in Chapter 1) as a guide to navigating the sometimes "gray" areas of cost accounting.

Exam Questions

Multiple Choice
Choose the letter of the best answer to the questions listed below.

1. Identify which of the following is typically listed on a purchase order form.
   a. Date ordered
   b. Item name and quoted price
   c. Vendor Information
   d. All of the above
   e. Only a. and b. above
   Correct answer is d (See: Preparing The Purchase Order)

2. Inventory levels are not determined by which of the following:
   a. Operating calendar
   b. Product name or specification number
   c. Storage capacity
   d. Potential savings from increased purchase size
   e. Vendor delivery schedule
   Correct answer is b (See: Determining Inventory Levels)

3. What is the formula for calculating the popularity index of a menu item?
   a. Total number of a specific menu item sold / total number of all menu items sold
   b. Total number of all menu items sold / Total number of a specific menu item sold
   c. Popularity of menu item X number of menu items
   d. Popularity of menu item / number of menu items
   e. None of the above
   Correct answer is a (See: Menu Item Forecasting)

4. Which of the following are factors that influence the number of guests you can expect to serve on any given day?
   a. Competition and weather
   b. Quality of service and operational consistency
   c. Your own promotions and your competitors' promotions
   d. All of the above
   e. Only a. and b. above
   Correct answer is d (See: Menu Item Forecasting)

5. Standardized Recipes should contain which of the following:
    a. Item name and ingredient list
    b. Number of servings and portion size
    c. Cooking time and temperature
    d. All of the above
    e. Only a. and c. above
    Correct answer is d (See: Standardized Recipes)

6. The textbook listed several common excuses for not using standard recipes. Which of the following describes these excuses?
    a. Accurate purchasing is possible without the existence and use of standardized recipes.
    b. It is easy to match food used to cash sales without standardized recipes.
    c. They take too long to write up and they are too hard to read.
    d. All of the above
    e. Only b. and c. above
    Correct answer is c (See: Standardized Recipes)

7. Purchasing ethics were discussed in the textbook. Which of the following questions is part of the self-test?
    a. Is it legal?
    b. Does it hurt anyone?
    c. Would I care if it happened to me?
    d. Would I publicize my action?
    e. All of the above
    Correct answer is e (See: Purchasing Ethics)

8. Calculate the cost of food sold based on the following information: Beginning inventory $5,000, ending inventory $2,000, purchases $1,500, employee meals $500.
    a. $1,000
    b. $2,500
    c. $4,000
    d. $4,500
    e. Cannot be determined
    Correct answer is c (See: Determining Actual Food Expense)

9. In the receiving area proper training should be in which of the following areas?
    a. Quantity and quality measurements
    b. Price measurement
    c. Weight measurement
    d. All of the above
    e. Only a. and c. above
    Correct answer is d (See: Proper Training)

10. When using the _____ storage system, the storeroom operator intends to use the most recently delivered product before he or she uses any part of that same product previously on hand.
   a. FIFO
   b. LIFO
   c. Both a. and b. above
   d. None of the above
   Correct answer is b (See: Methods of Storage)

11. The textbook discussed two methods for changing a recipe to produce a different number of portions. Which of the following best describes these methods?
   a. The factor method and the percentage technique
   b. FIFO and LIFO methods
   c. The six-column method and the inventory value method
   d. None of the above
   Correct answer is a (See: Standardized Recipes)

12. To assure a steady supply it is important that a foodservice operator remember which of the following points?
   a. Suppliers have many prices, not just one.
   b. Suppliers reward volume guests.
   c. Cherry pickers are serviced last.
   d. Vendors can help reduce costs.
   e. All of the above
   Correct answer is e (See: How Can a Steady Supply Be Assured?)

Questions 13 and 14 are based on the following information:

Menu Item	Number Sold	Popularity Index	Forecast # Guests	Forecast Item Sold
Steamed Fish	75			
Seafood Hot Pot	125			
Vegetable Lo Mein	100			
Total			500	

13. What is the popularity index for Vegetable Lo Mein?
   a. 0.2500
   b. 0.3333
   c. 0.4167
   d. 0.5000
   e. Cannot be determined
   Correct answer is b (See: Menu Item Forecasting)

14. Based on your calculations, what is the approximate number of Seafood Hot Pots that will be sold (please round up to the nearest whole item)?
    a. 125
    b. 167
    c. 209
    d. 500
    e. Cannot be determined
    Correct answer is c (See: Menu Item Forecasting)

15. Please calculate the order amount given the following information: par level 6 cases, currently on hand 2 cases, special order 4 cases.
    a. 6 cases
    b. 8 cases
    c. 10 cases
    d. 12 cases
    e. Cannot be determined
    Correct answer is b (See: Daily Inventory Sheet)

16. A variety of factors come together to influence the number of guests you can expect to serve on any specific day. Which is not one of these factors?
    a. Competition
    b. Quality of service
    c. Weather
    d. Number of employees
    Correct answer is d (See: Menu Item Forecasting)

17. What is the formula for calculating the order amount?
    a. Par value – on hand + special order
    b. Par value + special order
    c. On hand + special order
    d. None of the above
    Correct answer is a (See: Daily Inventory Sheet)

18. What method of storage is widely used among the restaurant industry?
    a. LIFO
    b. Inventory Valuation
    c. Padded Inventory
    d. FIFO
    Correct answer is d (See: Methods of Storage)

19. Calculate food cost percentage given the following information: Beginning inventory = $24,000, Ending inventory = $18,000, Purchases = $21,000, Employee Meals = $5000, Transfers from Kitchen = $2,000, Transfers to Kitchen = $2,500, Sales = $75,000.
    a. 28.7%
    b. 30.0%
    c. 33.3%
    d. 27.3%
    e. None of the above
    Correct answer is b (See: Determining Actual Food Expense)

20. Cherry Pickers are
    a. People that grow their own fruits and vegetables for use in their restaurants
    b. A vendor who ignores his small clients while servicing his larger accounts
    c. Buyers who get bids from multiple vendors, then buy only those items each vendor has on sale or for the lowest price
    d. None of the above
    Correct answer is c (See: How Can a Steady Supply Be Assured?)

21. Which of the following software programs can assist in areas like reporting par stock levels, reporting daily storeroom issues, reporting daily product usage, maintaining perpetual inventory, and computing LIFO or FIFO inventory values?
    a. Storage/Inventory Assessment Programs
    b. Receiving Software
    c. Purchasing Software
    d. Cost of Goods Sold Programs
    Correct answer is a (See: Technology Tools)

22. Please calculate the order amount given the following information: par level 10 cases, currently on hand 6 cases, special order 4 cases.
    a. 4 cases
    b. 8 cases
    c. 10 cases
    d. 20 cases
    e. Cannot be determined
    Correct answer is b (See: Daily Inventory Sheet)

True/False
Choose the letter of the best answer to the questions listed below.

23. Standardized recipes ensure that customers receive the same type and quality of an item every time they order that item.
    a. True
    b. False
    Correct answer is a (See: Standardized Recipes)

24. Working stock refers to the amount of inventory that will be used during a particular shift or work period.
    a. True
    b. False
    Correct answer is b (See: Inventory Control)

25. Foodservice operators should not order in quantities so large that they overload storage capacity, no matter how much money they would save.
    a. True
    b. False
    Correct answer is a (See: Determining Inventory Levels)

26. There are no costs associated with purchasing in extra-ordinary large quantities—if you have the room, you will always save money by buying in bulk.
    a. True
    b. False
    Correct answer is b (See: Value of Inventory Dollars to the Operator)

27. Foodservice operators typically use either the "as needed" or "par level" methods of ordering inventory.
    a. True
    b. False
    Correct answer is a (See: Setting the Purchase Point)

28. A product spec is simply a detailed description of an ingredient or menu item.
    a. True
    b. False
    Correct answer is a (See: What Should Be Purchased?)

29. An operator's food purveyor can be his or her best ally in controlling costs.
    a. True
    b. False
    Correct answer is a (See: How Can a Steady Supply Be Assured?)

30. Foodservice operators who give all their business to one supplier will probably see a rise in their cost.
    a. True
    b. False
    Correct answer is b (See: How Can a Steady Supply Be Assured?)

31. The cost of food consumed is the dollar amount of all food sold.
    a. True
    b. False
    Correct answer is b (See: Determining Actual Food Expense)

32. The shelf life is the amount of time that a particular food item is stored before it is used.
    a. True
    b. False
    Correct answer is b (See: Determining Inventory Levels)

33. The smallest order that can be placed with a vendor who delivers is called the maximum order amount.
    a. True
    b. False
    Correct answer is b (See: What is the Best Price to Pay?)

34. Recipe Software programs can assist chefs with suggested selling prices and alternative cooking methods.
    a. True
    b. False
    Correct answer is a (See: Technology Tools)

35. Farm to Fork refers to the path food follows from those who grow or raise it, to those who will prepare and serve it. Ideally, this path would be short, to maximize freshness, minimize health risks and be environmentally friendly.
    a. True
    b. False
    Correct answer is a (See: Green and Growing)

36. Source reduction is utilized by suppliers to minimize the amount of resources initially required to package, store and ship the items they sell.
    a. True
    b. False
    Correct answer is a (See: Green and Growing)

Chapter 4

Managing the Cost of Beverages

Learning Outcomes

At the conclusion of this chapter, you will be able to:

- Use sales histories and standardized drink recipes to develop a beverage purchase order.
- Compute the dollar value of bar transfers both to and from the kitchen.
- Compute an accurate cost of goods sold percentage for beer, wine, and spirits.

Lecture Outline

1. Serving Alcoholic Beverages

- **Alcoholic beverages** are those products that are meant for consumption as a beverage, and that contain a significant amount of ethyl alcohol.
- Alcoholic beverages are generally classified as beer, wine, or spirits.
- **Beer** is a fermented beverage made from grain and flavored with hops.
- **Wine** is a fermented beverage made from grapes, fruits, or berries.
- **Spirits** are fermented beverages that are distilled to increase the alcohol content of the product.
- These products will be specified, ordered, received, and stored much like food products. However, there are control issues that are much more difficult to handle.
- Such controls must be modified to meet the characteristic and inherent increased responsibility created by the sale of alcoholic beverages.
- There are two primary classifications of establishments that serve alcohol: restaurants that use it as an accompaniment to food, and those locations whose primary offering is alcohol.
- In moderate doses, ethyl alcohol is a mild tranquilizer; in excessive doses, it can become toxic.
- While the special requirements involved in serving alcoholic beverages are many, the control of beverage costs is similar to that of food-related costs.
- **Dramshop laws**, passed in many states, shift the liability for acts committed by an individual under the influence of alcohol from that individual to the server or operation that supplied the intoxicating beverage.

- In all states, the sale of alcoholic beverages is regulated either by the licensing of establishments that are allowed to sell alcoholic beverages **(license states)** or by direct control and sale of the products by the state **(control states)**.

2. Forecasting Beverage Sales

- Due to the limitless possibilities, forecasting customer item selection is difficult.
- Forecasting beer sales is basically the same as forecasting any regular menu item. By using sales histories, operators can determine what percentage of their customers will order beer, and which kind of beer and in what packaging format they will prefer their beer.
- **Keg beer** is also known as **draft beer**, or beer in a form of packaging in which the beer is shipped to you in multi-gallon units for bulk sale.
- Forecasting wine sales is divided into two parts: forecasting bottled-wine sales and forecasting wine-by-the-glass sales.
- When forecasting sales by the bottle, treat a bottled wine just like an individual menu item.
- While bottled wine is not highly perishable, all wine products are perishable to some degree; thus, excessive inventory of some wine types can result in increased product loss through oxidation (deterioration) and/or theft.
- Generally, forecasting the sale of **house wines**, includes those wines served to a guest who does not stipulate a specific brand when ordering, as well as those named wines offered by the glass.
- While the number of guests who order a mixed drink can be tracked, the exact item the guests request is very difficult to determine.
- One method categorizes all drinks based on the spirit that forms the base of the drink.
- Spirit sales can also be tracked by generic product name, specific product name, or specific drink requested.
- Obviously, different methods have varying degrees of accuracy. Operators must decide which is best for their establishment based on the cost effectiveness involved.

3. Standardized Drink Recipes and Portions

- Control is more important at the bar than in the kitchen because the potential for waste and employee theft is greater.
- However, it is still unrealistic to expect a bartender to consult a standardized recipe for every drink.
- Operators should remember: beverage operations are subject to tax audits, beverage operations can be closed down for violations, employees may bring in their own products to sell and keep sales revenue, and detecting the disappearance of small amounts of beverage products is very difficult.

- The following is the beverage cost % formula:

> **Cost of Beverage Sold**
> **Beverage Sales**　　　　= **Beverage Cost %**

- While standardized recipes (including step-by-step prep methods) may only be necessary for only a few types of drinks, standardized recipes that detail the quantity of beverage product predetermined by management as appropriate should be strictly adhered to.
- To insure that liquor is poured accurately, a **jigger**, a tool for measuring liquid, or an automated device programmed to dispense these predetermined amounts should be used.
- A standardized recipe sheet should be prepared for each drink item for costing purposes.

4. Purchasing Beverage Products

- While food products only require one level of quality per item, several levels of quality are chosen for alcoholic beverages.
- Beer is the most highly perishable of beverage products, with a **pull date**, or expiration date of only a few months. Operators must, therefore, carefully select brand and packaging methods.
- Generally, geographic location, clientele, ambiance, and menu help determine what beer product will be selected.
- Bartenders should maintain a beer **product request log** so that guest requests that cannot be filled are noted and monitored by management.
- Beer is typically sold in cans, bottles, or kegs.
- Draft beer (beer from kegs) is often the preferred choice and cheaper for operators to serve. However, special equipment and serving techniques are required.
- The shelf life of keg beer is the shortest of all packaging types, ranging from 30 to 45 days for an untapped keg, that is, one that has not yet been opened by the bartender, and even fewer days for a **tapped** (opened) keg.
- Wine must also be selected according to product and packaging.
- Operators generally sell wine by the glass, bottle, and split or half bottle.
- If wine is also purchased for cooking, it will be bought from the beverage wholesaler also, but generally not of the same quality as that purchased for drinking.
- As a good manager, you will build a **wine list**, the term used to describe your menu of wine offerings, that fits your own particular operation and guest expectations.
- In developing a **wine list**, operators must offer choices for guests who want to spend a lot or a little.
- A **vintner** is a wine producer.
- Wines that either complement the food or, in the case of a bar, are popular with the guests must be available.

- However, avoid the temptation to offer too many wines on a wine list.
- Wait staff should be trained to be knowledgeable but not intimidating to guests.
- Generally, if operators are having trouble selling wine, the difficulty lies in the delivery of the product rather than with the product selected.
- Distilled spirits have an extremely long shelf life; therefore, a wrong purchase is not usually a disaster.
- While packaging is not a major concern of the operator selecting a spirit product, brand quality is crucial.
- In general, operators will select spirits in two major categories, well and call liquors.
- **Well liquors** are those spirits that are poured when the customer does not specify a particular brand name when ordering.
- **Call liquors** are those requested by brand name; extremely expensive call liquors are sometimes referred to as **premium liquors**.
- Operators generally charge a higher price for call or **premium liquors**.
- Remember, guests who order well liquors may be price conscious, but that does not mean they are not quality conscious also.
- Quality spirit products at fair prices build customer loyalty.
- Depending on the state and county, special laws may influence how beverage purchases are to be made or paid for.
- The goal in purchasing beverages is to have an adequate, but not excessive, amount of product on hand at all times.
- Available organic spirits products include Vodka, Gin, Tequila, Scotch and Rum. While more expensive than non-organic versions of the same product, these items are increasingly available for purchase from main-line beverage distributors. Organic wines and beers are also becoming increasingly common.
- Concerns about costs can plague green beverage initiatives because organic product costs are historically higher, and in the past, the number of interested customers has been smaller. Today, however, using seasonal and local produce and juices for drink production can help moderate every operation's costs while increasing quality.
- A **broken case** occurs when several different brands or products are used to completely fill the case.
- As a general rule, wine, beer, and spirits are purchased by the case.

5. Receiving Beverage Products

- Since beverage products do not vary in quality, as does food, skill required to receive beverages is somewhat less than what is needed for receiving food.
- As with food, the receiving clerk needs a proper location, tools, and equipment.
- Proper delivery schedules must be maintained.
- When matching the purchase order to the vendor invoice, only quantity ordered and price must be verified.

- If beer is **fresh dated**, that is, a date is stamped on the product to indicate its freshness, very little inspection is required to ensure that the product is exactly what was ordered.
- Key beverage receiving checkpoints are: correct brand, correct bottle size, no broken bottles, freshness dates (beer), correct vintage (wine), correct unit price, correct price extension, and correct invoice total.
- If errors are detected, a credit memo should be filled out and signed by both the delivery person and the receiving clerk.
- A credit memo is an addendum to the vendor's delivery invoice that reconciles differences between the purchase order and the delivery invoice.

6. Storing Beverage Products

- Storage areas should be clean, free of infestation, and large enough to allow for easy rotation of stock.
- Security is crucial. A **two-key system** is often used to control access to beverage storage areas. The individual responsible for the beverage area has one key while the other key is kept in a sealed envelope in a secured area. In the event of emergency, the envelope can be opened.
- Spirits should be stored in a relatively dry storage area between 70 and 80°F (21 to 27°C).
- Beer in kegs or unpasteurized containers should be stored at refrigeration temperatures of 36 to 38°F (2 to 3°C).
- Canned beer should be covered when stored to eliminate the chance of dust or dirt settling on the rims of the cans.
- Pasteurized beer should be stored in a cool dark room at 50 to 70°F (10 to 21°C).
- Product rotation is critical if beer is to be served at its maximum freshness.
- The three components critical to wine storage are temperature, light, and cork condition.
- Generally, wines should be stored at a temperature of 50 to 65°F (10 to 18°C).
- Heat is an enemy of effective wine storage.
- When storing wine, it should be exposed only to the minimum amount of light necessary.
- The cork protects wine from its greatest enemy, oxygen. **Oxidation** occurs when oxygen comes in contact with bottled wine; you can detect a wine that has been overly oxidized because it smells somewhat like vinegar. Oxidation deteriorates the quality of bottled wines.
- Wine should always be stored in such a way, usually on its side, so that the cork remains in contact with the wine to stay moist.
- Storage should keep the cork, and thus the wine, cool, dark and moist.

7. Bar Transfers

- The great majority of product cost related to bar operations is alcoholic beverages.

- As far as spirits are concerned, nonalcoholic food products may be served as a part of the drink order and must be transferred from the kitchen to bar.
- If transfers are not controlled and recorded, the restaurant's food cost percentage will be artificially inflated while the total beverage cost percentage in the bar will be understated.
- Likewise, bar items may be used in the kitchen and must also be properly noted.
- The control procedure for kitchen and bar transfers is actually quite simple, requiring only consistency.

8. Computing Cost of Beverages

- When computing the beverage cost percentage, there is only one difference from computing the food cost percentage; there is no equivalent for "employee meals" since employees should not be drinking.

> **Beginning Inventory**
> **PLUS**
> **Purchases**
> **= Goods Available for Sale**
> **LESS**
> **Ending Inventory**
> **LESS**
> **Transfers from Bar**
> **PLUS**
> **Transfers to Bar**
> **= Cost of Beverage Sold**

9. Special Features of Liquor Inventory

- Unopened containers of beer, wine, and spirits can, of course, be counted. Opened containers, however, must be valued also. Three inventory methods are commonly in use to accomplish this goal. They are:

  1. Weight
  2. Count
  3. Measure

10. Sales Mix

- **Sales mix** is defined as the series of guest purchasing decisions that result in a specific food or beverage cost percentage.
- Guests can contribute to major changes in the food or beverage cost percentages, due to sales mix.

- To analyze the beverage sales mix, the item % of total beverage sales must be calculated, as follows:

Item Dollar Sales	
Total Beverage Sales	**= Item % of Total Beverage Sales**

11. Technology Tools

- For those operations that sell a significant amount of alcoholic beverage products, there are a variety of programs designed to discourage theft and carefully monitor product sales and expenses.
- In fact, the software and hardware available to help you in the beverage service area is generally more sophisticated than that found in most food-related areas.
- Programs available in the beverage area include those that can help you:

1. Monitor product sales.
2. Monitor product (inventory) usage.
3. Calculate actual and targeted pour percentages.
4. Adjust product costs for happy hours and specials, as well as product transfers to and from the kitchen.
5. Maintain adequate levels of product inventory.
6. Establish par stock quantities and values.
7. Generate purchase orders.
8. Schedule employees based on forecasted sales levels.
9. Create and print customized wine lists and specials menus.
10. Maintain sales histories.
11. Maintain drink recipe files.
12. Project the impact of sales mix on beverage cost percentages.

- It is important to realize that some bar-related software may be dependent on specific and sometimes expensive automated beverage dispensing systems.
- Other software is either stand-alone or designed to operate in conjunction with many of the basic POS systems currently on the market.

Consider The Cost

"You really need to add the Merlot, the Cabernet Franc, and the Chenin Blanc," said Guy Smiley, the salesperson for Abboit Wines. "Look, you have a Texas theme. These are Texas wines from Pheasant Ridge winery. We just got them in. They are really modestly priced. Your customers will love them. You add these wines, and you'll see your wine sales increase, I'll promise you that!"

Guy was attempting to convince Judith Fornes, manager of the Austin Limits steakhouse, that she should significantly increase the number of wines offered to the guests of the restaurant, which was located in a suburb of Atlanta, Georgia.

"I don't know Guy," replied Judith. "We already have nine good reds, six whites, and two blush wines on the menu now. Additional choices may just confuse our guests. Or those that want wine with dinner may just switch from their current wine selection to a different wine. That doesn't mean increased sales…just increased inventory."

Assume that you were Judith:

1. Other than recommendations of your salesperson, what factors would you assess regularly to determine if a new product should be added to your wine list?

2. What signs might suggest to you that the number of wines offered on your menu is already too large, and thus should be reduced?

3. Would you question the wisdom of Guy's advice in this case? Explain your answer.

Answers: This case is designed to make students think about the relationship between increased beverage inventory size and increased costs. As the number of items offered in a beverage operation increases, the size of beverage inventory and its associated costs increase as well. For this reason, operators must carefully consider all of the costs associated with product offering expansion. Expansion of beverage inventory may result in increased inventory carrying costs, storage costs, spoilage and menu reprint costs, to name a few.

1. While the advice of salespersons can be helpful, experienced operators should rely most on customer feedback, industry consumption trends, and their own feel for their specific market when determining whether to expand their product offerings. In this case, the fact that the items are from "Texas" may result in some purchases by curious wine drinkers. Whether this would encourage net incremental wine sales, of course, is the most important question.

2. Those beverage operators who encounter extremely slow moving inventory items would do well to evaluate the wisdom of keeping such items on their menus. For this reason, it is important that accurate inventories be taken regularly. Where beverage products are concerned, it is very costly to have an inventory so large that 100% of all drink requests can be filled with a specific "call" brand of beer, wine, or liquor. Those items that move very slowly (sell very little) should be continually evaluated for removal from the menu.

3. Information from a beverage (or other) vendor can be very useful. This information generally should not, however, take the form of, "You need to buy this product," but rather it should relate to product consumption trends, cost-per-serving information, and product availability and cost. These objective factors help beverage decision makers better do their jobs, an important part of which is addressing the very subjective question of when to carry new menu items.

Apply What You Have Learned

Assume you are the manager of a restaurant (serving casual Italian food) that is part of a national chain. Beverage sales account for 35% of your total sales with one half of those sales coming from diners, and one half from guests drinking in the bar area. An e-mail message from your supervisor arrives asking your opinion about the company converting from the manual bartending system currently in use to one that is fully automated. The system (similar to the one you can see at www.easybar.com) essentially controls and accounts for the quantity of alcohol poured when making drinks, or serving beer or wine. Your written response to the following questions is requested.

1. How would such a system specifically affect the controls procedures in place at your restaurant?

   Answer: A fully automated beverage system would positively affect the controls procedures at a restaurant in the areas of quality assurance and portion controls, and would provide uniform operating and controlling systems.

2. How would guests sitting at the bar likely perceive the system?

   Answer: Most guests would see a fully automated system providing them constant quality and quantity. Moreover, it is more likely that the guests will receive consistent drinks and correct bills, thus making them happy. However, guests who regularly tip bartenders extra for extra liquor in their drinks without being charged may not like the system.

3. How would the system likely be perceived by your bartenders?

   Answer: As bartenders, they would like using the system since each item of the menu is stored as a recipe in the system and can be produced from every bartender at any time in the same quality and quantity. The fully automated system also provides a better working environment for employees because employees can access available coordinated information anytime they want. However, unscrupulous bartenders who make extra tips by adding extra liquor to guests' drinks may not welcome the system.

Test Your Skills

1. Gil Bloom is planning for the wedding of the mayor's daughter in his hotel. The reception, to be held in the grand ballroom, will be attended by 1,000 people. From his sales histories of similar events, Gil knows that the average drinking habits of those attending receptions of this type are as follows:

   25% select champagne
   50% select white wine
   25% select spirits

Assuming three drinks per person and a portion size of 3 ounces for champagne, 4 ounces for wine, and 1 ounce for spirits, how much of each product, in 750-ml bottles, should Gil order? (Multiply fluid ounces by 29.57 to convert to milliliters.) Spreadsheet hint: Use the ROUNDUP function in the **Total Bottles** column to determine number of full bottles to order.

If you were Gil, would you order more than you think you would need? Why or why not? If so, how much more would you order?

Beverage Selection	Percent Selecting	Total Guests	# of Guests Selecting	# of Drinks per Guest	# of Portions	Portion Size (oz.)	Amount Needed (oz.)	Total Milliliters	Total Bottles (750 ml)
Champagne	0.25	1000	250	3	750	3	2,250	66,532.50	89
Wine	0.50	1000	500	3	1,500	4	6,000	177,420.00	237
Spirits	0.25	1000	250	3	750	1	750	22,177.50	30

Answer: Gil should order 1½ to 2 times the amount predicted. First, since this is in a hotel, the inventory will be used. Second, if the wedding for the mayor's daughter was not run perfectly, it would hurt the hotel and probably cost Gil his job. Therefore, it is better to be safe than sorry.

2. Jim Heeb operates a magical restaurant called Shazam! In it, he features both excellent food and magic shows. The lounge is popular since that is where the magic is viewed. Help Jim first calculate his transfers to and from the bar and then help him compute his cost of beverage sold percentage using the following data for the month of January:

Sales	$52,214
Beginning inventory	15,000
Purchases	11,000
Ending inventory	13,500

Date	Item	Quantity	Product Value To Bar	From Bar	Issued By	Received By
1/1	Lemons	200	$12.00		T.A.	B.P.
1/6	Coffee	60 lb.	126.00		T.A.	B.P.
	Cream	10 qt.	8.00		T.A.	B.P.
1/11	Chablis	5 gal.		$31.20	B.P.	T.A.
	Ice Cream	3 gal.	16.65		T.A.	B.P.
1/13	Pineapple Juice	5 gal.	15.00		T.A.	B.P.
	Sherry	3 gal.		42.60	B.P.	T.A.
1/17	Celery	5 cs.	48.60		T.A.	B.P.
1/22	Olives	5 gal.	42.50		T.A.	B.P.
1/27	Brandy	5 btl. (750 ml.)		60.00	B.P.	T.A.
Total			268.75	133.80		

Beverage Sales =	$52,214

Beginning Inventory	Purchases	Ending Inventory	Transfers to Bar	Transfers from Bar	Cost of Beverage Sold	Beverage Cost %
$15,000.00	$11,000.00	$13,500.00	268.75	133.80	$12,634.95	24.2%

3. Mary Louise operates a popular French restaurant in a large Midwestern city of the United States. Her establishment is a favorite both for its cozy cocktail area and for its superb cuisine, patterned after that of the Nantes area of France. Mary Louise keeps excellent records on all of her product usage. She wishes to compute, for the month of January, cost of goods sold in the food, beer, wine, and spirits areas. In effect, she desires a separate product cost percentage for each of these four areas. In addition, she has determined that the value of all transfers from the kitchen to the bar will be assigned to the "spirits" area for cost purposes.

    a.   Given the following data, compute these four cost percentages.

Sales
    Food $175,000
    Beer $ 12,000
    Wine $ 45,000
    Spirits $ 51,000

Employee Meals $ 3,500

Transfers from Bar	
Beer	$ 125
Wine	$ 1,800
Spirits	$ 425

Transfers to Bar	$ 960

Beginning Inventory

Food	$ 45,800
Beer	$ 4,500
Wine	$ 65,000
Spirits	$ 6,400

Ending Inventory

Food	$ 41,200
Beer	$ 4,400
Wine	$ 66,900
Spirits	$ 8,050

Purchases

Food	$ 65,400
Beer	$ 2,900
Wine	$ 15,400
Spirits	$ 11,850

Sales	
Food	$175,000.00
Beer	12,000.00
Wine	45,000.00
Spirits	51,000.00
Total Beverage	108,000.00
Employee Meals	3,500.00
Transfers From Bar	
Beer	$125.00
Wine	1,800.00
Spirits	425.00
Transfers to Bar (Spirits)	$960.00

	Beginning Inventory	Purchases	Ending Inventory	Employee Meals	Transfers from Bar	Transfers to Bar	Cost of Goods Sold	Cost %
Food	$45,800.00	$65,400.00	$41,200.00	$3,500.00	$2,350.00	$960.00	$67,890.00	38.8%
Beer	4,500.00	2,900.00	4,400.00	0	$125.00	0	2,875.00	24.0%
Wine	65,000.00	15,400.00	66,900.00	0	1,800.00	0	11,700.00	26.0%
Spirits	6,400.00	11,850.00	8,050.00	0	425.00	$960.00	10,735.00	21.0%
Total Beverage							25,310.00	23.4%

b. Calculate Mary Louise's Sales Mix (sales percentages) for beer, wine, and spirits. Then, create, either manually or electronically, a pie chart like the following that shows these percentages.

Sales		%
Beer	12,000.00	11%
Wine	45,000.00	42%
Spirits	51,000.00	47%
Total Beverage Sales	108,000.00	100%

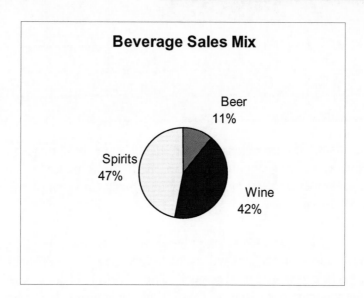

4. Maureen is the manager of a very popular nightspot. She and her bartender, Leon, have created a new drink called "The Midnight Triple". It includes Gin, pineapple juice and soda. Assume Maureen wants to sell the drink for $7.00. Using the data below, compute her beverage cost percentage if she and Leon make the drink according to the following recipes. (Spreadsheet hint: Use the ROUND function in the **Cost per Ounce** column and the **Total Cost** column.)

Recipe 1. 1 oz. Gin, 3 oz. pineapple juice, 2 oz. soda water

Recipe 2. 2 oz. Gin, 3 oz. pineapple juice, 2 oz. soda water

Recipe 3. 1 oz. Gin, 1 oz. pineapple juice, 4 oz. soda water

Recipe 4. 1.5 oz. Gin, 1.5 oz. pineapple juice, 2 oz. soda water

Recipe 5. 2 oz. Gin, 1 oz. pineapple juice, 3 oz. soda water

Cost of Gin   **$9.50 per 750 ml** (750 ml = 25.35 oz.)
Pineapple juice   **$2.50 per quart**
Soda water   **$0.06 per ounce**

Product	Unit	Cost	Cost per Ounce
Gin	750 ml	$9.50	$0.37
Pineapple Juice	quart	$2.50	$0.08
Soda Water	ounce	$0.06	$0.06

Recipe	Ounces of Gin	Ounces of Pineapple Juice	Ounces of Soda Water	Total Cost	Selling Price	Beverage Cost %
1	1	3	2	$0.73	$7.00	10.43%
2	2	3	2	$1.10	$7.00	15.71%
3	1	1	4	$0.69	$7.00	9.86%
4	1.5	1.5	2	$0.80	$7.00	11.43%
5	2	1	3	$1.00	$7.00	14.29%

Which recipe has the lowest beverage cost %? If Maureen chooses the recipe with the lowest beverage cost %, would the recipe be likely to make her guests happy? If not, what other recipe(s) might most satisfy her guests and still prove to be cost effective for Maureen?

Answer: Recipe 3 has the lowest beverage cost %. Recipe 3 would probably not make her guests happy because it will taste "watered down." Probably the best recipe for Maureen to choose would be Recipe 4. The beverage cost % is still low, and the drink has more balance to it. Recipe 1 would not be a good choice because it has the same problem as Recipe 3; it will taste "watered down."

How would Maureen's decision be affected by the sizes of glassware she has available to her?

Answer: If she only has small glasses, she will be forced to pick the recipe with the smallest amount of liquid; if she only has large glasses, she will be forced to pick the recipe with the largest amount of liquid.

5. Jana Foster is the General Manager for a new restaurant in the Champos Restaurants chain. This new facility is located in a beachfront resort town, and sales there are excellent. The problem, according to Jana's Regional Manager, is that the new operation is consistently operating at a beverage cost percentage higher than the company average. Jana's Regional Manager has flown to Jana's town to see why her beverage cost percentage is too high. The prices set by the company for all restaurants are $3.00 for beer, $3.50 for wine, $5.00 for spirits (nonfrozen specialty drinks), and $7.00 for frozen specialty drinks.

Help Jana compare her beverage cost percentages with the company averages below.

Company Averages

Product	Product Mix	Cost of Beverages	Beverage Sales	Beverage Cost %
Beer	30%	24,336	121,680	20.0%
Wine	20%	20,280	81,120	25.0%
Spirits (non-frozen specialty drinks)	30%	30,420	121,680	25.0%
Spirits (frozen specialty drinks)	20%	24,336	81,120	30.0%
Total	100%	99,372	405,600	24.5%

Beachfront Restaurant

Product	Product Mix	Cost of Beverages	Beverage Sales	Beverage Cost %
Beer	15%	14,700	73,500	20.0%
Wine	5%	6,125	24,500	25.0%
Spirits (non-frozen specialty drinks)	15%	18,375	73,500	25.0%
Spirits (frozen specialty drinks)	65%	95,550	318,500	30.0%
Total	100%	134,750	490,000	27.5%

Look at the sales mixes and the beverage cost percentages of both the company and the beach-side restaurant. Explain why Jana's total beverage cost percentages are consistently higher than the company averages. What would you advise Jana to tell her Regional Manager?

Answer: Although Jana's total beverage cost percentage is a bit too high, her individual product cost percentages are the same as the overall company. Her total beverage cost percentage is higher due to a different product mix than the company.

Since her restaurant is located in a beachfront resort town, Jana's guests order many more frozen specialty drinks than the average restaurant in the company at 65% product mix versus 20% product mix. These drinks are also the highest priced at $7.00. Because of this, her total sales are much higher than the company average.

I would advise Jana to tell her Regional Manager that she is actually doing a good job for the reasons stated above. Also, Jana should explain that because of her location on the beachfront, she will probably continue to sell more of the high priced (and higher cost) frozen specialty drinks.

6. Jack Stills operates the Spartan Restaurant. He is taking the month-end inventory in the restaurant's bar. When calculating the value of his spirits, he uses the "tenths" method of estimating product value. He has accounted for all of the spirits product held in his liquor storage area, and is now calculating the value of his "behind the bar" inventory. He has completed this process for all of the products he serves except Gin. Help him arrive at the ending inventory value for Gin by completing the following portion of his Spirits inventory value sheet.

Product	Cost per 750 ml. bottle	Amount On Hand (750 ml.)	Product Value
Seagram's	$11.50	2.3	$26.45
Well Gin	$7.50	4.6	$34.50
Bombay	$17.50	2.2	$38.50
Bombay Sapphire	$19.50	2.9	$56.55
Tanqueray	$16.50	1.0	$16.50
Tanqueray Ten	$19.00	1.7	$32.30
Tanqueray Rangpur	$19.00	2.3	$43.70
Gordon's	$10.75	1.5	$16.13
White Satin	$22.50	0.8	$18.00
Total Value			$282.63

7. Increasingly, some local and state governments are defining the phrase "drinking and driving" in a way that would prevent any individual who has consumed an alcoholic beverage from operating a motor vehicle. In 2008, in Massachusetts, legislation was proposed that would reduce the current 0.08 blood-alcohol limit recognized nationwide as the standard for being legally intoxicated to 0.02. Federal government research indicates a 160- to 240-pound man would register 0.02 sipping one glass of wine over the course of an hour. As a hospitality professional, would you support the proposed legislation? What specific operating cost-related beverage issues would be affected if such proposed laws became widely adopted?

Answer: The sale of alcoholic beverages is highly regulated. In the US and other parts of the world, increased concerns about "drinking and driving" have lead some to propose that any driving of a motor vehicle in combination with alcohol consumption should be illegal. Student opinions in favor or against such legislation will vary based upon a variety of personal factors (personal history with alcohol, religious beliefs, and social activism are likely examples of these factors).

Regardless of individual student views, such laws would prevent drivers from consuming a glass of wine with a nice dinner. It would also effectively eliminate the sale of alcoholic beverages in any venue in which individual buyers arrive by car. These include stadiums, concert halls, amusement parks, and many restaurants.

Increased costs likely to be experienced by operators should such legislation become widespread include increased liquor liability insurance costs (because the thresholds for potential liability will be reduced), increased employee training (to determine if drinkers will be driving), and increased costs related to providing taxis or access to public transportation for those who purchase alcohol. The most likely case is that these costs would be passed on to all consumers (drinkers and non-drinkers alike) because currently the profit margins on alcohol help keep food menu prices low (by providing operators with higher than average profit margins from the sale of alcoholic beverages).

Exam Questions

Multiple Choice
Choose the letter of the best answer to the questions listed below.

1. Which of the following are considered when developing a wine list?
   a. Wines that complement the food of the establishment and/or are popular.
   b. Alternatives for the price conscious and those guests who prefer the best.
   c. Can your staff effectively market this wine?
   d. All of the above
   e. None of the above
      Correct answer is d (See: Wine List)

2. Proper wine storage can be achieved if which of the following factors are monitored?
   a. Light
   b. Temperature
   c. Cork condition
   d. All of the above
   e. Only a. and c. above
      Correct answer is d (See: Wine Storage)

3. _____ are those spirits that are requested by name, such as Jack Daniel's.
   a. Beers
   b. Well
   c. Call
   d. All of the above
      Correct answer is c (See: Call Liquors)

4. Which of the following is not one of the primary classifications of beverages?
   a. Beer
   b. Wine
   c. Spirits
   d. Soft drinks
      Correct answer is d (See: Serving Alcoholic Beverages)

5. _____ shift the liability for acts committed by an individual under the influence of alcohol from that individual to the server or operation which supplied the intoxicating beverage.
   a. Control states
   b. Dramshop laws
   c. License states
   d. All of the above
   e. None of the above
      Correct answer is b (See: Responsible Alcoholic Beverage Service)

6. What are the three inventory methods commonly used to determine the value of open beverage containers?
   a. Weight, count, and measure
   b. LIFO, FIFO, and weighted average
   c. Well, call, and premium
   d. All of the above
   e. None of the above
      Correct answer is a (See: Special Features of Liquor Inventory)

7. What is the main difference between computing cost of beverage sold and cost of food sold?
   a. Employee meals
   b. Ending inventory
   c. Beginning inventory
   d. None of the above
      Correct answer is a (See: Computing Cost of Beverages)

8. A fermented beverage made from grain and flavored with hops is called:
   a. Beer
   b. Wine
   c. Vodka
   d. Tequila
      Correct answer is a (See: Classifications of Alcoholic Beverages)

9. Keg beer is also known as:
   a. Draft beer
   b. Bottled beer
   c. Canned beer
   d. Glass beer
   Correct answer is a (See: Forecasting Beer Sales)

10. Calculate food cost percentage and beverage cost percentage given the following:
   Food costs = $30,000, Beverage costs = $28,000, Food sales = $100,000, Beverage sales = $140,000, Total sales = $240,000.
   a. Food cost% = 20%; Beverage cost% = 30%
   b. Food cost% = 24%; Beverage cost% = 33%
   c. Food cost% = 12.5%; Beverage cost% = 11.7%
   d. Food cost% = 30%; Beverage cost% = 20%
   Correct answer is d (See: Standardized Drink Recipes and Portions)

11. Several Key Beverage Receiving Checkpoints for beverages were discussed in the textbook. Which of the following is included in these checkpoints?
   a. Correct brand and bottle size
   b. Correct unit price, price extension, and invoice total
   c. Freshness dates (beer) or year produced (wine)
   d. All of the above
   Correct answer is d (See: Receiving Beverage Products)

12. Which one of the following systems helps managers control the access of beverage storage areas?
   a. Cork Control System
   b. One-key System
   c. Two-key System
   d. Revenue Control System
   Correct answer is c (See: Storing Beverage Products)

13. For operations that sell a significant amount of alcoholic beverage products, there are a variety of software programs designed to help with which of the following:
   a. Maintain drink recipe files
   b. Monitor product sales
   c. Calculate actual and targeted pour percentages
   d. All of the above
   Correct answer is d (See: Technology Tools)

14. Calculate food cost percentage and beverage cost percentage given the following:
   Food costs = $20,000, Beverage costs = $25,000, Food sales = $90,000, Beverage sales = $120,000, Total sales = $210,000.
   a. Food cost% = 20%; Beverage cost% = 22%
   b. Food cost% = 9.5%; Beverage cost% = 11.9%
   c. Food cost% = 12%; Beverage cost% = 28%
   d. Food cost% = 22%; Beverage cost% = 21%
   Correct answer is d (See: Standardized Drink Recipes and Portions)

True/False
Choose the letter of the best answer to the questions listed below.

1. The potential for employee theft and waste is greater in the bar than in the kitchen.
    e. True
    f. False
        Correct answer is a (See: Standardized Drink Recipes and Portions)

2. Alcoholic beverages are generally classified as beers, cordials, or hard liquors.
    a. True
    b. False
        Correct answer is b (See: Classifications of Alcoholic Beverages)

3. Forecasting customer item selection is actually easier for alcoholic beverages than food, since the number of choices is limited.
    a. True
    b. False
        Correct answer is b (See: Forecasting Beverage Sales)

4. Standardized recipes, including step-by-step methods of preparation, should be used for all drinks to ensure the highest level of consistency and control.
    a. True
    b. False
        Correct answer is b (See: Standardized Drink Recipes and Portions)

5. Beer is the most highly perishable of beverage products.
    a. True
    b. False
        Correct answer is a (See: Determining Beer Products to Carry)

6. Bartenders should all be trained to keep a product request log so that management can monitor customer requests.
    a. True
    b. False
        Correct answer is a (See: Determining Beer Products to Carry)

7. When drafting a wine list, operators should avoid the temptation to limit the number of choices they offer.
    a. True
    b. False
        Correct answer is b (See: Determining Wine Products to Carry)

8. The skill required to receive beverage products is greater than what is needed to receive food.
    a.   True
    b.   False
    Correct answer is b (See: Receiving Beverage Products)

9. A credit memo is an addendum to the delivery invoice, designed to correct any differences between the purchase order and the delivery slip.
    a.   True
    b.   False
    Correct answer is a (See: Receiving Beverage Products)

10. Keg beer should be stored between 45 to 52°F, so it does not frost or crystallize.
    a.   True
    b.   False
    Correct answer is b (See: Storing Beverage Products)

11. A tremendously underutilized bottle size for wine is the split.
    a.   True
    b.   False
    Correct answer is a (See: Storing Beverage Products)

12. Wine should be stored so that the liquid does not come into contact with the cork and cause mold.
    a.   True
    b.   False
    Correct answer is b (See: Storing Beverage Products)

13. Since the amount of food items used in the production of beverages is minimal, it is not worth the time to conduct transfers from one area to another.
    a.   True
    b.   False
    Correct answer is b (See: Bar Transfers)

14. When computing the cost of beverages, consumption by employees is documented the same way as employee meals.
    a.   True
    b.   False
    Correct answer is b (See: Computing Cost of Beverages)

15. Sales mix is defined as the series of consumer purchasing decisions that result in a specific food or beverage cost percentage.
    a.   True
    b.   False
    Correct answer is a (See: Sales Mix)

16. The software and hardware available to help management in the beverage service area is generally less sophisticated than that found in most food-related areas.
    a. True
    b. False
    Correct answer is b (See: Technology Tools)

17. Using seasonal and local produce and juices for drink production can help moderate an operation's costs but also decrease quality.
    a. True
    b. False
    Correct answer is b (See: Green and Growing)

18. Spirits should be stored in a relatively dry storage area between 70 and 80°F (21 to 27°C).
    a. True
    b. False
    Correct answer is a (See: Storing Beverage Products)

Chapter 5

Managing the Food and Beverage Production Process

Learning Outcomes

At the conclusion of this chapter, you will be able to:

- Use management techniques to control the costs of preparing food and beverages for guests.
- Compute the actual cost of producing a menu item and compare that cost against the cost you planned to achieve.
- Recognize and be able to apply various methods to reduce the cost of goods sold percentage.

Lecture Outline

1. Managing the Food and Beverage Production Process

- The most important function of management is controlling the food and beverage production process.
- Fundamentally, each foodservice manager is in charge of kitchen production.
- Planning daily production schedules is important because you will want to have both the products and staff needed to properly service your guests.
- Ideally, the process of determining how much of each menu item to prepare on a given day would look as follows:

> **Prior Day's Carryover + Today's Production
> = Today's Sales Forecast +/– Margin of Error**

- Regardless of the type of operation you manage, you will likely find that some of your menu items simply do not retain their quality well when they are carried over.
- Some foodservice managers pre-print their production sheets listing all menu items and thus ensure that production levels for each major menu item are considered on a daily basis. Others prefer to use the production sheet on an "as needed" basis.

- When your kitchen production staff knows what you want them to produce for a given meal period, they can move to the next logical step which is to **requisition**, or request, the inventory items they must have to produce the menu items indicated on your production schedule.
- These inventory items are then **issued,** that is, taken from storage and placed into the food and beverage production areas.

2. Product Issuing

- Often, foodservice managers create difficulties for their workers by developing a requisition system that is far too time-consuming and complicated.
- The difficulty in such an approach usually arises because management hopes to equate products *issued* with products *sold* without taking a physical inventory.
- Maintaining product security can be achieved if a few principles are observed:

  1. Food, beverages, and supplies should be requisitioned only as needed based on approved production schedules.
  2. Required items (issues) should be issued only with management approval.
  3. If a written record of issues is to be kept, each person removing food, beverages, or supplies from the storage area must sign, acknowledging receipt of the products.
  4. Products that do not ultimately get used should be returned to the storage area, and their return recorded.

- Some larger operators who employ a full-time storeroom person prefer to operate with advance requisition schedules.
- Sometimes products are even weighed and measured for kitchen personnel; here, the storeroom is often called an **ingredient room**.
- The total cost is arrived at by computing the value of the issued amount, not the requisitioned amount.
- It is vital that a copy of the storeroom requisition form be sent to the purchasing agent after it has been prepared so that this individual will know about the movement of products in and out of the storage areas.
- The basic principles of product issuing which apply to food and supplies also apply to beverages.
- Beverage issues are generally one of two types: liquor storeroom issues, wine cellar issues.
- The **empty for full system** of liquor replacement requires bartenders to hold empty liquor bottles in a bar or a closely adjacent area; at a designated time each empty liquor bottle is replaced with a full one.
- All liquor issued from the liquor storage area should be marked or stamped in such a manner that is not easily duplicated.
- The issuing of wine from a wine cellar is a special case of product issuing because these sales cannot be predicted as accurately as sales of other alcoholic beverage products.

- If the wine storage area contains products valuable enough to remain locked, it is reasonable to assume that each bottled wine issued should be noted.
- In the case of transfers to the kitchen or the bar, it should be noted that the product has been directed to one of these two locations rather than having been assigned to a guest transaction number (maintained by the POS system) or a guest check number (when using a manual system).
- In an issues system, the dollar amount of issues is used to form the basis of the estimate.
- The six-column form requires only that the manager divide today's issues by today's sales to arrive at the today estimate as follows:

$$\frac{\text{Issues Today}}{\text{Sales Today}} = \text{Beverage Cost Estimate Today}$$

- The 'to date' columns represent cumulative totals of both issues and sales. Therefore, add today's issues to the issues total of the prior day and do the same with the sales figures to calculate the beverage cost estimate to date as follows:

$$\frac{\text{Issues to Date}}{\text{Sales to Date}} = \text{Beverage Cost Estimate to Date}$$

- These estimates will be extremely close to the actual cost of goods sold percentage if bar inventory remains constant or nearly constant in total dollar value from month to month.
- Adjust issues back to actual inventory levels at the end of the accounting period. If ending inventory is lower than beginning inventory, the difference between the two numbers is *added* to the issues total. If ending inventory is higher than beginning inventory, the difference in these two numbers will be *subtracted* from the issues total. Cost of beverage sold can be computed as follows:

$$\frac{\text{Issues to Date} + \text{Inventory Adjustment}}{\text{Sales to Date}} = \text{Cost of Beverage Sold}$$

- Inventory levels can vary based on delivery days of vendors, the day of the week inventory is taken, and even the seasonality of some businesses. Because of this variability, it is critical that you perform the month-end inventory adjustment.

3. Inventory Control

- Regardless of the methods used by employees to requisition food and beverage products, or management to issue these, inventory levels will be affected. It will be your responsibility and that of your purchasing agent to monitor this movement and purchase additional products, as needed.

- Restocking the inventory is critical if product shortages are to be avoided and if product necessary for menu item preparation is to be available.
- A **physical inventory** is one in which an actual, physical count and valuation of all inventory on hand is taken at the close of each accounting period.
- A **perpetual inventory** system is one in which the entire inventory is counted and recorded, then additions to and deletions from total inventory are recorded as they occur.
- The physical inventory, if properly taken, is the most accurate of all, since each item is actually counted and then valued.
- The perpetual inventory is especially popular in the area of liquor and wine.
- A **bin card** is simply an index card (or line on a spreadsheet) that details additions to and deletions from a given product's inventory level.
- **Perpetual inventory cards** are simply bin cards, but they include the product's price. A new perpetual inventory card or spreadsheet line is created each time the product's purchase price changes, with the quantity of product on hand entered on the new card.
- In the foodservice industry, it is not wise to depend exclusively on a perpetual inventory system.
- The ABC inventory system was designed to combine both the physical and perpetual inventory systems. It separates inventory items into three main categories:

  Category A items are those that require tight control and the most accurate record keeping. Those are typically high-value items, and while few in number, they can make up 70% to 80% of the total inventory value.

  Category B items are those that make up 10% to 15% of the inventory value and require only routine control and record keeping.

  Category C items make up only 5% to 10% of the inventory value. These items require only the simplest of inventory control systems.

- To develop the A, B, and C categories, you simply follow these steps.

  1. Calculate monthly usage in units (pounds, gallons, cases, etc.) for each inventory item.

  2. Multiply total unit usage times purchase price to arrive at the total monthly dollar value of product usage.

  3. Rank items from highest dollar usage to lowest.

- It is not necessary that the line between A, B, and C products be drawn at any given point. A common guideline is:

  Category A, top 20% of items
  Category B, next 30% of items
  Category C, next 50% of items

- It is important to note that while the percentage of items in category A is small, the percentage of total monthly product cost the items account for is large. Conversely, while the number of items in category C is large, the total dollar value of product cost the items account for is small.
- The ABC inventory system attempts to direct management's attention to the areas where it is most needed, especially of high cost.
  - Regardless of the inventory system used, management must be strict in monitoring both withdrawals from inventory and the process by which inventory is replenished.
  - You compute your **category food cost %**, that is, a food cost percentage computed on a portion of total food usage, by using the cost of food sold/sales formula.

  The proportion of total cost percentages is developed by the formula:

$$\frac{\text{Cost in Product Category}}{\text{Total Cost in All Categories}} = \text{Proportion of Total Product Cost}$$

4. Managing the Food Production Area

- Often, those individuals who manage restaurants do so because they relish managing the **back of the house**, or kitchen production area, of the food facility.
- Managing the food production process entails control of the following five areas: waste, overcooking, overserving, improper carryover utilization, and inappropriate make or buy decisions.
- Food losses through simple product waste can play a large role in overall excessive cost situations.
- In general, it can be said that food waste is the result of poor training or management inattentiveness.
- Increased cooking time or temperature can cause product shrinkage that increases average portion cost.
- To control loss due to overcooking, management must strictly enforce standardized recipe cooking times.
- Overportioning has the effect of increasing operational costs, and may cause the operation to mismatch its production schedule with anticipated demand.
- Overportioning must also be avoided because guests want to feel that they have received fair value for their money. Consistency is a key to operational success in foodservice.
- In most cases, tools are available that will help employees serve the proper portion size.

- Management should have a clear use in mind for each menu item that may have to be carried over, and those items should be noted on production schedules so they don't get stored and lost in freezers or refrigerators.
- It is important to understand that **carryover** foods seldom can be sold for their original value.
- Nearly all foodservice operations today use food products that are prepared in some fashion, called **convenience** or **ready foods**.
- Convenience or ready foods can save dollars spent on labor, equipment, and hard-to-secure food products to your operations. However, these items tend to cost more on a per-portion basis.
- In general, the following guidelines may be of value when determining whether to adopt the use of a convenience product.

  1. Is the quality acceptable?
  2. Will the product save labor?
  3. Would it matter if the guest knew?
  4. Does the product come in an acceptable package size?
  5. Is storage space adequate?

5. Managing the Beverage Production Area

- Controlling the amount of the product that actually is served to the guest is more complex with alcoholic beverages than with food.
- In its simplest, but least desired form, beverage production can consist of a bartender **free-pouring**, which is, pouring liquor from a bottle without carefully measuring the poured amount. In a situation such as this, it is very difficult to control product costs.
- Unlike food production, the beverage manager has a greater choice in automated equipment to help with controls.
- A **jigger** is a device (like a small cup) used to measure alcoholic beverages, typically in ounces, and fraction of ounce quantities.
- In some situations, you may determine that a **metered bottle** or other metered dispensing unit makes sense. In this case, a predetermined portion of product is dispensed whenever the bartender is called upon to serve that product.
- In some large operations, beverage "guns" are connected directly to liquor products. The gun may be activated by pushing a mechanical or electronic button built into the gun or POS.
- The most expensive, but also the most complete solution, a **total bar system** combines sales information with product dispensing information to create a complete revenue and product management system.

- Depending on the level of sophistication and cost, the total bar system can perform one or all of the following tasks:

    1. Record beverage sale by brand.
    2. Record who made the sale.
    3. Record sales dollars and/or post the sale to a guestroom folio (bill) in a hotel.
    4. Measure liquor.
    5. Add predetermined mixes to drink.
    6. Reduce liquor from inventory.
    7. Prepare liquor requisition.
    8. Compute liquor cost by brand sold.
    9. Calculate gratuity on check.
    10. Identify payment method, that is, cash, check, credit card.
    11. Record guest sale (check) number.
    12. Record date and time of sale.

- Other issues of beverage production management that should be of concern to the effective beverage manager are in-room mini-bars, bottle sales, open bars, and banquet operations.
- The control issue with mini-bars in hotel rooms is one of matching requests by housekeeping for replenishment bottles with guest usage of product.
- When liquor sales are made by the bottle, either through room service or at a reception area, the control issue is one of verifying bottle count.
- **Open bars** are ones in which no charge is made for the individual drinks at the time they are served.

The production control issues associated with open bars fall into one of two main categories: portion size and accountability.

- Some managers have virtually eliminated the open bar concept, preferring to go to a coupon system where each coupon issued is good for one drink. This way, the number of coupons issued, rather than the number of drinks, can be controlled.
- With states holding liquor sellers responsible for the actions of their patrons through the enactment of dramshop legislation, the entire concept of reasonable and prudent care in beverage operations is called into question.
- The sale of alcoholic beverages during a banquet usually takes the form of bottled-wine sales.
- If the payment is based on the number of bottles served, the bottles should be marked and the empties made available for inspection by either the guest or the banquet captain.

6. Employee Theft

- Loss of product can happen when control systems do not prevent employee theft.
- Bar theft is one of the most frequent types of thefts in the foodservice industry.
- While it may be impossible to halt all kinds of bar theft, management should check periodically the following areas: order filled but not rung up, bringing in extra product, over – and underpouring, incorrect change making, dilution of product, product theft, and product substitution.
- Proper portion size in the spirits area is ensured through the enforced use of jiggers, metered devices, or other mechanical or electronic equipment. In the case of draft beer, **head size**, that is the amount of foam on top of the glass, directly affects portion size and portion cost and, thus it too must be controlled.
- Since each alcohol product has a particular specific gravity or weight associated with it, you may also check for product dilution through the use of a **hydrometer**, which identifies specific gravity.
- Management should watch the bar area carefully, or enlist the aid of a **spotter**, a professional who will observe the bar operation with an eye toward reporting any unusual or inappropriate behavior by the bartender.
- Theft may also occur in the area of receptions and special events.
- Remember, anytime the same individual is responsible for both the preparation of a product and the collection of money for its sale, the opportunity for theft is greatly increased.
- Most kitchen-related theft deals with the removal of products from the premises, since few kitchen production workers also handle cash.
- The following product security tips are helpful when designing control systems to ensure the safety and security of food (and beverage) products.

Product Security Tips

1. Keep all storage areas locked and secure.
2. Issue food only with proper authorization and management approval.
3. Monitor the use of all carryovers.
4. Do not allow food to be prepared unless a guest check or written request precedes the preparation.
5. Maintain an active inventory management system.
6. Ensure that all food received is signed for by the appropriate receiving clerk.
7. Do not pay suppliers for food products without an appropriate and signed invoice.
8. Do not use "petty cash" to pay for food items unless a receipt and the product can be produced.
9. Conduct systematic physical inventories of all level A, B, and C products.
10. Do not allow employees to remove food from the premises without management's specific approval.

7. Determining Actual and Attainable Product Costs

- Knowledge of actual product cost begins with a standardized recipe cost for each menu item.
- The **standardized recipe cost sheet** is a record of the ingredient costs required to produce an item sold by your operation.
- When costing standardized recipes, many foodservice managers prefer to use whole cent figures rather than fractions of a cent.
- **AP** or **As Purchased** state refers to the weight or count of a product, as delivered to the foodservice operator.
- **EP** or **Edible Portion** refers to the weight of a product after it has been cleaned, trimmed, cooked, and portioned.
- A **yield test** is a procedure used for computing your actual EP costs on a product that will experience weight or volume loss in preparation.
- **Waste %** is the percentage of product lost due to cooking, trimming, portioning, or cleaning.

$$\textbf{Waste \%} = \frac{\textbf{Product Loss}}{\textbf{AP Weight}}$$

- Once waste % has been determined, it is possible to compute the yield %.
- **Yield %** is the percentage of product you will have remaining after cooking, trimming, portioning, or cleaning.

$$\textbf{Yield \%} = \textbf{1.00} - \textbf{Waste \%}$$

- If we know the yield % we can compute the A.P. weight needed to yield the appropriate E.P. weight required, by using the following formula:

$$\frac{\textbf{EP Required}}{\textbf{Yield \%}} = \textbf{AP Required}$$

- To check your figures to see if you should use a particular yield % when purchasing an item, you can proceed as follows:

$$\textbf{EP Required} = \textbf{AP Required} \times \textbf{Yield \%}$$

- Good vendors are an excellent source for providing tabled information related to trim and loss rates for standard products they carry.
- Another way to determine net product yield % is to compute it directly using the following formula:

$$\frac{\textbf{EP Weight}}{\textbf{AP Weight}} = \textbf{Product Yield \%}$$

To compute actual EP cost, use the following formula:

$$\frac{\text{AP Price per Pound}}{\text{Product Yield \%}} = \text{EP Cost (per pound)}$$

- A carbon footprint has been defined as a measure of the impact human activities have on the environment in terms of the amount of greenhouse gases (carbon dioxide) produced.
- Examples of activities in which foodservice operations engage to help reduce their carbon footprint include: buying food products locally, monitoring efficient energy usage regularly, avoiding the sale of bottled waters where the packaging and shipping of these items result in the unnecessary production of carbon dioxide, using cold water for cleaning when practical and sanitary, and reduce, reuse, and recycle.
- If you are to draw reasonable conclusions regarding operational efficiency, you must be able to compare how well you are doing with how well you should be doing.
- This process begins with determining **attainable product cost**. Attainable product cost is defined as that cost of goods sold figure that should be achievable given the product sales mix of a particular operation.
- The formula for the operational efficiency ratio is as follows:

$$\frac{\text{Actual Product Cost}}{\text{Attainable Product Cost}} = \text{Operational Efficiency Ratio}$$

- You would know your attainable food cost percentage through the use of the following formula:

$$\frac{\text{Cost as per Standardized Recipes}}{\text{Total Sales}} = \text{Attainable Product Cost \%}$$

- This cost excludes any losses due to overcooking, overportioning, waste, theft, etc. Therefore, the attainable food cost is rarely achieved.
- While it is not possible to determine one range of variance acceptability that is appropriate for all food facilities, it is important for you to establish acceptability ranges for your own facility.

8. Reducing Overall Product Cost Percentage

- While we must remember to guard against inappropriate cost cutting, management can find itself in a position where food and beverage production costs must be reduced.

- The food cost percentage equation is deceptively easy to understand. In its simplest form, it can be represented as:

$$\frac{A}{B} = C$$

where

A = **Cost of Goods Sold**
B = **Sales**
C = **Cost Percentage**

- In general, the rules of algebra say the following things about the A/B = C formula:

  1. If *A* is unchanged, and *B* increases, *C* decreases.
  2. If *A* is unchanged, and *B* decreases, *C* increases.
  3. If *A* increases at the same proportional rate *B* increases, *C* remains unchanged.
  4. If *A* decreases while *B* is unchanged, *C* decreases.
  5. If *A* increases and *B* is unchanged, *C* increases.

- Put into foodservice management terms, these five algebraic statements can be translated, as follows:

  1. If costs can be kept constant but sales increase, the cost percentage goes down.
  2. If costs remain constant but sales decline, the cost percentage increases.
  3. If costs go up at the same rate sales go up, the cost of goods sold percentage will remain unchanged.
  4. If costs can be reduced while sales remain constant, the cost percentage goes down.
  5. If costs increase with no increase in sales, the cost percentage will go up.

The six approaches to reducing overall product cost percentage are:

Reducing Overall Product Cost Percentage

1. **Decrease portion size relative to price.**
2. **Vary recipe composition.**
3. **Adjust product quality.**
4. **Achieve a more favorable sales mix.**
5. **Ensure that all product purchased is sold.**
6. **Increase price relative to portion size.**

9. Technology Tools

- In the past, restaurants were slow to install working computer terminals and other technological tools in kitchen areas where production staff could easily use them. Increasingly, however, these installations are being made.

- In a professional kitchen, cost control efforts are often shared between management and the production staff. Advanced technology programs available for kitchen production use include those that can help both you and your production staff members:

  1. Perform nutrition-related analysis of menu items.
  2. Develop production schedules based on forecasted sales.
  3. Create product requisition (issues) lists based on forecasted sales.
  4. Compute actual versus ideal costs based on product issues.
  5. Estimate and compute daily food cost.
  6. Maintain physical or perpetual inventory; compute inventory turnover rates.
  7. Maintain product usage record.
  8. Compare portions served to portions produced to monitor over portioning.
  9. Suggest usage for carryover products.
  10. Conduct "make versus buy" calculations to optimize employee productivity and minimize costs.

Consider The Cost

"How many dozen should I put in the proofer?" asked Elizabeth, the new baker at the Sands Cafeteria.

Rami El-Hussieny was the day shift operations manager and, unfortunately, he did not know how to answer Elizabeth's question. What she wanted to know was simple enough: How many dozen rolls should be placed in the proofer in anticipation of tonight's dinner business?

The problem was that the frozen dinner roll dough used at the Sands Cafeteria needed to proof for at least two hours prior to being baked for fifteen minutes. If too many rolls were proofed ahead, they would never be used and would have to be baked and made into bread dressing or tossed out. If too few dozen were proofed and the night was busier than anticipated, they would run out of "Fresh Baked Rolls" (one of the restaurant's signature items) and Rami knew that the night manager would be really upset. It was a daily guess, and sometimes Rami missed the guess!

He wondered if a pre-baked roll with a shelf-life of three or four days would, despite not having been baked on site, be the best solution to this problem.

1. What do you think is the main cause of Rami's difficulty?

2. Most foodservice managers would agree that fresh baked goods are very high quality and greatly enjoyed by their guests, yet many of these bake few, if any, products on-site. What are two specific reasons why higher quality, made "on-site" items are often not produced?

3. What is the relationship between product quality and product cost in this case study? Which product characteristic do you think is more important from the guest's point of view?

Answers:

This case requires students to consider two issues. The first is the importance of production schedules in ensuring cost-effective production planning. The second is the "quality/cost" relationship between producing menu items "in-house" versus purchasing "pre-made" items.

1. The main cause of Rami's difficulty appears to be the lack of a firm production schedule. If Rami's operation is maintaining sales histories, he will be in a better position to properly estimate the "right" number of rolls to proof given historical business patterns. Without those histories, Rami truly is "guessing" about the creation of a proper production schedule and in such a case, some of those guesses will indeed prove to be inaccurate. If production schedules are in place, Rami should have a good understanding from his own boss (or the restaurant's owner) about the desired trade-off between excess production and the potential harm caused by running out of a key menu item during a busy meal period.

2. Fresh baked products can be produced on sight. This is especially so when using, as in this case, pre-prepared dough or, in the case of many muffins and cookies, scoop and bake products. Mrs. Fields and Subway are both examples of foodservice organizations that have mastered on-site baking issues. Many organizations, however, do little baking on-site. Some specific reasons commonly given for purchasing pre-baked products include:

    - Lack of proper proofing or baking equipment
    - Difficulty in production planning/estimating (as in this case)
    - Lack of trained personnel to perform on-site baking tasks
    - Excessive product loss resulting from over-production
    - Excessive production time between knowing customer demand has exceeded forecasted levels and the ability to prepare and serve the additionally required baked products.

3. In this case, as in many others faced by foodservice operators, the "best" product is likely one produced, to the greatest degree possible, "in house." It is hard to deny that the aroma of fresh baked breads is one of the very "best" that could possibly be encountered by a restaurant guest upon entering a restaurant. The trade-off for producing such high quality items is that they are likely more difficult to produce and may cost more. In most cases, these additional costs must be passed on to consumers in the form of higher selling prices. Students considering their responses to the questions posed in this case should be reminded that some foodservice customers will, depending upon the type of operation they frequent, be more cost sensitive than others. In other cases (for example, government operated institutions such as schools, colleges, health care, and correctional facilities) fixed "per meal served" budget constraints may heavily influence "quality versus cost" decision making. Guests themselves can also make "quality versus cost" decisions difficult because, while many guests prefer higher quality items, some are unwilling to pay the higher prices associated with those higher quality levels. The general rule, however, is that consumers seek not low price, but good value (a high quality level relative to the price paid).

Apply What You Have Learned

Thandi Tye is the manager of a cafeteria chain that serves a variety of menu items, but is famous for its cream gravy and chicken fried steak (a beef steak, seasoned, breaded, and then pan fried). As food and labor costs on the item have risen, Thandi is considering whether this dish, which has previously been made on-site at each cafeteria, should be purchased pre-breaded and frozen. The cost of the same sized convenience item is 15% more than the prepared on-site item.

1. What issues should Thandi consider prior to making this decision?

   Answer: In deciding whether to adopt the use of this convenience item or not, Thandi should consider:
   - Whether the quality of the convenience item is acceptable.
   - Whether the use of a convenience item indeed saves labor costs.
   - Whether guests may react negatively to the use of a convenience item.
   - Whether a convenience item comes in an acceptable package size.
   - Whether her storage space is adequate to store the convenience item.

2. What would you advise Thandi to do?

   Answer: After taking the above issues into consideration, Thandi should come up with pros and cons for adopting the use of a convenient product for chicken fried steak. She should compare the costs associated with the convenience item (such as increased purchase price, preparation, and storage) with the costs associated with making the item from scratch (such as raw materials and labor). She must do this comparison before she can make a good recommendation for each cafeteria.

3. If the decision were made to use the convenience item, how would guests likely respond to the change if it were known? Should it be made known?

Answer: If the cafeteria chain has already built a positive image with made-on-site items, guests may react negatively when they know that the cafeteria chain now uses the pre-breaded, frozen chicken fried steak. The menu item does not need to be advertised as a convenience item (or a scratch item either), but guests should be told the truth if they ask.

Test Your Skills

1. Loralei owns Loralei's Electra Club, a nightclub in a mid-sized coastal city. She has set a standard beverage cost of 27% for her club, and she wants to make sure that her beverage costs are in line with her standard. Loralei wants to estimate her beverage cost after the first 10 days of the month. Since she doesn't have time to take a physical inventory, she decides to use her issues to estimate her costs. Help Loralei complete her six-column beverage cost estimate.

Unit Name: Loralei's Electra Club   **Date: 1/1 to 1/10**

Date	Issues		Sales		Beverage Cost Estimate	
	Today	**To Date**	**Today**	**To Date**	**Today**	**To Date**
1/1	$701.89	$701.89	$2,232.56	$2,232.56	31.4%	31.4%
1/2	650.21	1,352.10	2,536.56	4,769.12	25.6%	28.4%
1/3	857.96	2,210.06	2,764.23	7,533.35	31.0%	29.3%
1/4	852.65	3,062.71	2,656.82	10,190.17	32.1%	30.1%
1/5	1,223.35	4,286.06	6,123.54	16,313.71	20.0%	26.3%
1/6	1,300.50	5,586.56	6,445.36	22,759.07	20.2%	24.5%
1/7	785.56	6,372.12	2,545.87	25,304.94	30.9%	25.2%
1/8	1,200.80	7,572.92	3,568.91	28,873.85	33.6%	26.2%
1/9	655.85	8,228.77	2,258.75	31,132.60	29.0%	26.4%
1/10	601.25	8,830.02	2,379.96	33,512.56	25.3%	26.3%
Total	$8,830.02		$33,512.56		26.3%	

Based on the first 10 days of the month, is her beverage cost within acceptable limits?

Answer: Based on the first 10 days of the month her beverage cost is within acceptable limits.

2. Guests come from all over the county to sample the surf and turf special at Mike's Seaside Café. However, Mike is concerned about his food cost %. He thinks that his seafood costs may be causing the problem. Help him calculate his category food cost percentages and his product usage ratios (portion of total cost).

Monthly Food Cost Category Percentage/Proportion

Unit Name: Mike's Seaside Café

Sales: $271,795

Category	Cost of Food Consumed	Food Cost %	Portion of Total Cost
Seafood	$38,500	14.2%	44.1%
Meat	25,850	9.5%	29.6%
Dairy	6,145	2.3%	7.0%
Produce	12,500	4.6%	14.3%
Other	4,315	1.6%	4.95%
Total	87,310	32.1%	100.0%

List six suggestions for Mike to help him lower his food cost %.

Answer: To reduce his food cost %, Mike can do the following:

1. Decrease portion size relative to price.
2. Vary recipe composition.
3. Adjust product quality.
4. Achieve a more favorable sales mix.
5. Ensure that all product purchased is sold.
6. Increase price relative to portion size.

3. Dave would like to add a new menu item to his standard menu. Upper management has approved such an addition if his total product cost percentage does not exceed 31.5% of his allowable selling price. The selling price allowed is $9.75.

Standardized Recipe Cost Sheet

Menu Item: Dave's Pork Surprise

	Recipe Number:	15
Special Notes:	Recipe Yield:	24
Boston butt net	Portion Size:	5 oz
All ingredients weighed as EP	Portion Cost:	$2.60

Ingredients			Ingredient Cost		
Item	**Amount**	**Unit**	**Unit Cost**	**Unit**	**Total Cost**
Boston Butt	10	lb	$5.90	lb	$59.00
Jones Spicy Sauce	4	oz	8.00	lb	$2.00
Onion	8	oz	1.20	lb	$0.60
Water	¼	C	N/A	N/A	$0.00
Salt	2	T	0.40	lb	$0.03
Pepper	1	t	12.00	lb	$0.06
Garlic	1	clove	0.60	clove	$0.60
Pineapple Juice	½	C	3.78	gal	$0.12
Total					$62.41

Total Recipe Cost:	$62.41			
Portion Cost:	$ 2.60		Date Costed:	4/13
Previous Portion Cost:	N/A		Previous Date Costed:	N/A

Selling Price: $ 9.75
Food Cost Percentage (by portion): 26.7%
Food Cost Percentage Goal: 31.5%

Using the standardized recipe cost sheet below, can Dave add the new menu item?

Answer: This item should be added.

4. Elaine is the Director of Foodservice at a large retirement center and she has asked Jerry, one of her managers, to investigate the costs involved in adding a carving station to the regular Sunday brunch menu. Jerry is trying to decide which carved meats could be served. She must first determine the EP costs and yields of the various kinds of meats. Help her calculate the EP cost and yield of the inside round.

Butcher's Yield Test Results

Unit Name: Elaine's   Date Tested: May 20

Item: Inside Round
Specification: # 138
AP Amount Tested: 20 lb.
Price per Pound AP: $6.00

Loss Detail	lb.	Oz.	Total Ounces	% of Original
AP Weight	20	0	320	100.0%
Fat Loss	3	6	54	16.9%
Bone Loss	2	4	36	11.3%
Cooking Loss	1	12	28	8.8%
Carving Loss	0	8	8	2.5%
Total Production Loss			126	39.4%
EP Weight			194	60.6%

Net Product Yield: 60.6%
Yield Test Performed by: G.W.
EP Cost: $9.90

5. Liza operates a lunchroom in a large, exclusive health club. The members demand high-quality service and are especially concerned about reducing fat in their diets. They like high-protein items for their lunches, which are light and generally consumed prior to or immediately after a workout. The menu in Liza's restaurant consists of five main lunch specials. Each meat, poultry, or fish item is purchased by the pound (using product specifications), then prepared and served in a 4-ounce portion (EP), according to the standardized recipe. Liza keeps excellent sales records and, thus, knows her % selecting figures, which are tabulated as follows. She also carefully monitors waste % data, which are tabulated for each item. How much of each item should Liza order for next week, given that she expects 500 customers for lunch next week, each of whom will order one of her five menu items?

    What should the total of Liza's purchases for these items be next week, if she buys at the purchase prices listed?

    Do you think Liza should buy these items on a par or as needed basis? Why?

Item	% Selecting	Waste	Purchase Price/lb.
Beef	0.21	0.30	$3.20
Pork	0.18	0.25	1.70
Chicken	0.15	0.10	0.89
Sole	0.30	0.10	3.20
Tuna	0.16	0.05	4.10

Item	Total Served	Percent Selected	# of Servings	Oz. per serving	Total Weight of Servings (oz.)	Yield	Purchase Weight (oz.)	Oz. Per Pound	Purchase Weight (lb.)	Purchase Price	Total Purchases
Beef	500	0.21	105	4	420	0.70	600.00	16	37.50	$3.20	$120.00
Pork	500	0.18	90	4	360	0.75	480.00	16	30.00	$1.70	$51.00
Chicken	500	0.15	75	4	300	0.90	333.33	16	20.83	$0.89	$18.54
Sole	500	0.30	150	4	600	0.90	666.67	16	41.67	$3.20	$133.33
Tuna	500	0.16	80	4	320	0.95	336.84	16	21.05	$4.10	$86.32

Answer: Liza might look at purchasing her fish items on an as needed basis, since freshness is critical with these items. But, all of her other meats are easily stored and should be bought on a par basis.

6. Kathey operates a takeout cookie store in the mall. Business is good, and guests seem to enjoy the products. Her employees, mostly young teens, are a problem since they seem to like the products also. Kathey takes a physical inventory on a weekly basis. This week, her total cost of goods sold figure was $725.58. Kathey has determined that this week she will also compute her attainable food cost and her operational efficiency ratio. Help Kathey by completing the following information using the attainable food cost form.

Attainable Food Cost

Unit Name: Kathey's

Date Prepared: 1/8   Time Period: 1/1 to 1/7

Prepared By: S.L.

Item	Number Sold in Dozens	Cost per Dozen	Total Cost	Menu Price per Dozen	Total Sales
Chocolate Chip	85	$1.32	$112.20	$3.40	$289.00
Macadamia	60	$1.61	$96.60	$4.10	$246.00
Coconut Chip	70	$0.83	$58.10	$2.95	$206.50
Fudge	141	$1.42	$200.22	$3.80	$535.80
M & M	68	$1.39	$94.52	$3.40	$231.20
Soft Drinks	295	$0.16	$47.20	$0.85	$250.75
Coffee	160	$0.09	$14.40	$0.75	$120.00
Attainable Product Cost			$623.24		$1,879.25

Actual Product Cost: $725.58

Attainable Product Cost: $623.24

Operational Efficiency Ratio: 116.42%

Attainable Food Cost %:   33.2%

After completing the form, give Kathey five suggestions to keep her employees from eating all of her profits.

Answer: Students can choose five of the following ten product security tips:

1. Keep all storage areas locked and secure.
2. Issue food only with proper authorization and management approval.
3. Monitor the use of all carryovers.
4. Do not allow food to be prepared unless a guest check or written request precedes the preparation.
5. Maintain an active inventory management system.
6. Ensure that all food received is signed for by the appropriate receiving clerk.
7. Do not pay suppliers for food products without an appropriate and signed invoice.
8. Do not use "petty cash" to pay for food items unless a receipt and the product can be produced.
9. Conduct systematic physical inventories of all level A, B, and C products.
10. Do not allow employees to remove food from the premises without management's specific approval.

7. Shingi Rukunia operates a small home-style restaurant with a limited menu but extremely good food. Given the data below, help Shingi compute her entrée food cost % in the first and second weeks of the month.

Item	Item Cost	Selling Price	Week One Number Sold	Week Two Number Sold
Sirloin Steak	$5.50	$18.95	25	20
Grilled Chicken	$2.50	$12.50	20	25
Broiled Cod	$3.95	$17.95	45	30
Beef Ragout	$1.95	$11.50	10	25
Total			100	100

Week One Food Cost %

	Number Sold	Item Cost	Total Cost	Selling Price	Total Sales	Food Cost %
Sirloin Steak	25	$ 5.50	$ 137.50	$ 18.95	$ 473.75	29.0%
Grilled Chicken	20	$ 2.50	$ 50.00	$ 12.50	$ 250.00	20.0%
Broiled Cod	45	$ 3.95	$ 177.75	$ 17.95	$ 807.75	22.0%
Beef Ragout	10	$ 1.95	$ 19.50	$ 11.50	$ 115.00	17.0%
Total			$ 384.75		$1,646.50	**23.4%**

Week Two Food Cost %

	Number Sold	Item Cost	Total Cost	Selling Price	Total Sales	Food Cost %
Sirloin Steak	20	$ 5.50	$ 110.00	$ 18.95	$ 379.00	29.0%
Grilled Chicken	25	$ 2.50	$ 62.50	$ 12.50	$ 312.50	20.0%
Broiled Cod	30	$ 3.95	$ 118.50	$ 17.95	$ 538.50	22.0%
Beef Ragout	25	$ 1.95	$ 48.75	$ 11.50	$ 287.50	17.0%
Total			$ 339.75		$1,517.50	**22.4%**

Shingi served the same total number of guests and used the same standardized recipes and portion sizes both weeks. Why did her total food cost % change from week one to week two?

Answer: Shingi sold less of the higher cost items and more of the lower cost items in week two. Because her sales mix changed, her total food cost % changed.

8. Lebron operates "Ham in Heaven," a sandwich shop specializing in slow roasted spicy ham sandwiches. Currently, Lebron buys bone-in hams and roasts them in-house. These hams cost $2.99 per pound and produce a 58% usable yield. Semi-boneless hams of the same quality cost $3.99 per pound with a 78% yield. Boneless hams of the same quality would cost $6.99 per pound and produce a 96% yield. Calculate the E.P. cost per pound of each alternative.

Ham in Heaven			
	AP Price per lb.	Yield	EP Cost per lb.
Bone-in Ham	$2.99	58%	$5.16
Semi-boneless Ham	$3.99	78%	$5.12
Boneless Ham	$6.99	96%	$7.28

Choose the alternative you would recommend to Lebron and explain your reason for choosing it. Specifically, what factors would influence your decision?

Answer: I would recommend the semi-boneless ham since it has a lower EP cost per pound than the other alternatives. Using semi-boneless ham may also reduce the cost of labor to prepare the meat than the bone-in ham.

9. This chapter introduced six different action steps managers could take to reduce their cost of food and cost of food percentages when they encounter rising costs. In some foodservice settings, such as schools, colleges, correctional, and health care facilities, however, managers are allotted a fixed amount of money to spend per meal served and this amount may only be adjusted on an annual basis. Thus, managers of these facility types cannot readily increase their prices in the face of rising costs. Review the six alternative cost reduction strategies presented in the chapter and identify three specific actions you would recommend such managers take to stay within their budgets during times of rapidly rising product costs.

Answer: When a foodservice operation is responsible for the nutritional needs of those it serves, decreasing the portion size of items served often is not a viable cost reduction strategy. Varying recipe composition, while still meeting nutritional needs of those served, however, is a very viable option.

While reducing product quality is likely a poor choice for reducing costs in institutional settings, varying the menu mix to include a higher percentage of lower cost menu items on an increased basis would likely be a very effective strategy.

Finally, while increasing price relative to portion size is not likely a viable option, taking all possible steps to ensure that all product purchased is sold would very likely be the most effective cost-reduction strategy that could be undertaken by foodservice managers in these special institutional settings.

Exam Questions

Multiple Choice
Choose the letter of the best answer to the questions listed below.

1. _____ items are those that require tight control and the most accurate record keeping. These are typically high value items, which can make up 70% to 80 % of the total inventory value.
   a. Category "A" (items of the ABC inventory system)
   b. Category "B" (items of the ABC inventory system)
   c. Category "C" (items of the ABC inventory system)
   d. Category "Z" (items of the XYZ inventory system)
   e. None of the above
   Correct answer is a (See: Physical or Perpetual Inventory)

2. One of the advantages of the _____ inventory system is the ability of the purchasing agent to quickly note the quantity of product on hand.
   a. Physical
   b. ABC
   c. Perpetual
   d. XYZ
   e. LIFO
   Correct answer is c (See: Physical or Perpetual Inventory)

3. According to the textbook, managing the food production process entails control of five areas. Which of the following is one of these five areas?
   a. Overcooking and Overserving
   b. Improper carry-over utilization
   c. Inappropriate make or buy decisions
   d. All of the above
   e. Only b. and c. above
   Correct answer is d (See: Managing the Food Production Area)

4. The textbook discussed several guidelines to consider when determining whether to adopt the use of a convenience product. Which of the following best describes one or more of these guidelines?
   a. Is the quality acceptable?
   b. Would it matter if the guest knew?
   c. Will the product save labor?
   d. All of the above
   e. Only a. and c. above
   Correct answer is d (See: Inappropriate Make or Buy Decisions)

5. The production control issues associated with open bars fall into one of two main categories. What are those categories?
    a. Accountability and portion size
    b. Free pouring and the use of a rigger
    c. Incorrect change making and dilution of product
    d. All of the above
    e. Only b. and c. above
    Correct answer is a (See: Open Bars)

6. What is the formula for operational efficiency ratio?
    a. Actual product cost/attainable product cost
    b. Price per pound/product yield
    c. Attainable product cost/actual product cost
    d. Product cost/current yield
    Correct answer is a (See: Determining Attainable Product Cost)

7. What is the formula for calculating the waste percentage of a product?
    a. Total number of a specific menu item sold / total number of all menu items sold
    b. Yield desired / current yield
    c. Ingredient weight / total recipe weight
    d. Product loss / as purchased weight
    e. None of the above
    Correct answer is d (See: Product Yield)

8. What is the formula for calculating the As Purchased weight?
    a. Product loss / as purchased weight
    b. 1.00 - waste %
    c. As purchased weight required X yield %
    d. Edible portion weight required / yield %
    e. As purchased weight required / edible portion cost per serving
    Correct answer is d (See: Product Yield)

9. If the yield percentage is 80% and you have 100 pounds of As Purchased beef in your refrigerator. How many 8-ounce portions of beef can you serve?
    a. 80
    b. 120
    c. 160
    d. 192
    e. Cannot be determined
    Correct answer is c (See: Product Yield)

10. According to the text, what is the definition of edible portion?
   a. It refers to the weight of a product after it has been cleaned, trimmed, cooked, and portioned.
   b. It refers to the weight or count of a product as delivered to the foodservice operator.
   c. It refers to the portion wasted after the product has been cleaned, trimmed, and cooked.
   Correct answer is a (See: Product Yield)

11. What is the formula for yield %?
   a. Product loss / A. P. weight
   b. A. P. weight / Product loss
   c. 1.00 – waste %
   d. 1.00 + waste %
   Correct answer is c (See: Product Yield)

12. You purchase 20 pounds of brisket. If after cooking, trimming, and portioning, you find that you have 12 pounds 8 ounces remaining, what is your waste percentage?
   a. 37.5%
   b. 40.0%
   c. 62.5%
   d. 60.0%
   e. None of the above
   Correct answer is a (See: Product Yield)

13. If a chef requires 30 pounds of ribs (edible portion) and the yield percentage is 60%, how many pounds of ribs (as purchased) should he order?
   a. 30 lbs.
   b. 45 lbs.
   c. 18 lbs.
   d. 50 lbs.
   Correct answer is d (See: Product Yield)

14. You have collected data from your standardized recipe cost sheets and you determine that the weekly attainable cost for your menu is $1,500. At the end of the week you find that your actual cost is $1,750. What is your operational efficiency ratio? From a cost perspective, does this number indicate efficiency?
   a. 1.17; yes
   b. 0.86; yes
   c. 1.17; no
   d. 0.86; no
   Correct answer is c (See: Determining Attainable Product Cost)

15. What are some of the areas that advanced software programs can do to help kitchen staff be more efficient?
    a. Maintain product usage record
    b. Suggest usage for carryover products
    c. Estimate and compute daily food cost
    d. Develop production schedules based on forecasted sales
    e. All of the above
    Correct answer is e (See: Technology Tools)

16. If a chef requires 50 pounds of ribs (edible portion) and the yield percentage is 40%, how many pounds of ribs (as purchased) should he order?
    a. 30 lbs.
    b. 15 lbs.
    c. 180 lbs.
    d. 125 lbs.
    Correct answer is d (See: Product Yield)

True/False
Choose the letter of the best answer to the questions listed below.

17. Perpetual inventory control is one in which an actual physical count and valuation of all inventory on hand is taken at the close of each accounting period.
    a. True
    b. False
    Correct answer is b (See: ABC Inventory Control)

18. Requisitioning, the process of issuing food and supply products to employees, is usually a detailed and complicated process, and is therefore always left up to management.
    a. True
    b. False
    Correct answer is b (See: Product Issuing)

19. All liquor issued from storage should be stamped or marked in a manner that is easily duplicated to ensure uniformity throughout the stock.
    a. True
    b. False
    Correct answer is b (See: Product Issuing)

20. A bin card is used to record the number of each item on hand when taking a physical inventory.
    a. True
    b. False
    Correct answer is b (See: ABC Inventory Control)

21. The ABC inventory system attempts to separate inventory items into three main categories, based on cost.
    a. True
    b. False
    Correct answer is a (See: Physical or Perpetual Inventory)

22. In general, it can be said that food waste is the result of poor training or management inattentiveness.
    a. True
    b. False
    Correct answer is a (See: Managing the Food Production Area)

23. One example of bar related theft is a bartender who brings in his or her own liquor, and pockets the sales.
    a. True
    b. False
    Correct answer is a (See: Reducing Bar-Related Theft)

24. Yield tests are helpful, but not necessary to determine actual recipe costs.
    a. True
    b. False
    Correct answer is b (See: Yield Testing)

25. Increasing prices relative to portion size is one approach to reducing overall product cost percentage.
    a. True
    b. False
    Correct answer is a (See: Reducing Overall Product Cost Percentage)

26. The empty for full system of liquor issuing procedure requires that each empty bottle be replaced with a full one.
    a. True
    b. False
    Correct answer is a (See: Product Issuing: Special Concerns for Beverages)

27. Carryover foods seldom can be sold for their original value.
    a. True
    b. False
    Correct answer is a (See: Improper Carryover Utilization)

28. The opportunity for theft is greatly decreased anytime the same individual is responsible for the preparation of a product and the collection of money for its sale.
    a. True
    b. False
    Correct answer is b (See: Reducing Bar Related Theft)

29. One may check for product dilution through the use of a hydrometer, which identifies specific gravity.
    a. True
    b. False
    Correct answer is a (See: Reducing Bar Related Theft)

30. A jigger is another name for free pouring of alcoholic beverages.
    a. True
    b. False
    Correct answer is b (See: Managing the Beverage Production Area)

31. In a professional kitchen, cost control efforts are often shared between management and the production staff due to the installation of working computer terminals in the kitchen.
    a. True
    b. False
    Correct answer is a (See: Technology Tools)

32. A carbon footprint has been defined as a measure of the impact human activities have on the environment in terms of the amount of greenhouse gases (carbon dioxide) produced.
    a. True
    b. False
    Correct answer is a (See: Green and Growing)

33. Using cold water for cleaning when practical and sanitary is one of the examples of activities in which foodservice operations can engage to reduce their carbon footprint.
    a. True
    b. False
    Correct answer is a (See: Green and Growing)

Chapter 6

Managing Food and Beverage Pricing

Learning Outcomes

At the conclusion of this chapter, you will be able to:

- Choose and apply the best menu format to an operation.
- Identify the variables to be considered when establishing menu prices.
- Assign menu prices to menu items based on their cost, popularity, and ultimate profitability.

Lecture Outline

1. Menu Formats

- Menus are one of the most effective ways manager's can communicate with their guests. Regardless of the choice the business makes, the menu is an excellent opportunity to build impulse sales or to communicate special sales and services the facility has to offer.
- Menus in foodservice establishments generally fall into one of three major categories: standard, daily, or cycle.
- Menu **"tip-ons,"** which are smaller menu segments clipped on to more permanent menus, can prove very effective in influencing impulse buying.
- The **standard menu** is printed, displayed, recited by service staff, or otherwise communicated to the guest. The standard menu is fixed day after day.
- Standard menus simplify the ordering process; guests tend to have a good number of choices, and guest preference data can be easily obtained.
- But, standard menus do not utilize carryovers effectively, do not respond quickly to market changes, and do not allow easy seasonal adjustments.
- The **daily menu** changes every day. Management can respond quickly to changes in ingredient or item prices, and can use carryovers. But, planning is more difficult, as is collecting customer data.
- A **cycle menu** is a menu in effect for a specific time period. The length of the cycle refers to the length of time the menu is in effect.
- Typically, cycle menus are repeated on a regular basis.
- Cycle menus are often selected by managers whose guests dine frequently with them on a very regular basis, as a cycle menu provides a systematic means for incorporating variety into the menu.

- Production personnel can be trained to produce a wider variety of foods with a cycle menu than with a standard menu.
- With cycle menus, purchasing is simplified, inventory levels are easy to maintain, and carryovers are easily utilized.
- Regardless of the menu type used, you can generally incorporate minor menu changes on a regular basis. This is accomplished through the offering of daily or weekly **menu specials**, that is, menu items that will appear on the menu as you desire and be removed when they are either consumed or discontinued.
- Daily or weekly menu specials provide variety, low-cost raw ingredients, carryover utilization, or test-market potential for new menu items.

2. Factors Affecting Menu Pricing

- It is important to remember that revenue and price are not synonymous terms.
- **Revenue** means the amount spent by *all guests* while **Price** refers to the amount charged to *one guest*. Total revenue is generated by the following formula:

> **Price x Number Sold = Total Revenue**

- It is a truism that as price increases, the number of items sold will generally decrease.
- Guests demand a good **price/value relationship** when making a purchase.
- The price/value relationship simply reflects guests' view of how much value they are receiving for the price they are paying.
- It may be said that price is significantly affected by all of the following factors:

> **Factors Influencing Menu Price**
> 1. **Local competition**
> 2. **Service levels**
> 3. **Guest type**
> 4. **Product quality**
> 5. **Portion size**
> 6. **Ambience**
> 7. **Meal period**
> 8. **Location**
> 9. **Sales mix**

- Successful foodservice operators spend their time focusing on building guest value in their *own* operation, and not in attempting to mimic the efforts of the competition.
- Guests expect to pay more for the same product when service levels are higher.
- Some guests are simply less price sensitive than others. All guests, however, want value for their money.

- Foodservice operators should select the quality level that best represents their guests' anticipated desire as well as their goals, and then price the products accordingly.
- Portion size plays a large role in determining menu pricing.
- The proper dish size is just as critical as the proper size of scoop or ladle when serving the food.
- For the foodservice operator who provides an attractive ambience, menu prices can be increased. However, excellent product quality with outstanding service goes much further over the long run than do clever restaurant designs.
- In some cases, diners expect to pay more for an item served in the evening than for that same item served at a lunch period. You must exercise caution in this area. Guests should clearly understand *why* a menu item's price changes with the time of day.
- Location can be a major factor in determining price.
- There is no discounting the value of a prime restaurant location, which can influence price; it does not, however, guarantee success.
- Sales mix refers to the specific menu items selected by guests.
- Sales mix will most heavily influence the menu pricing decision, just as guest purchase decisions will influence total product costs.
- **Price blending** refers to the process of pricing products, with very different individual cost percentages, in groups with the intent of achieving a favorable overall cost situation.
- The formula for computing food cost percentage is as follows:

$$\frac{\text{Cost of Food Sold}}{\text{Food Sales}} = \text{Food Cost \%}$$

- This formula can be worded somewhat differently for a single menu item without changing its accuracy. Consider that:

$$\frac{\text{Costs of a Specific Food Item Sold}}{\text{Food Sales of That Item}} = \text{Food Cost \% of That Item}$$

- It is important to understand that the food sales value in the above formula is a synonymous term to the selling price when evaluating the menu price of a single menu item. The principles of algebra allow you to rearrange the formula as follows:

$$\frac{\text{Cost of a Specific Food Item Sold}}{\text{Food Cost \% of That Item}} = \text{Food Sales (Selling Price) of That Item}$$

- The Leadership in Energy and Environmental Design (LEED) rating system developed by the U.S. Green Building Council (USGBC) evaluates facilities on a variety of standards.

- The rating system considers sustainability, water use efficiency, energy usage, air quality, construction and materials, and innovation.

3. Assigning Menu Prices

- In general, menu prices are most often assigned on the basis of one of the following two concepts: product cost percentage or contribution margin.
- The **product cost percentage** is based on the idea that product cost should be a predetermined percentage of selling price.
- When management uses a predetermined food cost percentage to price menu items, it is stating its belief that product cost in relationship to selling price is of great importance.
- A cost factor or multiplier can be assigned to each desired food cost percentage as follows:

$$\frac{1.00}{\text{Desired Product Cost \%}} = \text{Pricing Factor}$$

- The pricing factor when multiplied by any product cost will result in a selling price that yields the product cost. The formula is as follows:

$$\text{Pricing Factor} \times \text{Product Cost} = \text{Menu Price}$$

- A **plate cost** is simply the sum of all product costs included in a single meal (or "plate") served to a guest.
- **Contribution margin** is defined as the amount that remains after the product cost of the menu item is subtracted from the item's selling price. Contribution margin is computed as follows:

$$\text{Selling Price} - \text{Product Cost} = \text{Contribution Margin}$$

- When this approach is used, the formula for determining selling price is:

$$\text{Product Cost} + \text{Contribution Margin Desired} = \text{Selling Price}$$

- The effective manager will view pricing as an important process with an end goal of setting a good price/value relationship in the mind of the guest.
- Regardless of whether the pricing method used is based on food cost percentage or contribution margin, the selling price selected must provide for a predetermined operational profit.

4. Special Pricing Situations

- Some pricing decisions faced by foodservice managers call for a unique approach. In many cases, pricing is used as a way to influence guests' purchasing decisions or to respond to particularly complex situations. The following are examples: coupons, value pricing, bundling, salad bars and buffets, bottled wine, beverages at receptions and parties.

- Coupons are a popular way to vary menu price. There are two types of coupons in use in the hospitality industry. The first type generally allows guests to get a free item anytime they buy another item. With the second type, some form of restriction is placed on the coupon's use.

- Coupons have the effect of reducing sales revenue from each guest in the hope that the total number of guests will increase to the point that total sales revenue increases.

- **Value Pricing** refers to the practice of reducing prices on selected menu items in the belief that, as in couponing, total guest counts will increase to the point that total sales revenue also increases.

- **Bundling** refers to the practice of selecting specific menu items and pricing them as a group in such a manner that the single menu price of the group is lower than if the items in the group were purchased individually.

- When bundling, as in couponing or value pricing, lower menu prices are accepted by management in the belief that this pricing strategy will increase total sales revenue and thus profit, by increasing the number of guests served.

- The difficulty in establishing a set price for either a salad bar or buffet is that total portion cost can vary greatly from one guest to the next.

- The secret to keeping the selling price low in a salad bar or buffet is to apply the ABC inventory approach. That is, A items should comprise no more than 20% of the total product available; B items, no more than 30%; and C items, 50%.

- Use the following formula to determine buffet product cost per guest:

$$\frac{\text{Total Buffet Product Cost}}{\text{Guests Served}} = \text{Buffet Product Cost per Guest}$$

- Few areas of menu pricing create more controversy than that of pricing wines by the bottle. The reason for this may be the incredible variance in cost among different **vintages** or years of production, as well as the quality of alternative wine offerings.

- How you decide to price the bottled wine offerings on your menu will definitely affect your guest's perception of the price/value relationship offered by your operation.

- The **price spread** is defined as the range between the lowest and highest priced menu item.

- Pricing beverages for open-bar events can be difficult, since each consumer group can be expected to behave somewhat differently when attending an open bar or hosted bar function.

- When charging on a per person, per hour basis you must have a good idea of how much the average attendee will consume during the length of the party or reception so that an appropriate price can be established.
- Also, maintaining past events and records of what the average consumption for each group of guests has been previously can help you establish an appropriate price.

5. Technology Tools

- In this chapter you learned about the menu formats you most often encounter as hospitality managers, as well as the factors affecting menu prices, and the procedures used to assign individual menu item prices based on cost and sales data.
- The mathematical computations required to evaluate the effectiveness of individual menu items and to establish their prices can be complex, but there are a wide range of software products available that can help you:

  1. Develop menus and cost recipes.
  2. Design and print menu "specials" for meal periods or happy hours.
  3. Compute and analyze item contribution margin.
  4. Compute and analyze item and overall food cost percentage.
  5. Price banquet menus and bars based on known product costs.
  6. Evaluate the profitability of individual menu items.
  7. Estimate future item demand based on past purchase patterns.
  8. Assign individual menu item prices based on management-supplied parameters.

- Menu analysis and pricing software is often packaged as part of a larger software program. It is an area that will continue to see rapid development in the future as software makers seek additional ways to improve their products.

Consider The Cost

"We have to lower our price or we'll just get killed," said Hoyt Jones, Director of Operations for the seven-unit Binky's Sub shops. Binky's was known for its modestly priced, but very high quality sandwiches and soups. Business and profits were good. But now, Hoyt and Rachel, who served as Binky's Director of Marketing, were discussing the new $4.99 "Foot Long Deal" sandwich promotion that had just been rolled out by their major competitor, an extremely large chain of sub shops that operated over 5000 units nationally and internationally.

"They just decided to lower their prices to appeal to value-conscious customers," said Hoyt. "But how can they do that and still make money?" asked Rachel.

"There's always a less expensive variety of ham and cheese on the market," replied Hoyt. "They use lower quality ingredients than we do. We charge $6.99 for our foot-long sub. That wasn't bad when they sold theirs at $5.99. Our customers know we are worth the extra dollar. Now that they are at $4.99...I don't know, but I think they are going to kill us in the market. We need to do something. Fast."

1. How large a role do you believe "costs" likely played into the decision of this competitor to reduce its sandwich prices? Explain your answer.

2. Do you think the typical foodservice customer will consistently pay a higher price for better quality food and beverage products? Give a specific example to support your answer.

3. Assume you were the President of Binky's Subs. What steps would you instruct Hoyt and Rachel to take to address this specific pricing challenge?

Answers:

In this case, Hoyt and Rachel face a challenge that is continually present in the operation of a foodservice unit or company. That is the challenge of balancing product quality and selling price when creating and marketing menu items.

1. It is very likely that costs played only a minor role in the decision of Hoyt and Rachel's competitor to lower its prices. The decision appears to be marketing (not cost) based. This case illustrates the fact that customers care very little about the "costs" incurred by a foodservice operation. Instead, they care about the costs they themselves incur when paying for menu items. The important point for foodservice professionals to remember is that an increase in their own operating cost does not immediately result in willingness by customers to higher prices. Menu prices must reflect high levels of customer's perceived value, regardless of the operator's costs.

2. The answer to this question is often determined by a foodservice operation's target customer. There are indeed some customers who seek only to pay the lowest possible price. These customers, however, are very hard to retain over time because it is nearly always possible for a foodservice operator's competitor to offer a "cheaper" (and lower quality) product. If target customers have a "cheapest is best" mentality, they will not exhibit the type of customer loyalty sought by the operator who provides good quality at a fair price. Experienced foodservice managers know that seeking to be "cheapest," at the expense of quality, is usually a poor long-term marketing strategy for a foodservice company.

3. Student answers will vary greatly here; however, as the individual responsible for food production, Hoyt could be assigned by the President to identify one or more sandwich items whose price could be reduced to match the competitor's new menu price. This would be the strategy to employ if the President of Binky's wished to directly compete with the competitor on the basis of price, rather than quality. Alternatively, Rachel, the Director of Marketing, might be assigned the task of creating an ad campaign that emphasized the superior "quality" of Binky's products and reinforced the message that value received for the price paid always has been, and still is, highest at Binky's. The fact that Hoyt does not currently appear to truly believe in the value proposition offered to Binky's customers ("We'll just get killed.") may be the President of this company's biggest challenge!

Apply What You Have Learned

Dominic Carbonne owns Hungry Henry's pizza, a four-unit chain of take-out pizza shops in a city of 60,000 people (with an additional 25,000 college students attending the local State University). Recently, a new chain of pizza restaurants has opened in town. The products sold by this chain have lesser quality and use lesser quantity of ingredients (cheese, meat and vegetable toppings, etc.), but are also priced 25% less than Hungry Henry's equivalent size. Dominic has seen his business decline somewhat since the new chain opened. This is especially true with the college students.

1. How would you evaluate the new competitor's pricing strategy?

   Answer: The new competitor's pricing strategy can be evaluated as follows:
   - It sells a lesser quality pizza for a lesser price.
   - It targets college students who are more price sensitive than other groups of people.

2. What steps would you advise Dominic to take to counter this competitor?

   Answer: In order to counter this new competitor, Dominic may need to develop a new pricing strategy to attract college students. For example, he might offer coupons, value priced or combo pizza/breadstick meals, and daily or weekly menu specials.

3. Describe three specific strategies restaurants can use to communicate "quality", rather than "low price" to potential guests.

   Answer: Restaurants can communicate "quality" to potential guests by developing advertising and promotion programs that highlight menu items that are heart healthy or nutritious, items with fresh ingredients, items with a special quality grade such as Certified Angus Beef, etc. This can be communicated on the menu, in advertisements, and on the restaurant website.

Test Your Skills

1. Bill owns Bill's Burger Barn, and he is dissatisfied with his consistently high food cost percentage. In an effort to drop his food cost % *below* 35%, he has decided to incorporate price blending into his pricing strategy. He has developed three combo items, and he wants to find out if his food cost % has been lowered after the first week of sales. Help Bill calculate the food cost % for his combo items below.

Price Blending

Bills Burger Barn Combo

Item	Number Sold	Item Cost	Total Cost	Selling Price	Total Sales	Food Cost %
Hamburger	200	$1.50	$300.00	$3.49	$698.00	43.0%
French Fries (large)	185	0.40	$74.00	1.60	$296.00	25.0%
Soft Drink (16 oz.)	190	0.20	$38.00	1.35	$256.50	14.8%
Total	575		$412.00		$1,250.50	32.9%

Bill's Bacon Cheeseburger Combo

Item	Number Sold	Item Cost	Total Cost	Selling Price	Total Sales	Food Cost %
Bacon Cheeseburger	160	$1.65	$264.00	$4.29	$686.40	38.5%
Onion Rings	135	0.30	$40.50	1.40	$189.00	21.4%
Soft Drink (16 oz.)	155	0.20	$31.00	1.35	$209.25	14.8%
Total	450		$335.50		$1,084.65	30.9%

Bill's Chicken Sandwich Combo

Item	Number Sold	Item Cost	Total Cost	Selling Price	Total Sales	Food Cost %
Chicken Sandwich	75	$1.10	$82.50	$3.15	$236.25	34.9%
French Fries (large)	75	0.40	$30.00	1.60	$120.00	25.0%
Soft Drink (16 oz.)	75	0.20	$15.00	1.35	$101.25	14.8%
Total	225		$127.50		$457.50	27.9%

Should Bill continue with this pricing strategy?

Answer: Yes, Bill should continue this pricing strategy because the food cost percentages for all three combos are below 35%.

2. Tonekwa has priced her menu items using the product cost percentage method in the past. She has asked her evening shift manager to price new menu items, and she believes that he will feel more comfortable using the factor method to price the new items. Help Tonekwa convert her desired product cost percentages to factors. (Spreadsheet hint: Use the ROUND function for the "Factor" column to three decimal places.)

Pricing Factor Table

Desired Product Cost	Factor
18%	5.556
21%	4.762
22%	4.545
24%	4.167
26%	3.846
31%	3.226
32%	3.125
36%	2.778
37%	2.703
41%	2.439
42%	2.381
44%	2.273
46%	2.174

3. Bess and David own two small diners in a mid-sized city in Oklahoma. Bess has primary responsibility for the diner in the suburbs, and David has primary responsibility for the diner in the inner city. The menu items and product costs are the same in both diners, but the market in the inner city demands lower menu prices than that in the suburbs. So, Bess has set her desired product cost percentage to 40%, and David's desired product cost percentage is 42% since he can't charge as much as Bess. Bess likes to use the product cost percentage method to price menu items, and David likes to use the factor method. Help both of them determine their selling prices.

Bess and David's Diner – Suburbs (Bess)

Desired Product Cost Percentage: 40%

Product Cost Percentage Method

Item	Cost of Product	Desired Product Cost Percentage	Selling Price
Chicken Breast Dinner	$2.25	40%	$5.63
Seafood Platter	3.45	40%	$8.63
Steak Dinner	4.99	40%	$12.48
Turkey Sandwich	1.25	40%	$3.13
Pork Chop	2.45	40%	$6.13
Hamburger	1.50	40%	$3.75
Cheeseburger	1.75	40%	$4.38
Fries	0.45	40%	$1.13
Meat Loaf	1.25	40%	$3.13
Small Drink	0.35	40%	$0.88

Bess and David's Diner – Inner City (David)

Desired Product Cost Percentage: 42%

Factor Method

Item	Cost of Product	Factor	Selling Price
Chicken Breast Dinner	$2.25	2.381	$5.36
Seafood Platter	3.45	2.381	$8.21
Steak Dinner	4.99	2.381	$11.88
Turkey Sandwich	1.25	2.381	$2.98
Pork Chop	2.45	2.381	$5.83
Hamburger	1.50	2.381	$3.57
Cheeseburger	1.75	2.381	$4.17
Fries	0.45	2.381	$1.07
Meat Loaf	1.25	2.381	$2.98
Small Drink	0.35	2.381	$0.83

133

4. Frankie Marie owns Frankie's Cafeteria in a small southern town. She has decided to price her menu items using the contribution margin method. She has determined the following contribution margins for her food categories:

Contribution margins:
Salads: $1.20
Entrees: $4.25
Desserts: $1.50
Drinks: $1.10

Help her price her menu items below.

Item	Product Cost	Desired Contribution Margin	Selling Price
Salads			
Dinner Salad	$0.30	$1.20	$1.50
Macaroni Salad	$0.55	$1.20	$1.75
Potato Salad	$0.65	$1.20	$1.85
Carrot and Raisin Salad	$0.40	$1.20	$1.60
Bavarian Salad	$0.60	$1.20	$1.80
Entrees			
Liver and Onions	$2.50	$4.25	$6.75
Steak Patty	$2.75	$4.25	$7.00
Meat Loaf	$2.85	$4.25	$7.10
Chicken Fried Steak	$2.10	$4.25	$6.35
Fried Catfish	$2.35	$4.25	$6.60
Chicken Casserole	$2.25	$4.25	$6.50
Turkey and Dressing	$2.55	$4.25	$6.80
Desserts			
Chocolate Cream Pie	$0.75	$1.50	$2.25
Coconut Cream Pie	$0.75	$1.50	$2.25
Pecan Pie	$1.25	$1.50	$2.75
Chocolate Cake	$0.60	$1.50	$2.10
Pudding	$0.20	$1.50	$1.70
Jello	$0.20	$1.50	$1.70
Carrot Cake	$0.70	$1.50	$2.20
Drinks			
Coffee	$0.15	$1.10	$1.25
Tea	$0.15	$1.10	$1.25
Soft Drink	$0.15	$1.10	$1.25

5. Gabriel Hinojosa owns Gabriel's Tex-Mex Restaurant, an extremely popular, 250-seat establishment in a large California city. Gabriel has decided to offer a four-hour Sunday brunch buffet for his guests because he thinks he can achieve a guest count of 625 (2 ½ turns). Last Sunday, June 1, he offered the buffet for the first time, and he charged $12.00 per guest. However, he only served 400 people. He thinks that maybe he could attract more guests if he offered the buffet at a lower price. He collected information on last Sunday's buffet product usage, and he used the ABC method to put his menu items into categories. His desired food cost percentage is 40%. Help him complete the buffet product usage report.

After completing this analysis, what should be Gabriel's selling price? If he uses this new selling price and he serves 625 guests next Sunday, June 8, will his total revenue increase? If so, how much? (Spreadsheet hint: Use the ROUND function for "Cost per Guest" and "Desired Selling Price Based on Cost".)

Buffet Product Usage (Sunday, June 1): Gabriel's Tex-Mex Restaurant

Item	Category	Unit	Beginning Amount	Additions	Ending Amount	Total Usage	Unit Cost	Total Cost
Steak Fajitas	A	lb.	20	60	6	74	4.50	$333.00
Chicken Fajitas	A	lb.	15	70	10	75	4.00	$300.00
Carne Asada	A	lb.	10	50	4	56	4.25	$238.00
Cheese Enchiladas	B	lb.	2	80	15	67	2.00	$134.00
Beef Enchiladas	B	lb.	3	60	10	53	2.50	$132.50
Enchiladas Verde	B	lb.	1	70	8	63	2.00	$126.00
Chili Rellenos	B	lb	10	45	5	50	2.75	$137.50
Tacos	C	each	0	150	20	130	0.30	$39.00
Bean Chalupas	C	each	0	175	5	170	0.25	$42.50
Tortilla Soup	C	gal.	2	10	4	8	0.30	$2.40
Spanish Rice	C	lb.	5	70	12	63	0.20	$12.60
Refried Beans	C	lb.	15	75	6	84	0.20	$16.80
Sopapillas	C	each	25	200	30	195	0.15	$29.25
Total Product Cost								$1,543.55
Guests Served:	400		Desired Food Cost %:	40%				
Total Product Cost:	$1,543.55		Desired Selling Price Based on Cost:	$9.65				
Cost Per Guest:	$3.86							
Revenues, June 1:	$4,800.00		Projected Revenues, June 8:	$6,031.25		Difference:	$1,231.25	

Answer: Gabriel's selling price should be $9.65. If he uses this new selling price and he serves 625 guests next Sunday, June 8, his total revenue will increase by $1,231.25

6. JoAnna is the Foodservice Director at Reading Hospital. She has just started a new menu program to offer those guests visiting hospitalized patients "guest trays", so the patients and their guests can eat together. She has been offering her "guest tray" program for one month, and it has been popular. She would like to know her average selling price per guest (check average) to see if she needs to change the price of her menu items. She would like to keep her average selling price above $11.50. Given the information below, and the fact that JoAnna has determined that she should achieve an $8.00 per guest tray contribution margin, calculate her average selling price for the month.

   Did JoAnna achieve her desired average selling price per guest? Does she need to change her prices?

Menu Item	Number Sold	Product Cost	Contribution Margin	Selling Price	Total Sales
Hunter's Chicken	2560	$3.50	$8.00	$11.50	$29,440.00
Jambalaya	750	$3.75	$8.00	$11.75	$8,812.50
Grilled Salmon	1200	$4.50	$8.00	$12.50	$15,000.00
Beef Tenderloin	500	$8.50	$8.00	$16.50	$8,250.00
Vegetarian Cheese Bake	1210	$2.75	$8.00	$10.75	$13,007.50
Total	6220				$74,510.00

   Average Selling Price: $11.98

   Answer: Yes, JoAnna did achieve her desired average selling price per guest. At $11.98, she is above her target selling price of $11.50. She does not need to change her prices.

7. Ming has recently inherited the Quick Wok restaurant started by her parents. It is located in a busy strip shopping area surrounded by many office complexes, but it is also near many quick-service restaurants. The Quick Wok has been successful because of the quality of its food, but Ming feels that it could do even better at lunchtime if she could create a "Value Meal" option to appeal to the price conscious consumer. Because there exists both a McDonald's and a Wendy's within a quarter mile of her store, she has determined that her Value Meal needs to be priced at $1.00. She creates a stir-fry dish that, when served with white rice, has a portion cost of 65 cents. Her beverages have a cost of 20 cents. The beverages already sell for $1.00 each and she does not want to raise this price.

   She believes she could sell 75 of the new Value Meals per day if she offers the stir-fry dish at $1.00. As well, she seeks an overall product cost percentage of 35%. From historical data she knows that 80% of her customers purchase a drink with their meals.

Value Meal and Beverage

Item	Number Sold	Item Cost	Total Cost	Selling Price	Total Sales	Food Cost %
Stir Fry Dish	75	$0.65	$48.75	$1.00	$75.00	65.0%
Beverage	60	$0.20	$12.00	$1.00	$60.00	20.0%
Total	135		$60.75		$135.00	45.0%

Number of Beverages to Achieve Target Overall Product Cost Percentage

Item	Number Sold	Item Cost	Total Cost	Selling Price	Total Sales	Food Cost %
Stir Fry Dish	75	$0.65	$48.75	$1.00	$75.00	65.0%
Beverage	150	$0.20	$30.00	$1.00	$150.00	20.0%
Total	225		$78.75		$225.00	35.0%

Based on the information given, calculate the overall product cost percentage of the Value Meals and beverages. Would you advise Ming to "go for it"? Why or why not?

Answer: I would not advise Ming to "go for it" because her overall product cost percentage would be 45%. This would be 10% above her target of 35%.

How many beverages must be sold in addition to the Value Meals if Ming is to achieve her target food cost percentage goal? Is this number feasible?

Answer: She would have to sell 150 beverages in order to meet her 35% overall product cost percentage target. This means that each customer would have to buy 2 beverages! This is definitely not feasible.

8. Jackson Daniels is the Director of Food and Beverage at the Foxfire Country Club. In June, Jackson's Club hosted three weddings. Each wedding featured a 4-hour hosted bar paid for by the bride and groom. The consumption data from each event is listed below. Complete the missing data in the report, and then help Jackson answer the questions that follow.

	Number of Guests Served	Beer Cost	Wine Cost	Spirit Cost	Total Cost	Cost per Guest
June 07	250	$500	$400	$600	$1,500	$6.00
June 14	500	650	1,225	1,000	2,875	5.75
June 21	400	525	1,000	675	2,200	5.50
Total	1,150	1,675	2,625	2,275	6,575	5.72

i. What do you think should be Jackson's "best estimate" of the cost, to the Club, of providing a 4-hour hosted bar at weddings?

    Answer: Jackson's best estimate of the cost would be $5.72 per person. This cost would be multiplied by the anticipated number of guests to arrive at the total cost of a 4-hour hosted bar.

ii. If Jackson seeks to ensure a 20% beverage cost, what should be his selling price, per guest, for a 4-hour hosted bar?

    Answer: His selling price per guest would be $5.72/20% = $28.60.

iii. Would you recommend Jackson charge 1/2 of the amount in the answer in b. above for a 2-hour hosted bar? Explain your answer.

    Answer: No! Consumption of alcohol at a hosted bar starts quickly, and then tapers off. As a result, the cost to provide a 2-hour hosted bar is MORE than one half the amount of a 4-hour hosted bar. This question provides a good example of why food and beverage cost control requires both knowledge of mathematics **and** of consumer behavior.

9. One criticism of both the Food Cost Percentage and Contribution Margin methods of determining menu price is that both are based primarily on the cost of "food," and ignore the cost of labor. In many foodservice operations, however, the cost of labor equals or even exceeds the cost of food. Do you foresee the cost of labor playing an increasing role in the calculation of menu prices? Explain your answer.

    Answer:

    With the continually increasing cost of salaries, wages, and benefits, the prices paid for fixed and variable labor will likely play an increasingly important role in determining menu prices. It is for that reason the authors will introduce (in Chapter 10: Planning for Profits), Goal Value Analysis, a method of considering the cost of labor (and other non-food expenses) when evaluating the effectiveness of a menu's pricing structure.

    As food becomes ever less costly (relative to the cost of labor) it is inevitable that the price paid for workers will take on a more significant role in determining menu prices. This may also be a good point in the course for Instructors to discuss the pros and cons of "Guest Worker" programs implemented by the Federal government and the direct impact on the foodservice industry.

Exam Questions

Multiple Choice
Choose the letter of the best answer to the questions listed below.

1. Which of the following describes the practice of selecting menu items and pricing them as a group?
   a. Bundling
   b. Couponing
   c. Value pricing
   d. All of the above
   e. None of the above
   Correct answer is a (See: Special Prices Situations)

2. Which of the following is an advantage of the standard menu?
   a. It simplifies your ordering process.
   b. Guest preference data is easily obtained.
   c. It can respond quickly to market changes and product cost changes.
   d. All of the above
   e. Only a. and b. above
   Correct answer is e (See: Menu Formats)

3. Which menu type is most commonly used in traditional restaurants?
   a. Cycle menu
   b. Daily menu
   c. Standard menu
   d. Rotating menu
   e. None of the above
   Correct answer is c (See: Menu Formats)

4. Menu prices are affected by several factors. Which of the following best describes these factors?
   a. Portion size and product quality
   b. Local competition and service levels
   c. Guest type and location
   d. Ambience and meal period
   e. All of the above
   Correct answer is e (See: Factors Affecting Menu Pricing)

5. Which term is used to describe menu items that will appear on the menu as the operator desires and will be removed when they are either consumed or discarded?
    a. Cycle menu
    b. Standard menu
    c. Menu specials
    d. All of the above
    e. Only a. and b. above
    Correct answer is c (See: Menu Formats)

6. How does one determine the pricing factor in the factor method approach to menu item pricing?
    a. Desired product cost / 1
    b. 1 / desired product cost
    c. 1 – desired product cost
    d. Desired product cost / 3
    e. None of the above
    Correct answer is b (See: Assigning Menu Prices)

7. Using the factor method, determine the sales price given the following: desired product cost % of 20%, product cost $1.00, covers served 200.
    a. Sales price = $5.00
    b. Sales price = $2.50
    c. Sales price = $40.00
    d. Cannot be determined from the information given
    Correct answer is a (See: Assigning Menu Prices)

8. _____ refers to the practice of reducing all or most prices on the menu in the belief that total guests will increase to the point that total sales revenue also increases.
    a. Bundling
    b. The Factor Method
    c. Couponing
    d. Value pricing
    e. None of the above
    Correct answer is d (See: Special Pricing Situations)

9. Factors influencing menu pricing include all of the following except:
    a. Local competition
    b. Service levels
    c. Guest type
    d. Weather
    e. Location
    Correct answer is d (See: Factors Affecting Menu Pricing)

10. Menu specials are used for what purpose?
    a. Provide variety
    b. Take advantage of low-cost raw ingredients
    c. Utilize carryover products
    d. Only a. and b.
    e. All of the above
    Correct answer is e (See: Menu Formats)

11. The EP cost of your steak dinner menu item is $4.00 and your desired food cost percentage is 40%. Using either the factor method or the product cost percentage method for pricing, what should the price be?
    a. $16.00
    b. $10.00
    c. $ 8.00
    d. $20.00
    Correct answer is b (See: Assigning Menu Prices)

12. Which of the following software functions can help management evaluate the effectiveness of individual menu items and establish their prices?
    a. Develop menus and cost recipes
    b. Evaluate the profitability of individual menu items
    c. Estimate future item demand based on past purchase patterns
    d. All of the above
    Correct answer is d (See: Technology Tools)

13. The EP cost of your lamb dinner menu item is $7.00 and your desired food cost percentage is 50%. Using either the factor method or the product cost percentage method for pricing, what should the price be?
    a. $16.00
    b. $14.00
    c. $ 9.00
    d. $26.00
    Correct answer is b (See: Assigning Menu Prices)

True/False
Choose the letter of the best answer to the questions listed below.

14. A cycle menu contains menu items that will appear on the menu as the operator desires and will be removed when they are either consumed or discarded.
    a. True
    b. False
    Correct answer is b (See: Menu Formats)

15. A standard menu is in effect for a specific time period.
    a. True
    b. False
    Correct answer is b (See: Menu Formats)

16. Revenue refers to the amount spent by all customers, while price refers to the amount charged to one customer.
    a. True
    b. False
    Correct answer is a (See: Factors Affecting Menu Pricing)

17. Local competition cannot be monitored too closely.
    a. True
    b. False
    Correct answer is b (See: Factors Affecting Menu Pricing)

18. Customers are willing to pay more for increased service levels.
    a. True
    b. False
    Correct answer is a (See: Factors Affecting Menu Pricing)

19. Contribution margin can be defined as the profit that remains after product cost is subtracted from an item's selling price.
    a. True
    b. False
    Correct answer is a (See: Assigning Menu Prices)

20. Price spread is defined as the range between the lowest and highest priced menu item.
    a. True
    b. False
    Correct answer is a (See: Special Pricing Situations)

21. The Leadership in Energy and Environmental Design (LEED) rating system developed by the U.S. Green Building Council (USGBC) evaluates facilities on a variety of standards, such as sustainability.
    a. True
    b. False
    Correct answer is a (See: Green and Growing)

22. Currently, the maximum LEED score that can be achieved is 80 points.
    a. True
    b. False
    Correct answer is b (See: Green and Growing)

Chapter 7

Managing the Cost of Labor

Learning Outcomes

At the conclusion of this chapter, you will be able to:

- Identify the factors that affect employee productivity.
- Develop labor standards and employee schedules used in a foodservice operation.
- Analyze and evaluate actual labor utilization.

Lecture Outline

1. Labor Expense in the Hospitality Industry

- In today's market, labor is so expensive, a manager cannot over staff to meet demand. Other methods must be used to accomplish necessary tasks and stay within the allotted labor budget.
- In some foodservice establishments, the cost of labor actually exceeds the cost of food and beverage products.
- Today's shrinking workforce indicates that managers will find it more difficult to recruit, train, and retain an effective group of employees.
- **Labor Expense** includes salaries and wages, but it consists of other labor-related costs as well.
- Other items included under labor expense vary from operation to operation, but may include such items as: FICA taxes, FUTA (Federal unemployment taxes) and state unemployment taxes, worker's compensation, group life insurance, health insurance, pension plan payments, employee meals, employee training, employee transportation, employee uniforms, employee housing, vacation/sick leave, tuition reimbursement programs, and employee incentives and bonuses.
- **Payroll** refers to the gross pay received by an employee in exchange for his or her work.

A **salaried employee** receives the same income per week or month regardless of the number of hours worked.

- Salaried employees are actually more accurately described as an **exempt employee** because their duties, responsibilities, and level of decisions make them "exempt" from the overtime provisions of the federal government's Fair Labor Standards Act (FLSA).

- **Minimum staff** is used to designate the least number of employees, or payroll dollars, needed to operate a facility or department within the facility.
- **Fixed Payroll** refers to the amount an operation pays in salaries.
- **Variable Payroll** consists of those dollars paid to hourly employees.
- Variable payroll is added only when management feels it is necessary to provide extra employees in anticipation of an increase in the number of guests to be served.
- Management has little control over fixed labor expense, but nearly 100% control over variable labor expense.
- Labor expense refers to the total of all costs associated with maintaining a foodservice workforce.
- Total labor expense will always exceed that of payroll.
- Payroll is considered a "controllable" labor expense, unlike FICA taxes and insurance premiums. But, in reality, managers may even be able to influence some of the no controllable labor expenses, such as providing a training program to reduce injuries and insurance premiums.

2. Assessing Labor Productivity

- Productivity is the amount of work performed by an employee in a fixed period of time.
- There are many ways to assess labor productivity. In general, productivity is measured in terms of the **productivity ratio** as follows:

$$\frac{\text{Output}}{\text{Input}} = \text{Productivity Ratio}$$

- There are several ways of defining foodservice output and input; thus, there are several types of productivity ratios.
- Foodservice operators must develop their own methods for managing payroll because every food service unit is different.

3. Maintaining a Productive Workforce

- The following are ten key employee-related factors that affect employee productivity:

10 Key Factors Affecting Employee Productivity
1.   **Employee Selection**
2.   **Training**
3.   **Supervision**
4.   **Scheduling**
5.   **Breaks**
6.   **Morale**
7.   **Menu**
8.   **Convenience vs. Scratch Preparation**
9.   **Equipment/Tools**
10.   **Service Level Desired**

- Choosing the right employee is vital in developing a highly productive workforce. The process begins with the development of the job description and job specification.
- A **job description** is a listing of the tasks that must be accomplished by the employee hired to fill a particular position.
- A **job specification** is a listing of the personal characteristics needed to perform the tasks contained in a particular job description.
- When actually beginning to select employees for vacancies, one or more of the following selection aids are normally used: applications, interviews, preemployment testing, and background/reference checks.
- The employment application is a document completed by the candidate for employment.
- Job interviews, if improperly performed, can subject an employer to significant legal liability.

Preemployment testing is a common way to help improve employee productivity.

- **Skills tests** can include activities such as typing tests, and computer application tests. **Psychological testing** can include personality tests, tests designed to predict performance, or tests of mental ability. **Preemployment drug testing** is used to determine if an applicant uses drugs.
- Increasingly, hospitality employers are utilizing background checks prior to hiring employees in selected positions.
- Not conducting background checks on some positions can subject the employer to potential litigation under the doctrine of **negligent hiring**, that is, a failure on the part of an employer to exercise reasonable care in the selection of employees.
- No area under management control holds greater promise for increased employee productivity than job improvement through training.
- Effective training will improve job satisfaction and instill in employees a sense of well-being and accomplishment. It will also reduce confusion, product waste, and loss of guests.
- Effective training begins with a good **orientation program**.

- **Task training** is the training undertaken to ensure an employee has the skills to meet productivity goals.
  - The first step in developing a training program is determining how the task is to be done. Once a method for completing a task is developed, it should be strictly enforced unless a better way is developed. Discipline should be administered positively.
  - The second step in developing a training program is planning the training session. Taking time to plan the session lets employees know that management is taking it seriously.
  - The third step is presenting the training session. Present sessions with enthusiasm. Always make sure that training is presented not because employees "don't know" but rather because management wants them to "know more."
  - The fourth step is evaluating the session's effectiveness. Evaluation can be as simple as observing employee behavior or as detailed as preparing written questions, but it must be done to ensure the employees learned.
  - The fifth step is retraining at the proper intervals. Employees must be retrained and reminded constantly if their productivity or their skill levels are to remain high.
- All employees require proper supervision.
- Proper supervision means assisting employees in improving productivity.
- When supervision is geared toward helping, the guest benefits and, thus, the operation benefits. This is why it is so important for managers to be **on the floor**, in other words, in the dining area, during meal periods.
- When employees can please both the guests and the manager at once, productivity rises; if employees feel that they can only satisfy the guest *or* the operation, difficulties will arise.
- Even with highly productive employees, poor employee scheduling by management can result in low productivity ratios.
- Proper scheduling ensures that the correct number of employees is available to do the necessary amount of work.
- Scheduling efficiency can often be improved through the use of the **split-shift**, a technique used to match individual employee work shifts with peaks and valleys of customer demand.
- Employees have both a physical and a mental need for breaks from their work.
- Employees need to know that management cares enough to establish a break schedule and stick to it.
- Management should view breaks as a necessary part of maintaining a highly productive workforce, not as lost or wasted time.
- Management must create a fun, motivating environment for employees to work in.
- Motivated groups usually work for a management team that has created a vision, communicated the vision to employees, and ensured that employees share the vision.
- Creating a vision is nothing more than finding a "purpose" for the workforce.

- A shared purpose between management and employees is important for the development and maintenance of high morale.
- Employee turnover *is* high in some sections of the hospitality industry. By some estimates, it exceeds 200% per year. You can measure your turnover by using the following formula:

Employee Turnover Rate =	Number of Employees Separated
	Number of Employees in Workforce

- **Separated** is the term used to describe employees who have either quit, been terminated, or in some other manner have "separated" themselves from the operation.
- Some foodservice operators prefer to distinguish between voluntary and involuntary separation.
- A **voluntary separation** is one in which the employee made the decision to leave the organization.
- An **involuntary separation** is one in which management has caused the employee to separate from the organization.
- The turnover formula can be modified to create these two ratios:

Involuntary Employee Turnover Rate =	Number of Employees Involuntarily Separated
	Number of Employees in Workforce
Voluntary Employee Turnover Rate =	Number of Employees Voluntarily Separated
	Number of Employees in Workforce

- Turnover is expensive. This expense is comprised of actual and hidden costs. Actual costs include interviewing and training time, while hidden costs refer to the number of dishes broken by a new dishwasher, etc.
- A major factor in employee productivity is the foodservice operation's actual menu.
- In general, the more variety of items a kitchen is asked to produce, the less efficient that kitchen will be.
- Menu items must also be selected to complement the skill level of the employees and the equipment available to produce the menu item.
- Since most foodservice operations change their menus infrequently, it is critical that the menu items selected can be prepared efficiently and well.
- The decision of whether to "make" or "buy" involves two major factors, the product quality and the product cost.
- It is important to remember that make or buy decisions affect both food and labor costs.
- Management, often in consultation with kitchen production staff, must resolve make or buy decisions.

- Generally, foodservice productivity ratios have not increased as have those of other businesses, since foodservice is a labor-intensive, rather than machine-intensive industry.
- But, it is critical for the foodservice manager to understand the importance of a properly equipped workplace to improve productivity.
- Equipment should be properly maintained and updated if employees are to be held accountable for productivity standards or gains.
- Today's guest expects and demands higher levels of service than ever before, which requires management to become creative in order to still improve employee productivity.
- When management varies service levels, it varies employee productivity ratios.
- The key to knowing "how many employees are needed" to effectively operate the foodservice unit lies in developing productivity standards.
- The best productivity measure for any unit is, of course, the one that makes the most sense for that unique operation.

4. Measuring Current Labor Productivity

- There are a variety of ways to measure productivity in the hospitality industry such as: labor cost percentage, sales per labor hour, labor dollars per guest served, guests served per labor dollar, guests served per labor hour, revenue available seat hour (RevPASH).
- A very commonly used measure of employee productivity in the foodservice industry is the labor cost percentage.
- The labor cost percentage is computed as follows:

$$\frac{\text{Cost of Labor}}{\text{Total Sales}} = \text{Labor Cost \%}$$

- It is important to realize that there are several ways to define cost of labor.
- Controlling the labor cost percentage is extremely important in the foodservice industry since it is the most widely used measure of productivity and thus is often used to determine the effectiveness of a manager.
- Labor cost percentage varies with changes in the price paid for labor. Because of this, labor cost percentage by itself is not a complete measure of workforce productivity.
- The most perishable commodity any foodservice operator buys is the labor hour. When not productively used, it disappears forever.
- This is why many foodservice operators prefer to measure labor productivity in terms of the amount of sales generated for each labor hour used.

$$\frac{\text{Total Sales}}{\text{Labor Hours Used}} = \text{Sales per Labor Hour}$$

- Sales per labor hour will vary with changes in menu selling price, not with changes in the price paid for labor.
- However, sales per labor hour neglects to consider the amount paid to employees per hour to generate the sales.

$$\frac{\text{Cost of Labor}}{\text{Guests Served}} = \text{Labor Dollars per Guest Served}$$

- With labor dollars per guest served, the cost of labor represents all the labor required to serve the guest.
- Labor dollars per guest served varies based on the price paid for labor.

$$\frac{\text{Guests Served}}{\text{Cost of Labor}} = \text{Guests Served per Labor Dollar}$$

- As a measure of productivity, guests served per labor dollar expended has advantages. It is relatively easy to compute, and can be used by foodservice units, such as institutions, that do not routinely record dollar sales figures.

$$\frac{\text{Guests Served}}{\text{Labor Hours Used}} = \text{Guests Served per Labor Hour}$$

- Guests served per labor hour is a powerful measure of productivity, not a measure of either cost and productivity or sales and productivity.
- It is extremely useful in comparing similar units in areas with widely differing wage rates or selling prices.
- The managers who use this figure do so because they like the focus of emphasizing service levels and not just reducing costs.
- **Revenue Per Available Seat Hour (RevPASH)** helps managers evaluate how much guests buy and how quickly they are served. It does so primarily by assessing the duration of guests' dining experiences. Duration is simply the length of time customers sit at a table.

$$\frac{\text{Revenue}}{\text{Available Seat Hours}} = \text{Revenue Per Available Seat Hour (RevPASH)}$$

- Many operators prefer to compute their productivity measures on a daily, rather than on a weekly or monthly basis. This can easily be done by using a six-column form with cost of labor, sales, and labor cost %.
- Many operators find that a single measure of their labor productivity is insufficient for their needs.
- Therefore, an operator may establish labor subcategories such as production, service, sanitation, and management.

- When determining labor productivity measures by subcategory remember the following: be sure to include all the relevant data, use the same method to identify the numerator and denominator for each category, compute an overall total to ensure that the sum of the categories is consistent with the overall total.
- Labor costs for each subcategory can be estimated. By following the rules of algebra and adding the word "estimated," the guests served per labor dollar formula can be restated as follows:

$$\frac{\text{Number of Estimated Guests Served}}{\text{Guests Served Per Labor Dollar}} = \text{Estimated Cost of Labor}$$

5. Managing Payroll Costs

- Essentially, the management of payroll costs is a four-step process, which includes the following factors:

    1. Determine productivity standards.
    2. Forecast sales volume.
    3. Schedule employees using productivity standards and forecasted sales volume.
    4. Analyze results.

- A **productivity standard** is defined as management's view of what constitutes an appropriate productivity ratio in a specific foodservice operation.
- Productivity standards represent what you should reasonably expect in the way of output per unit of labor input.
- Productivity standards are typically based on the following types of information: unit history, company average, industry average, management experience, or a combination of some or all of the above.
- A **franchisor** is the entity responsible for selling and maintaining control over the franchise brand's name.
- Sales volume forecasting, when combined with established labor productivity standards, allows a foodservice operator to determine the number of employees needed to effectively service your guests.
- You can establish a labor budget using your productivity standards, your sales forecast, and the labor cost percentage formula you have already learned. Remember that the labor cost percentage formula is defined as:

$$\frac{\text{Cost of Labor}}{\text{Total Sales}} = \text{Labor Cost \%}$$

- If you include the words "forecasted", "standard", and "budget", and follow the rules of algebra, the labor cost percentage formula can be restated as follows:

Forecasted Total Sales x Labor Cost % Standard = Cost of Labor Budget

- You can establish a budget for total number of labor hours needed to service your establishment. Remember, that guests served per labor hour formula is defined as:

$$\frac{\text{Guests Served}}{\text{Labor Hours Used}} = \text{Guests Served per Labor Hour}$$

- If you include the words "forecasted," "standard," and "budget," and follow the rules of algebra, the guests served per labor hour formula can be restated as follows:

$$\frac{\text{Forecasted Number of Guests Served}}{\text{Guests Served per Labor Hour Standard}} = \text{Labor Hours Budget}$$

- Because employee schedules are based upon the number of hours to be worked or dollars to be spent, an employee schedule recap form can be an effective tool in a daily analysis of labor productivity.
- Since labor is purchased on a daily basis, labor costs should be monitored on a daily basis.
- Some foodservice managers practice an **on-call** system whereby employees who are off duty are assigned to on-call status.
- Other managers practice a **call-in** system. In this arrangement, employees who are off duty are required to check in with management on a daily basis to see if the predicted sales volume is such that they may be needed.
- Schedule modifications should be done hourly, if necessary.
- It is critical to match labor usage with projected volume.
- To complete the job of managing labor-related expense, you should analyze your results by comparing actual labor cost to budgeted labor cost. To determine the percentage of budget, the following formula is used:

$$\frac{\text{Actual Amount}}{\text{Budgeted Amount}} = \text{\% of Budget}$$

- When referring to labor costs, some foodservice operators use the term **standard cost,** that is the labor cost needed to meet established productivity standards, rather than "budgeted cost."
- In the case of labor, we may still be within reasonable budget, though we may vary greatly from the standard. For this reason, the authors prefer the term **budgeted labor** rather than **standard labor**. Labor standards will always vary a bit unless guest counts can be predicted perfectly which, of course, is rarely the case.

6. Reducing Labor-Related Costs

- If management finds that labor costs are too high, problem areas must be identified and corrective action must be taken.
- Ways to reduce fixed labor costs include; improve productivity, increase sales volume, combine jobs to eliminate fixed positions, and reduce wages paid to the fixed payroll employees.
- Ways to reduce variable labor costs include; improve productivity, schedule appropriately to adjust to changes in sales volume, combine jobs to eliminate variable positions, and reduce wages paid to the variable employees.
- One way to increase productivity and reduce labor-related expense is through **employee empowerment**, involving employees in the decision-making process.
- Today, employees have come to realize there is more to life than work. Management, unable to always offer more money, has been forced to come up with new incentives.
- Employees are seeking job satisfaction in addition to salaries or wages.
- Consumers are increasingly aware that when they support businesses committed to sustainability, their dollars impact social and environmental concerns. So committed are they that they are, on average, willing to spend 20% more than the typical guest for products that meet their values and lifestyle.
- In a similar manner, environmentally conscious workers are increasingly becoming aware that a company's care for the environment most often is also reflected in care for its employees. As a result, those companies espousing genuine commitment to the environment attract a more committed and, as a result, a higher quality staff.

7. Technology Tools

- As labor costs continue to increase, and as labor cost management becomes increasingly important to the profitability of restaurateurs, the tools available to manage these costs have increased significantly also.
- Current software programs can help you manage and control labor costs including the following tasks:
  1. Maintain employment records such as:
     a. Required employment documents (i.e., applications, I-9s, W-2s, etc.)
     b. Tax data
     c. Pay rates
     d. Earned vacation or other leave time
     e. Department/cost center affiliation
     f. Benefits eligibility
     g. Training records
  2. Conduct and record the results of on-line or computer-based training programs.
  3. Compute voluntary and involuntary employee turnover rates by department.
  4. Track employee lost days due to injury/accident.
  5. Maintain employee availability records (requested days off, vacation, etc.).

6. Develop employee schedules and interface employee schedules with time clock systems.
7. Monitor overtime costs.
8. Maintain job descriptions and specifications.
9. Develop and maintain daily, weekly, and monthly productivity reports, including:
   a. Labor cost percentage
   b. Sales per labor hour
   c. Labor dollars per guest served
   d. Guests served per labor dollar
   e. Guests served per labor hour
   f. Optimal labor costs based on actual sales achieved
10. Interface employee scheduling component with forecasted sales volume software in the POS system.

Consider The Cost

"You wanted to see me, Sir?" said Francis to the clearly agitated guest seated at the six-top table in the corner of Chez Lapin, the upscale French Bistro-style restaurant that Francis managed.

"I've been waiting ten minutes for my waiter to bring us our check. And as slow as he's been, it will probably take another ten minutes to process my credit card. I just want to pay and leave. The food was fine, but this is ridiculous!"

"I'm really sorry Sir. I'll find your server," replied Francis as he glanced around the dining room. As he did, he noticed several unbussed tables that were littered with dirty dishes, as well as the Hostess stand where the line of guests waiting to be seated hadn't gotten any smaller in nearly an hour.

When Francis entered the kitchen looking for the disgruntled guest's server, he was surprised to see several of the line cooks relaxing on the production line.

"How's it going back here tonight?" asked Francis as he glanced around the kitchen.

"No problems. Just waiting for the orders to come in boss," replied Sasha, the Sous Chef in charge of the production line. "We're keeping up easily."

Assume that all of the workers at Chez Lapin are well-trained and highly motivated.

1. Do you think the servers are likely doing their best to provide good service to the restaurant's guests? If you believe so, then why was the guest in this scenario unhappy?
2. What do you think is the cause of a consistently long line of waiting diners when there are numerous vacant, but unbussed, tables in the dining room?
3. The Sous Chef in this case said, "We're keeping up easily." Do you think that means they are being very efficient and thus very productive? Explain your answer.

Answers:

In this case, Francis is having difficulty keeping the kitchen staff working at a 100% productivity level because the dining room is understaffed. As a result, the operation is serving fewer guests per hour of operation than it was designed to serve. The money Francis may be saving by scheduling fewer than the needed number of dining room staff is "costing" him in terms of unhappy guests and longer than desirable waiting times for vacant tables.

1. If they are well-trained and highly motivated, it is very likely that Francis' dining room staff is working hard. Perhaps too hard! They do not appear to have enough time to deliver the quality service levels Francis desires. As a result, service is slow, as evidenced by the unhappy guest in this scenario.

2. If Francis employs table bussers, too few have been scheduled. If wait staff are responsible for clearing their own tables, the number of servers scheduled is inadequate. In either case, the result is an excessive number of uncleared or dirty tables that should be ready for new guest seating, but are not.

3. The fact that the Sous Chef states, "We're keeping up easily," is not good. It is yet another indication to Francis that all is not well. In fact, with guests waiting in line, unbussed tables in the dining room, and a food production line operating at less than a 100% productivity level, Francis has several indications that his restaurant is not being operated very efficiently or productively when it comes to the proper scheduling of labor.

Apply What You Have Learned

Teddy Fields is the Kitchen Manager at the Tanron Corporation International Headquarters. The facility he helps manage serves 3000 employees per day. Teddy very much needs an additional dishwasher, and is interviewing Wayne, an excellent candidate with 5 years experience who is now washing dishes at the Roadway restaurant. Teddy normally starts his dishwashers at $9.00 per hour. Wayne states that he makes $10.00 per hour, a rate that is higher than all but one of Teddy's current dishwashers. Wayne states that he would not leave his current job to take a "pay-cut".

1. Should Teddy offer to hire Wayne at a rate higher than most of his current employees? Why or why not?

   Answer: Teddy should be hired because he is an excellent candidate with 5 years dishwashing experience. Because Wayne is expected to wash dishes for 3,000 employees per day, $10.00 per hour would be a reasonable rate for him. However, this may cause some issues with the other dishwashers.

2. Assume you answered "No" to question one above, what would you say to Wayne?

   Answer: I would say to Wayne that it is the company's policy to hire new dishwashers at $9.00 per hour. However, I would point out that the company offers good employee benefits, and I would also explain that he could receive a raise quickly because of his excellent work experience.

3. Assume you answered "Yes" to question one above, what would you say to your current dishwashing employees?

   Answer: I would explain to the current dishwashing employees that Wayne has 5 years experience working as a dishwasher, so his wage is fair. However, he is expected to work hard and get along well with other employees in the kitchen.

Test Your Skills

1. Rosa is the manager of a fine dining Italian restaurant in a large Midwest City. She has experienced high turnover with her hourly employees over the past several months because they say that she isn't paying competitive wages. More employees have threatened to leave if she doesn't give them a raise. She has determined that she can compete with local restaurants if she raises the hourly wage from $8.00 per hour to $8.50, a 6.25% increase. Rosa is concerned about what this will do to her labor cost percentage. Her current labor cost % is at 35%, and she has determined that 38% is the highest she can go and still make a profit. Using last month's data, help Rosa calculate the effect of a 6.25% increase in wages. Can she give the employees what they want and still make a profit?

Week	Original Cost of Labor	Raise in Dollars	Total Cost of Labor	Sales	Labor Cost %
1	$10,650	$665.63	$11,315.63	$27,600	41.0%
2	12,075	754.69	$12,829.69	32,250	39.8%
3	10,887	680.44	$11,567.44	28,650	40.4%
4	10,383	648.94	$11,031.94	37,200	29.7%
Total	43,995	$2,749.69	$46,744.69	$125,700	37.2%

Answer: Yes, she can still make a profit even with a 6.25% raise. Her labor cost % will be lower than 38%.

2. Jennifer operates Joe Bob's Bar-B-Q Restaurant in a quaint Southwestern city of the United States. She specializes in beef brisket and blackberry cobbler. Her operation is very popular. The following data are taken from her last month's operation. She would like to establish labor standards for the entire year based on last month's figures because she believes *that* month represents a good level of both guest service and profitability for her operation. Jennifer has an average guest check of $12 and an overall average payroll cost of $8 per hour.

a. Use Jennifer's last month's operating results to calculate the following productivity standards: labor cost percentage, sales per labor hour, labor dollars per guest served, guests served per labor dollar, guests served per labor hour. (Spreadsheet hint: Use the ROUND function to two decimal places for "Guests Served per Labor Hour.")

Operating Results for Joe Bob's

Week	Number of Guests Served	Labor Hours Used
1	7,000	4,000
2	7,800	4,120
3	7,500	4,110
4	8,000	4,450
Total	30,300	16,680

Calculate:

Average Guest Check	$12
Average Wage per Hour	$8
Total Sales	$363,600
Total Labor Cost	$133,440

Productivity Measurement	Productivity Standard
Labor Cost Percentage	36.7%
Sales per Labor Hour	$21.80
Labor Dollars per Guest Served	$4.40
Guests Served per Labor Dollar	0.23
Guests Served per Labor Hour	1.82

b. Jennifer has sub-divided her employees into the following categories: meat production, bakery production, salad production, service, sanitation, and management. She wants to develop a sales per labor hour standard for each of her labor categories. She believes this will help her develop future labor budgets based on forecasted sales. Help Jennifer calculate this below, based on her current usage of labor hours.

Labor Category	% of Labor Hours Used	Labor Hours	Sales per Labor Hour
Meat Production	25%	4,170	$87.19
Bakery Production	15%	2,502	$145.32
Salad Production	10%	1,668	$217.99
Service	20%	3,336	$108.99
Sanitation	20%	3,336	$108.99
Management	10%	1,668	$217.99
Total	100%	16,680	$21.80

c. Now that Jennifer has calculated her productivity standards she would like to use them to develop a labor hours budget for each day next week. She has forecasted 8,000 guests, and she wants to use the guests served per labor hour standard that was calculated in part a. Use this information to develop a labor hours budget for Jennifer.

Day	Forecasted Number of Guests Served	Guests Served per Labor Hour Standard	Labor Hours Budget
1	900	1.82	494.5
2	925	1.82	508.2
3	975	1.82	535.7
4	1,200	1.82	659.3
5	1,400	1.82	769.2
6	1,600	1.82	879.1
7	1,000	1.82	549.5
Total	8,000	1.82	4,395.6

3. Mikel owns Mikel's Steak House, a popular dining establishment just outside of town on a busy state highway. Mikel uses labor cost % as his productivity measure, but he has been calculating it only once per month. Since his monthly costs have been higher than he expected, Mikel has decided that he needs a *daily* measure of his labor cost % in order to control his costs better.

a. Calculate Mikel's daily labor cost % using the six-column daily productivity report which follows.

b. Mikel wants to keep his labor cost % at 37%. Given the results of his six-column daily productivity report for the first week of March, will he be able to achieve his labor cost % standard if he continues in the same manner for the remainder of the month? If not, what actions can he take to reduce both his fixed and variable labor-related expense?

Six-Column Labor Cost Percentage

Unit Name: Mikel's Steak House   Date: 3/1 – 3/7

Weekday	Cost of Labor		Sales		Labor Cost %	
	Today	To Date	Today	To Date	Today	To Date
1	$950	$950	$2,520	$2,520	37.7%	37.7%
2	$1,120	$2,070	$2,610	$5,130	42.9%	40.4%
3	$1,040	$3,110	$2,720	$7,850	38.2%	39.6%
4	$1,100	$4,210	$2,780	$10,630	39.6%	39.6%
5	$1,600	$5,810	$3,530	$14,160	45.3%	41.0%
6	$1,700	$7,510	$4,100	$18,260	41.5%	41.1%
7	$1,300	$8,810	$3,910	$22,170	33.2%	39.7%
Total	$8,810		$22,170		39.7%	

Answer: No, Mikel will not be able to achieve his 37% labor cost standard if he continues in the same manner for the remainder of the month since he is at 39.7%, currently. Actions he can take to reduce labor-related expense are as follows:

Category	Actions
Fixed	1. Improve productivity
	2. Increase sales volume
	3. Combine jobs to eliminate fixed positions
	4. Reduce wages paid to the fixed payroll employees
Variable	1. Improve productivity
	2. Schedule appropriately to adjust to changes in sales volume
	3. Combine jobs to eliminate variable positions
	4. Reduce wages paid to the variable employees

4. Jeffrey operates a high volume, fine dining restaurant called the Baroness. His labor productivity ratio of choice is guests served per labor hour. His standards for both servers and buspersons are as follows:

        A.   **Servers**   =   **10 guests per labor hour**
        B.   **Buspersons** =   **25 guests per labor hour**

On a busy day, Jeffrey projects the following volume in terms of anticipated guests. His projections are made in one-hour blocks. Determine the number of labor hours Jeffrey should schedule for each job classification for each time period.

How often in the night should Jeffrey check his volume forecast in order to ensure that he achieves his labor productivity standards and thus is within budget at the end of the evening?

Servers:	10	Guests Per Labor Hour	
Buspersons:	25	Guests Per Labor Hour	

Volume/Staff Forecasting for Saturday

The Baroness

Time	Forecasted Number of Guests Served	Server Hours Needed	Busperson Hours Needed
11:00 - 12:00	85	8.5	3.4
12:00 - 1:00	175	17.5	7.0
1:00 - 2:00	95	9.5	3.8
2:00 - 3:00	30	3.0	1.2
3:00 - 4:00	25	2.5	1.0
4:00 - 5:00	45	4.5	1.8
5:00 - 6:00	90	9.0	3.6
6:00 - 7:00	125	12.5	5.0
7:00 - 8:00	185	18.5	7.4
8:00 - 9:00	150	15.0	6.0
9:00 - 10:00	90	9.0	3.6
10:00 - 11:00	45	4.5	1.8
Total	1,140	114.0	45.6

Answer: Jeffrey should be checking his volume hourly. That way, if guests do not arrive as predicted, he can adjust his number of employees to save labor costs.

5. Steve is in trouble. He has never been a particularly strong labor cost control person. He likes to think of himself more as a "people person." His boss, however, believes that Steve must get more serious about controlling labor costs or he will make Steve an unemployed people person! Steve estimates his weekly sales, and then submits that figure to his boss, who then assigns Steve a labor budget for the week. Steve's operating results and budget figures for last month are presented below.

a. Compute Steve's % of budget figures for both sales and labor cost. Also compute Steve's budget and actual labor cost percentages per week and for the five-week accounting period.

Operating Results

Steve's Airport Deli

Week	Sales			Labor Cost			Labor Cost %	
	Budget	Actual	% of Budget	Budget	Actual	% of Budget	Budget	Actual
1	$2,500	$2,250	90%	$875	$900	103%	35%	40%
2	1,700	1,610	95%	595	630	106%	35%	39%
3	4,080	3,650	89%	1,224	1,300	106%	30%	36%
4	3,100	2,800	90%	1,085	1,100	101%	35%	39%
5	2,600	2,400	92%	910	980	108%	35%	41%
Total	$13,980	$12,710	91%	$4,689	$4,910	105%	34%	39%

b. Do you feel that Steve has significant variations from budget? Why do you think Steve's boss assigned Steve a lower labor cost % goal during week 3? How do you feel about Steve's overall performance? What would you do if you were Steve's boss? If you were Steve?

Answer: Steve's labor cost percentages are significantly higher than budgeted. In anticipation of negative performance by Steve, Steve's boss probably lowered his budgeted labor cost percentage in week three in case his actual labor cost percentages in the previous two weeks are high. This might help Steve to get back on track, if needed. Steve and his boss need to observe what is going on during the workday in operations. Steve may also need more guidance on how to schedule; he may not be setting expectations high enough for his employees.

6. Jordan is the new Western Regional manager for "The Lotus House" Asian buffet restaurant chain. Her territory consists of 12 stores in four states. Last week she received the following data from her stores. Compute Jordan's labor cost by store, by state, and for her region.

	Sales	Cost of Labor	Labor Cost %
California			
Store 1	$91,000.00	$34,500.00	37.91%
Store 2	$106,500.00	$38,750.00	36.38%
Store 3	$83,500.00	$31,500.00	37.72%
Total	$281,000.00	$104,750.00	37.28%
Oregon			
Store 1	$36,800.00	$12,250.00	33.29%
Store 2	$61,000.00	$18,750.00	30.74%
Store 3	$52,000.00	$17,500.00	33.65%
Total	$149,800.00	$48,500.00	32.38%
Washington			
Store 1	$47,500.00	$14,750.00	31.05%
Store 2	$46,500.00	$15,000.00	32.26%
Store 3	$45,500.00	$15,000.00	32.97%
Total	$139,500.00	$44,750.00	32.08%
Nevada			
Store 1	$53,000.00	$17,250.00	32.55%
Store 2	$56,000.00	$18,500.00	33.04%
Store 3	$55,100.00	$17,250.00	31.31%
Total	$164,100.00	$53,000.00	32.30%
Region	$734,400.00	$251,000.00	34.18%

Can Jordan compute the average labor cost percentage for her region by summing the labor cost percentages of the four states and dividing by four? Why or why not? How is the overall labor cost percentage for her region computed?

Answer: No, she cannot compute a simple average; she must compute a weighted average. If she simply takes the labor cost percentages of the four states and divides them by four, she will get 33.51%, which is inaccurate. Her overall labor cost percentage of the region is computed by dividing total labor cost for the region by total sales for the region.

7. Ravi Shah is the Food and Beverage Director at the St. Andrews Golf Course and Conference Center. The facility is a popular place for weddings and Ravi finds that, on many Friday and Saturday nights, the banquet space at St. Andrews is completely booked. That is good news, but Ravi now finds that Allisha, the one full-time (paid $20.00 per hour) employee he has utilized as a supervisor for the banquet area is now averaging 15 hours overtime per week.

    Ravi is considering three alternative courses of action. They are:

    1. Maintain the status quo and pay Allisha for 55 hours a week.

    2. Create a salaried position, schedule the employee who holds the position 55 hours per week, and pay that individual $50,000 per year.

    3. Split the job into two part-time positions of 30 and 25 hours per week and pay these employees $22.50 per hour.

    Assume the following:

    1. Overtime is paid at 1.5 times the normally paid rate.

    2. The operation's benefit package for part-time employees is 20% of the wages paid to them.

    3. The operation's benefit package for full-time employees is 35% of the wages paid to them.

    4. All full-time and part-time employees at the supervisor level or above receive two weeks paid vacation per year.

    Which of these three courses of action will cost the facility the most money? The least? If you were Ravi, which of these alternatives would you implement? Why?

    Answer: Alternative 1 would cost the facility the most money. Alternative 2 would cost the facility the least money. If I were Ravi, I would implement Alternative 2 because it is the least expensive and it provides continuity because it does not split the work between two people. I would offer the salaried position to Allisha or promote her.

	Hours Worked	Pay Per Hour	Pay Per Week	Weeks in a Year	Pay Before Benefits	Benefits	Annual Pay with Benefits
Alternative 1	40	$20.00	$800.00	52	$41,600.00	$14,560.00	$56,160.00
	15	30.00	450.00	52	23,400.00	8,190.00	31,590.00
Total	55		$1,250.00		$65,000.00	$22,750.00	$87,750.00
Alternative 2	55				$50,000.00	$17,500.00	$67,500.00
Alternative 3	30	$22.50	$675.00	52	$35,100.00	$7,020.00	$42,120.00
	25	$22.50	$562.50	52	$29,250.00	$5,850.00	$35,100.00
Total	55		$1,237.50		$64,350.00	$12,870.00	$77,220.00

8. Luis manages Havana, a 150-seat full-service restaurant featuring Cuban and other Caribbean-style menu items. His restaurant is open for dinner from 5:00 p.m. to 11:00 p.m. Luis was excited to read, in one of the industry publications to which he subscribed, an article explaining RevPASH. In the past, Luis used labor cost % to create his allowable labor cost budget. Luis now wants to calculate RevPASH, as well as continue to use labor cost % to establish his *hourly* allowable labor cost budget. He has created a form (below) to calculate each of these measures.

Luis is a good manager. When his dining room is slower, he encourages his servers to aggressively sell appetizers and desserts to increase his check average. When the restaurant is very busy, he encourages his servers to stress the quick turn of tables to minimize guest wait times and maximize the number of guests that can be served. As a result, and based on his historical records, when he serves 100 or less guests per hour, the restaurant achieves a $20.00 per guest check average. When 101 - 150 guests are served per hour, the check average drops to $18.00 per guest. When over 150 guests are served per hour, Havana achieves a $16.00 per guest check average.

Consider below Luis's forecast of the number of guests he will serve this coming Friday night; and then calculate his forecasted RevPASH for each hour he will be open. Next, help him know how much he can spend for labor for each hour he will be open. Assume Luis's target is a 30% labor cost at all times. (Spreadsheet hint: calculate Total Check Average AFTER Total Revenue and Total Guests Served have been calculated.)

Havana Forecast for: **This FRIDAY Night**

Hour	Available Seats	Guests Served	Check Average	Revenue	RevPASH	Allowable Cost Based on 30% Labor Cost
5- 6 p.m.	150	50	$20.00	$1,000	$6.67	$300.00
6- 7 p.m.	150	100	$20.00	$2,000	$13.33	$600.00
7- 8 p.m.	150	150	$18.00	$2,700	$18.00	$810.00
8- 9 p.m.	150	175	$16.00	$2,800	$18.67	$840.00
9-10 p.m.	150	125	$18.00	$2,250	$15.00	$675.00
10-11 p.m.	150	75	$20.00	$1,500	$10.00	$450.00
Total	900	675	$18.15	$12,250	$13.61	$3,675.00

% Seats Sold =   75%

a. What percentage of his total seats available does Luis believe he will fill on Friday night? What overall check average does he estimate he will achieve?

b. What would be Luis's forecast for his hourly and overall RevPASH on this day?

c. What would be Luis's labor budget for each hour his restaurant will be open, as well as the total amount that could be spent for labor that night?

d. What are some specific steps Luis might take to improve his RevPASH on Fridays from 5 - 6 p.m.? From 8 - 9 p.m.?

Answers:

a. 75% of total seats available; $18.15 overall check average

b. His hourly RevPASH can be seen in each of the hours from 5:00 p.m. to 11:00 p.m. in the grid above. His overall RevPASH is $13.61.

c. His budgeted hourly labor cost can be seen in each of the hours from 5:00 p.m. to 11:00 p.m. in the grid above. The total amount that could be spent for labor is $3,675.

d. From 5–6 p.m. Luis needs to attract more guests (fill more seats). One popular way restaurants do so is by offering "Early Bird" specials that discount food or offer special, lower cost menu items to those diners willing to eat at these slower demand times.

From 8–9 p.m. Luis needs to "turn" more seats. He should place heavy emphasis on cleaning dirty tables quickly, using a computerized table management seating system to ensure the maximum "fill" on his seats, and he should popularly price those menu items that can be produced, served and eaten fairly quickly, thus effectively reducing the duration (seating time) of each guest, without seeming to rush them.

9. In this chapter you learned about the importance of employee training when seeking to improve worker productivity. The old foodservice adage that "Training doesn't cost, it pays!" is true. With creative thinking, even the cost of acquiring quality training materials can be made very reasonable. Assume you were the Director of Foodservice for a school district that included 20 elementary, middle, and high schools. You seek to provide training to the 100 foodservice employees working in your district. Identify five specific steps you could take to identify and secure low-cost training materials so they can be utilized at a minimum "cost-per-employee" to be trained.

Answers:

Student answers will vary; however, the following steps could be reasonably taken by creative foodservice managers in any industry segment if they sought to secure low-cost but high quality training materials.

1. Contact the national headquarters for the professional foodservice trade association for the specific industry segment. In this scenario, contact the ASFSA (American School Food Service Association). Many trade associations prepare low cost training materials for their members.

2. Contact the state headquarters of the professional association for the specific industry. In this scenario, contact the state chapter of the ASFSA (American School Food Service Association). Many state associations purchase copies of nationally prepared training materials so they can be "loaned" to members of the state association.

3. Contact local area community colleges offering food service training programs. Such programs can help identify materials they own that may be available for lending on a short term basis.

4. Contact local or regional four-year universities offering hospitality education. In this example, both food service and nutrition/dietetics programs could be of assistance in providing training materials. This is especially true in those Land Grant colleges providing extension services to non-profit foodservice operations.

5. Contact the National Restaurant Association (NRA) for "generic" training materials that address general foodservice training issues.

6. Look for cost sharing opportunities inside the organization itself. In corporations operating multi-units, the organization may be willing to invest in training materials that can be shared across units. In this scenario, the director of foodservice could contact directors in nearby districts to share materials and/or coordinate training efforts to create low "cost-per-employee" training sessions.

Exam Questions

Multiple Choice
Choose the letter of the best answer to the questions listed below.

1. What is the correct order of the steps used to manage payroll costs?
   a. Analyze results, forecast sales volume, determine productivity standards, schedule employees using productivity standards and forecasted sales volume
   b. Forecast sales volume, determine productivity standards, schedule employees using productivity standards and forecasted sales volume, analyze results
   c. Determine productivity standards, forecast sales volume, schedule employees using productivity standards and forecasted sales volume, analyze results
   d. Schedule employees using productivity standards and forecasted sales volume, analyze results, forecast sales volume, determine productivity standards
   Correct answer is c (See: Managing Payroll Costs)

2. According to the text, which of the following is not a key factor affecting employee productivity?
   a. Training
   b. Employee selection
   c. Morale
   d. FICA
   Correct answer is d (See: Maintaining a Productive Workforce)

3. Which of the following items is included in the definition of labor expense?
   a. Salaries and wages
   b. Health insurance and workman's compensation
   c. Unemployment taxes
   d. All of the above
   e. Only a. and b. above
   Correct answer is d (See: Labor Expense Defined)

4. Which of the following does not describe empowerment?
   a. Employees have the "power" to get involved.
   b. Employees solve guest-related problems.
   c. Employee productivity is increased.
   d. Managers have more "power" over employees and cost of labor
   Correct answer is d (See: Employee Empowerment)

5. The labor dollars per guest served productivity measure:
   a. Cannot be used by non-revenue-generating units
   b. Does not vary with changes in menu selling price
   c. Does not vary with changes in the price of labor
   d. All of the above
   e. Only a. and c. above
   Correct answer is b (See: Productivity Measures Summary)

6. _____is defined as management's view of what constitutes an appropriate productivity ratio in a given foodservice unit or units.
   a. Productivity standard
   b. Task training
   c. Split-shift
   d. All of the above
   e. Only a. and b. above
   Correct answer is a (See: Step 1: Determine Productivity Standards)

7. A ____ is a listing of the tasks that must be accomplished by the employee hired to fill a particular position.
   a. Job specification
   b. Job description
   c. Employer selection
   d. All of the above
   e. Only b. and c. above
   Correct answer is b (See: Employee Selection)

8. Given the following information, calculate the labor cost percentage. Cost of labor $7,100, sales $34,000, number of employees 6.
   a. 20.9%
   b. 25.0%
   c. 4.8%
   d. 1.25%
   e. Cannot be determined from the information given
   Correct answer is a (See: Labor Cost Percentage)

9. _____ refers to the amount an operation pays in salaries. _____ consists of those dollars paid to hourly employees.
   a. Fixed payroll, variable payroll
   b. Variable payroll, fixed payroll
   c. Daily payroll, variable payroll
   d. Fixed payroll, daily payroll
   Correct answer is a (See: Payroll)

10. Which of the following is not a category of preemployment testing?
    a. Skill testing
    b. IQ testing
    c. Psychological testing
    d. Drug screening test
    Correct answer is b (See: Employee Selection)

Use the information below to answer Questions 11 through 15.

Use Robert's last month's operating results to calculate the following productivity standards: labor cost percentage, sales per labor hour, labor dollars per guest served, guests served per labor dollar, guests served per labor hour.

Operating Results for Robert's Cafe

Sales Week	# of Guests Served	Labor Hours Used
1	10,000	6,000
2	10,800	6,200
3	10,600	6,100
4	11,000	6,600
Total	**42,400**	**24,900**

Average Guest Check	$14
Average Wage per Hour	$9
Total Sales	
Total Labor Cost	

Productivity Measurement	Productivity Standard
Labor Cost Percentage	
Sales per Labor Hour	
Labor Dollars per Guest Served	
Guests Served per Labor Dollar	
Guests Served per Labor Hour	

11. Robert's Labor Cost Percentage is:
    a. 39.7%
    b. 37.8%
    c. 35.5%
    d. 32.4%
    Correct answer is b (See: Measuring Current Labor Productivity)

12. Robert's Sales per Labor Hour is:
    a. $23.84
    b. $28.57
    c. $20.15
    d. $25.42
    Correct answer is a (See: Measuring Current Labor Productivity)

13. Robert's Labor Dollars per Guest Served is:
    a. $6.50
    b. $5.75
    c. $5.29
    d. $7.48
    Correct answer is c (See: Measuring Current Labor Productivity)

14. Robert's Guests Served per Labor Dollar is:
    a. 0.23
    b. 0.19
    c. 0.16
    d. 0.12
    Correct answer is b (See: Measuring Current Labor Productivity)

15. Robert's Guests Served per Labor Hour is:
    a. 1.85
    b. 1.50
    c. 1.70
    d. 1.35
    Correct answer is c (See: Measuring Current Labor Productivity)

16. Which of the following is not a common verification point of employment?
    a. Family history
    b. Criminal background
    c. Social security number
    d. Name
    Correct answer is a (See: Employee Selection)

17. Employees that receive the same amount of income regardless of the number of hours worked are:
    a. Hourly employees
    b. Salary employees
    c. Variable employees
    d. Only a. and c.
    Correct answer is b (See: Payroll)

18. Cost of labor divided by total sales is equal to:
    a. Sales per labor hour
    b. Labor productivity
    c. Labor dollars per guest
    d. Labor cost percentage
    Correct answer is d (See: Labor Cost Percentage)

19. Which of the following steps is not part of developing a training program?
    a. Forecasting sales volume.
    b. Determining how the task is to be done.
    c. Planning the training session.
    d. Evaluating the session's effectiveness.
    Correct answer is a (See: Maintaining Productive workforce)

20. Which of the following software functions can help manage and control labor costs?
    a. Monitor overtime costs
    b. Track employee lost days due to injury/accident
    c. Maintain job descriptions and specifications
    d. All of the above
    e. None of the above
    Correct answer is d (See: Technology Tools)

21. Given the following information, calculate the labor cost percentage. Cost of labor $4,500, sales $9,000, number of employees 5.
    a. 50%
    b. 100%
    c. 5.4%
    d. 1.5%
    e. Cannot be determined from the information given
    Correct answer is a (See: Labor Cost Percentage)

22. Given the following information, calculate the sales per labor hour. Total sales $49,500, labor hours used 1,750.
    a. $39.50
    b. $28.29
    c. $40.35
    d. $35.35
    e. Cannot be determined from the information given
    Correct answer is b (See: Sales Per Labor Hour)

True/False
Choose the letter of the best answer to the questions listed below.

23. The cost of labor is always less than that of food and beverage products.
    a. True
    b. False
    Correct answer is b (See: Labor Expense in the Hospitality Industry)

24. Labor expense and payroll are synonymous.
    a. True
    b. False
    Correct answer is b (See: Labor Expense Defined)

25. Minimum staff payroll is the amount of labor expense that must be spent to minimally operate the business.
    a. True
    b. False
    Correct answer is a (See: Payroll)

26. The productivity ratio represents what output should be expected per unit of input.
    a. True
    b. False
    Correct answer is a (See: Assessing Labor Productivity)

27. Frequently, employees with low productivity ratios are simply lazy.
    a. True
    b. False
    Correct answer is b (See: Training)

28. Management should not worry about enforcing standard operating procedures if the employees have found an easier way to accomplish a task.
    a. True
    b. False
    Correct answer is b (See: Training)

29. All employees require proper supervision.
    a. True
    b. False
    Correct answer is a (See: Supervision)

30. Interviewing and training time are examples of the hidden costs of turnover.
    a. True
    b. False
    Correct answer is b (See: Morale)

31. Split-shifts match employee work shifts with guest demand.
    a. True
    b. False
    Correct answer is a (See: Scheduling)

32. Sales per labor hour, as a productivity measure, ignores price per hour paid for labor.
    a. True
    b. False
    Correct answer is a (See: Productivity Measures Summary)

33. Labor cost percentage varies does not vary with changes in the price of labor.
    a. True
    b. False
    Correct answer is b (See: Productivity Measures Summary)

34. Some foodservice managers use an on-call system to keep off-duty employees handy if they need them without scheduling them unnecessarily.
    a. True
    b. False
    Correct answer is a (See: Step 3. Schedule Employees Using Productivity Standards and Forecasted Sales Volume)

35. Increasing sales volume will reduce both fixed and variable labor costs.
    a. True
    b. False
    Correct answer is b (See: Reducing Labor-Related Costs)

36. Fixed payroll refers to the amount an operation pays in salaries.
    a. True
    b. False
    Correct answer is a (See: Payroll)

37. Labor expense refers to the gross pay received by an employee in exchange for his or her work.
    a. True
    b. False
    Correct answer is b (See: Payroll)

38. Software technology can help managers develop employee schedules and interface employee schedules with time clock systems, and interface the employee scheduling component with forecasted sales volume software.
    a. True
    b. False
    Correct answer is a (See: Technology Tools)

39. RevPASH helps managers evaluate how much guests buy and how quickly they are served. It does so primarily by assessing the duration of guests' dining experiences.
    a. True
    b. False
    Correct answer is a (See: Revenue Per Available Seat Hour)

40. One of the advantages of a commitment to sustainability is gaining the customers who are willing to spend, on average, 20% more than the typical guest for products that meet their values and lifestyle.
    a. True
    b. False
    Correct answer is a (See: Green and Growing)

Chapter 8

Controlling Other Expenses

Learning Outcomes

At the conclusion of this chapter, you will be able to:

- Categorize Other Expenses in terms of being fixed, variable, or mixed.
- Classify individual Other Expenses as either controllable or noncontrollable.
- Compute Other Expense costs in terms of both cost per guest and percentage of sales.

Lecture Outline

1. Managing Other Expenses

- **Other expenses** are those items that are neither food, beverage, nor labor.
- Other expenses can account for a significant amount of the total cost of operating your foodservice unit.
- You must look for ways to control all of your expenses, but sometimes the environment in which you operate will act upon your facility to influence some of your costs in positive or negative ways.
- In the past, serving water to each guest upon arrival in a restaurant was simply **SOP** (standard operating procedure) for many operations. The rising cost of energy has caused many foodservice operations to implement a policy of serving water on request rather than with each order.
- Energy conservation and waste recycling are two examples of attempts to control and reduce other expenses.
- Each foodservice operation will have its own unique list of required other expenses.
- Another expense can constitute almost anything in the foodservice business.
- If cost groupings are used, they should make sense to the operator and should be specific enough to let the operator know what is in the category.
- Operators can use their own categories, or follow those used in the *Uniform System of Accounts for Restaurants* (USAR).
- While there are many ways in which to assess other expenses, two different considerations of these costs are particularly useful for the foodservice manager. They are:
  1. Fixed, variable, or mixed
  2. Controllable or noncontrollable

2. Fixed, Variable, and Mixed Other Expenses

- A **fixed expense** is one that remains constant despite increases or decreases in sales volume.
- A **variable expense** is one that generally increases as sales volume increases, and decreases as sales volume decreases.
- A **mixed expense** is one that has properties of both a fixed and a variable expense.
- The following shows how fixed, variable, and mixed expenses are affected as sales volume increases:

Expense	As a Percentage of Sales	Total Dollars
Fixed Expense	Decreases	Remains the Same
Variable Expense	Remains the Same	Increases
Mixed Expense	Decreases	Increases

- If an operator feels that a fixed expense percentage is too high, he or she must either increase sales or negotiate better rates.
- Normal variations in expense percentage that relate *only* to whether an expense is fixed, variable, or mixed should not be of undue concern to management. It is only when a fixed expense is too high or a variable expense is out of control, that management should act. This is called the concept of **management by exception**.

3. Controllable and Noncontrollable Other Expenses

- A **noncontrollable expense** is one that the foodservice manager can neither increase nor decrease.
- A **controllable expense** is one in which decisions made by the foodservice manager can have the effect of either increasing or reducing the expense.
- Management should focus its attention on controllable rather than noncontrollable expenses.

4. Monitoring Other Expenses

- When managing other expenses, two control and monitoring alternatives are available. They are:

    1. Other expense cost %
    2. Other expense cost per guest

$$\frac{\text{Other Expenses}}{\text{Total Sales}} = \text{Other Expense Cost \%}$$

$$\frac{\text{Other Expense}}{\text{Number of Guests Served}} = \text{Other Expense Cost Per Guest}$$

- The other expense cost per guest formula is of value when management believes it can be helpful, or when lack of a sales figure makes the computation of other expense cost percentage impossible.
- Increasingly, foodservice managers are finding that creative "Green" initiatives benefit their operations in many ways, including those that reduce other expenses. "Trayless dining" is just such an example.
- Trayless operations experience a 30-50% reduction in food and beverage waste. Diners take less food (because they only want to carry what they know they will eat). Without trays to wash, water consumption is also decreased. The result is a decrease in other expenses such as water, utilities, and cleaning products.

5. Reducing Other Expenses

- It is useful to break down other expenses into four categories: food and beverage, labor, facility maintenance, and occupancy when developing strategies for reducing overall other expense costs.
- In general, fixed costs related to food and beverage operations can only be reduced when measuring them as a percentage of total sales. This can be done only by increasing the total sales figure.
- Labor related expenses can also be considered partially fixed and partially variable.
- To reduce costs related to labor, it is necessary to eliminate wasteful labor-related expense.
- However, if an operator attempts to reduce other expenses related to labor too much, he or she may find that the best workers prefer to work elsewhere.
- Reducing employee benefits while attempting to retain a well-qualified workforce is simply management at its worst.
- A properly designed and implemented preventative maintenance program can go a long way toward reducing equipment failure and thus decreasing equipment and facility-related costs.

- Proper care of mechanical equipment prolongs its life and reduces operational costs.
- One way to help ensure that costs are as low as possible is to use a competitive bid process before awarding contracts for services you require.
- In the area of maintenance contracts, for areas such as the kitchen or for mechanical equipment, elevators, or grounds, it is recommended that these contracts be bid at least once per year.
- Air-conditioning, plumbing, heating and refrigerated units should be inspected at least yearly, and kitchen equipment should be inspected at least monthly for purposes of preventative maintenance.
- **Occupancy costs** refer to those expenses incurred by the foodservice unit that are related to the occupancy of and payment for the physical facility it occupies.

6. Technology Tools

- Depending upon the specific food service operation, these costs can represent a significant portion of the operations total expense requirements. As a result, controlling these costs is just as important as controlling food and labor-related costs.
- Software and hardware that can be purchased to assist in this area include applications that relate to:

  1. Assessing and monitoring utilities cost
  2. Minimizing energy costs via the use of motion-activated sensors
  3. Managing equipment maintenance records
  4. Tracking marketing costs/benefits
  5. Menu and promotional materials printing hardware and software
  6. Analysis of communications costs (telephone tolls)
  7. Analysis of all other expense costs on a per-guest basis
  8. Analysis of all other expense costs on a "cost per dollar sale" basis
  9. Comparing building/contents insurance costs across alternative insurance providers
  10. Software designed to assist in the preparation of the income statement, balance sheet, and the statement of cash flows
  11. Income tax management
  12. Income tax filing

- At the minimum, most independent operators should computerize their records related to taxes at all levels to ensure accuracy, safekeeping, and timeliness of required filings.

Consider The Cost

"The piece looks great, but tell me about the prices one more time," said Nigel, the manager of the Old Dublin Pub. Nigel was talking to Alice Petoskey, the sales representative for Image Custom Printing.

Nigel had asked Alice for a quote on producing a flyer that would advertise the pub's St. Patrick's Day festivities to be held in just one month. Nigel planned to offer special menu items on that day as well as discounted prices on the Irish-made draft beers he offered on tap. He had also arranged to hire a band to play traditional Irish music. He was now considering how best to advertise the event and all of the special activities he had planned at the pub on that day.

He and Alice were discussing prices for printing the beautiful flyer Alice's company had designed for him.

"O.K." replied Alice, "There is a onetime design and set-up up fee of $300.00, no matter how many pieces we print. After that fee, they are $0.50 per copy if you buy 1 to 1,000 copies, $0.40 per copy if you buy 2,000 to 5,000 copies, and like I was telling you, the best deal for you is if you buy 10,000. Then the price per copy goes down to only $0.25!"

1. What would Nigel's total payment to Alice's company be if he purchases 1,000 flyers? 5,000 flyers? 10,000 flyers? Use the table below to help you with you answer.

Number of Copies	Cost per Copy	Set-Up Fee	Total Cost

2. What additional flyer-related costs will Nigel incur if he decides to purchase the advertising flyers from Alice?

3. Assume you were Nigel. What additional and potentially lower cost advertising alternatives would you want to consider prior to agreeing to buy the flyers from Alice's company?

Answers:

In this case, students are confronted with a very typical "other expense" control decision. In this scenario, the costs are related to an operation's marketing efforts and can be used to point out that in many cases other expenses related to food and beverage operations are incurred at the discretion of managers; who must make these expenditures wisely.

1.

Number of Copies	Cost per Copy	Set-Up Fee	Total Cost
1,000	$0.50	$300	$800
5,000	$0.40	$300	$2,300
10,000	$0.25	$300	$2,800

2. If the flyers are to be distributed to Pub patrons within the Pub, no additional costs will be incurred.

   Addressing and postage costs will be incurred if the flyers are to be mailed.

   Labor costs will be incurred if the flyer is to be distributed (passed out) manually at one or more locations not within the Pub.

3. Increasingly, e-mail distribution of information such as that likely contained on the flyer is practiced by restaurants. Posting on the Pub's website is also a viable option.

Apply What You Have Learned

Hyewon Kim owns her own catering business. She provides her full-time employees with good health insurance benefits. Part-time employees do not receive the benefit. This year, Hyewon's health insurer advises Hyewon that insurance rates for her employees will increase 25% next year.

Hyewon had planned on giving both full and part-time employees a wage increase on January 1, but finds that the increased cost of the health care premiums for her full-time employees will take all of the funds she had budgeted for the wage increases.

1. If you were Hyewon, would you give your part-time employees a wage increase? If so, how?

   Answer: Although the increased cost of health care premiums for full-time employees will take all of the budgeted funds for wage increases, I would try to give part-time employees a raise. This would probably be less expensive than turnover that might result in no wage increases. Since employees are our most valuable assets, we should try to make sure that they are reasonably compensated for their work. To provide the extra money, I would have to find other areas of the operation where I could cut costs without negatively impacting guests.

2. What specific types of employees value health insurance coverage more than hourly pay rate?

   Answer: Employees that have spouses and children who need health insurance coverage will value insurance over hourly pay rate.

3. What steps can Hyewon take next year to help control her health insurance coverage costs? For example, one Michigan company drew international attention for its new policy of refusing to allow its employees to use tobacco (smoke) while at work or while off the job. Random testing for tobacco use was instituted and those found to have violated the policy were terminated. The company maintained the policy was a way to help curtail rising health care costs and employees who disagreed with the policy were free to quit. Opponents claimed the company was infringing on their employees' rights to engage in lawful behavior when they were off the job. Do you agree with the company's policy? What other types of health-adverse behaviors might employers seek to monitor in the future? Should they do so?

Answer: Next year, Hyewon needs to make sure that she is providing a safe and healthy work environment for employees that may result in lower health insurance claims.

If students agree with the smoke-free policy:
Employers may decide to decrease their insurance premiums by mandating that their employees are "smoke-free"; however, these employers also must agree to incur increased costs of turnover for employees who quit due to this policy.

If students disagree with the smoke-free policy:
Employers who decide to mandate that their employees be "smoke-free" both on and off the job may incur lawsuits regarding employees' rights to engage in lawful behavior outside of work.

For other health-adverse behaviors in the future, employers may continue to use tests such as preemployment drug screening when hiring new employees.

Test Your Skills

1. Susie operates a restaurant in the Ski Resort town of Asvail. She has decided to group her other expense categories in terms of either fixed expense or variable expense. Place an "X" in the Variable Expense column for those expenses that vary with sales volume. For expenses that do not vary with sales, place an "X" in the Fixed Expense column.

Other Expenses	Variable Expense	Fixed Expense
Linen rental	X	
Piano rental		X
Ice	X	
Insurance		X
Pension plan payments		X
Snow shoveling fees (parking lot)		X
Paper products	X	
Kitchen equipment rental (mixer)		X
Long-term debt payment		X
Real estate tax		X

2. Tutti owns a fine dining restaurant in a suburb of a major coastal city. Last year, her sales were not as high as she would have liked. To help increase her sales volume, Tutti decided to hire a sales consultant, Tina Boniner, to help bring in more customers. Tutti hired Tina on a trial basis for the first six months of the year. Tina was paid a fixed fee of $1,000 per month and a commission of 1% of sales. At the end of June, Tutti wants to evaluate whether she should hire Tina for the next six months. Calculate Tutti's sales consultant cost %.

    a. Tutti has decided that she cannot spend more than 2.2% of total sales for Tina's services. Based on the six-month average cost %, can Tutti afford to hire Tina for another six months?

        Answer: Yes, Tutti can afford to hire Tina for another six months because her average cost % is 2.07% which is below her maximum allowable amount of 2.2%.

    b. Last year's average sales for the first six months was $80,000. Based on the sales data, did Tina do a good job at increasing sales? Should she be hired again?

        Answer: Tutti should be hired again because, based on the sales data, average sales have increased from $80,000 to $93,167.

Mixed Expense - Sales Consultant

For period: <u>1/1 to 6/30</u>

Month	Sales	Fixed Fee	1% Variable Expense	Total Expense	Cost %
January	$81,000	$1,000	$810	$1,810	2.23%
February	80,000	1,000	800	1,800	2.25%
March	88,000	1,000	880	1,880	2.14%
April	92,000	1,000	920	1,920	2.09%
May	110,000	1,000	1,100	2,100	1.91%
June	108,000	1,000	1,080	2,080	1.93%
6-Month Average	93,167	1,000	932	1,932	2.07%

3. John owns and operates the End Zone Steakhouse. He would like to turn the operation over to his son Zeke, a graduate of Spartacus High School. Zeke, however, has no foodservice background. Zeke would like to prove that he can effectively operate the restaurant and would be good at controlling costs. Operating cost categories for the restaurant, in terms of other expenses, are as follows. Place an "X" in the Controllable column for those operating expenses that Zeke could control. If he could not control the cost, place an "X" in the Noncontrollable column.

Other Expenses	Controllable	Noncontrollable
Real estate tax		X
Menu printing	X	
Professional musicians	X	
Interest on long-term debt		X
Charitable donations	X	
Cleaning supplies	X	
Flowers and decorations	X	
Licenses and permits		X

4. Shanna operates a lounge in an extremely popular downtown convention hotel. The hotel regularly operates around the 80% occupancy mark, and its lounge, Luigi's, is very often filled to capacity. On weeks when business at the hotel is slower, Shanna attempts to build local sales by scheduling a variety of popular bands to play on the stage. She must select one band to play on Saturday night, six weeks from now, when the hotel is not busy. She has kept records of the costs and sales volume of the last four bands she has booked.

a. Compute both band expense percent and cost per guest served. Based on the cost % of the bands, which one should Shanna select for booking?

Answer: Based on the cost % data, Shanna should select Tiny and the Boys since their cost % is lowest at 12.3%.

b. Would your answer change if you knew Shanna charged a $5.00 cover charge to enter the lounge on the nights she has a band, and the cover charge is reported separately from the lounge sales? If so, which band would you choose?

Answer: If Shanna charged a $5.00 cover charge, then she should choose Shakin' Bill and the Billfolds. This would give Shanna the highest total revenue.

	Expense % and Cost Per Guest Served – Bands	

Unit Name: <u>Luigi's Lounge</u>

Date	Band	Band Expense	Lounge Sales	Cost %	Number of Guests Served	Cost per Guest Served
1/1	Tiny and the Boys	$1,400	$11,400	12.3%	1,425	$0.98
2/1	Shakin' Bill and the Billfolds	1,900	12,250	15.5%	1,980	0.96
3/1	La Noise	2,000	12,000	16.7%	2,005	1.00
4/1	The Hoppers	2,000	10,250	19.5%	2,100	0.95

Date	Band	Number of Guests Served	Cover Charge per Guest	Total Cover Charges	Lounge Sales	Total Sales
1/1	Tiny and the Boys	1,425	$5.00	$7,125	$11,400	$18,525
2/1	Shakin' Bill and the Billfolds	1,980	$5.00	$9,900	$12,250	$22,150
3/1	La Noise	2,005	$5.00	$10,025	$12,000	$22,025
4/1	The Hoppers	2,100	$5.00	$10,500	$10,250	$20,750

5. Marjorie runs a 200-seat, white-tablecloth restaurant in a wealthy neighborhood. Since her guests expect her tablecloths and napkins to be *really* white, she sends her linens to a local laundry service daily. The laundry service charges her by the piece. She wants to keep track of her laundry cost per guest to see if she can use the information to control her laundry costs better. Help her complete her six-column cost per guest report. She has budgeted $0.60 per guest on average. How is she doing at controlling her costs?

Six-Column Cost Per Guest - Laundry Service

Unit Name: <u>Marjorie's</u>   Date: <u>5/1 - 5/7</u>

Weekday	Laundry Service Cost		Number of Guests Served		Cost Per Guest	
	Today	To Date	Today	To Date	Today	To Date
1	$225	$225	400	400	$0.56	$0.56
2	$204	$429	375	775	$0.54	$0.55
3	$200	$629	350	1,125	$0.57	$0.56
4	$240	$869	425	1,550	$0.56	$0.56
5	$275	$1,144	450	2,000	$0.61	$0.57
6	$300	$1,444	500	2,500	$0.60	$0.58
7	$230	$1,674	420	2,920	$0.55	$0.57
Total	$1,674		2,920		$0.57	

Answer: Marjorie is doing well at controlling her costs. At the end of one week, she is running a $0.57 cost per guest, which is lower than her budgeted amount of $0.60.

6. Josiam operates the foodservice at Springdale Valley school system. He has just been informed by City Power, the electrical company in his area that the rate per kilowatt hour (kwh) for the school system's kitchens will be rising from $0.085 per kwh to $0.092 per kwh beginning next academic year (September). Based on last year's bill, what was each kitchen's electricity usage?

School	Electricity Cost Last Year	Number of Kwh Used Last Year	Kwh Cost Estimate Next Year	Estimated Electricity Cost for Next Year
Springdale Elementary	$6,800.00	80,000	0.092	$7,360.00
Jefferson Elementary	$7,650.00	90,000	0.092	$8,280.00
Clinton Middle School	$10,200.00	120,000	0.092	$11,040.00
Tri-valley High School	$12,750.00	150,000	0.092	$13,800.00
Total	$37,400.00	440,000	0.092	$40,480.00

Assuming no operating changes, how much more will be spent next year?

Answer: He will spend $3,080 more for electricity next year.

Who are some of Josiam's best resources for discovering ways to limit electricity usage in the kitchens?

Answer: Josiam can solicit ideas for energy reduction from his kitchen equipment suppliers.

7. Enrique has located the perfect spot for his restaurant. It is 3,000 square feet in the local mall, and the mall managers have given him the following monthly lease options:

Option 1: Pay a flat fee of $2.00 per square foot per month

Option 2: Pay a flat fee of $3,000 per month and 5% of food sales

Enrique estimates that his sales for the coming year will be as follows. Calculate the monthly lease amount for both options.

Month	Sales Forecast	Option 1			Option 2		
		# of Square Feet	Flat Fee per Square Foot	Monthly Lease $	Flat Fee per Month	Five % of Sales	Monthly Lease $
Jan	$65,000	3,000	$2.00	$6,000	$3,000	$3,250	$6,250
Feb	$55,000	3,000	$2.00	$6,000	$3,000	$2,750	$5,750
Mar	$65,000	3,000	$2.00	$6,000	$3,000	$3,250	$6,250
April	$70,000	3,000	$2.00	$6,000	$3,000	$3,500	$6,500
May	$80,000	3,000	$2.00	$6,000	$3,000	$4,000	$7,000
June	$70,000	3,000	$2.00	$6,000	$3,000	$3,500	$6,500
July	$70,000	3,000	$2.00	$6,000	$3,000	$3,500	$6,500
Aug	$85,000	3,000	$2.00	$6,000	$3,000	$4,250	$7,250
Sept	$90,000	3,000	$2.00	$6,000	$3,000	$4,500	$7,500
Oct	$95,000	3,000	$2.00	$6,000	$3,000	$4,750	$7,750
Nov	$110,000	3,000	$2.00	$6,000	$3,000	$5,500	$8,500
Dec	$135,000	3,000	$2.00	$6,000	$3,000	$6,750	$9,750
Total	$990,000			$72,000	$36,000	$49,500	$85,500

Which lease option should Enrique choose? Why?

Answer: Enrique should choose Option 1 because it is less expensive than Option 2, assuming Enrique's sales projections are correct.

8. Libbey Hocking is the owner of the Hummingbird, an all-organic restaurant featuring fresh salads and a variety of vegetarian entrée dishes. As part of a dining room re-design, she is replacing all of the glassware in her 100-seat restaurant. Libbey would like to purchase 40 dozen glasses. Her glassware vendor has offered her similarly styled glassware at three different quality levels. The highest quality glassware would cost Libbey $50.00 per dozen. The average life expectancy of these glasses is 1,000 uses before they either break or chip. A lower priced, mid-quality glass sells for $35.00 per dozen and has an expected life of 750 uses. The least expensive glasses sell for $26.00 per dozen and have an expected life of 500 uses. Help Libbey get more information to assess her best purchase choice by completing the following product cost comparison worksheet. (Spreadsheet hint: format the "Per Use Cost" column to five decimal places.)

Hummingbird's Glassware Purchase Worksheet

Product Durability	Price per Dozen	Number of Dozens	Total Cost	Total Number of Glasses	Per Glass Cost	Estimated Uses Per Glass	Per Use Cost
Highest	$50.00	40	$2,000	480	$4.17	1,000	0.00417
Middle	$35.00	40	$1,400	480	$2.92	750	0.00389
Lowest	$26.00	40	$1,040	480	$2.17	500	0.00433

a. Based on cost per use only, which quality glass should Libbey purchase?

Answer: Libbey should purchase the mid-quality glass based on per use cost of 0.00389.

b. What non-purchase price factors might influence Libbey's choice of glassware?

Answer: Assuming the style and appearance of the glasses were similar, Libbey's major concern would be her ability to fund the initial purchase. The lowest cost alternative is priced at about 50% of the highest cost alternative. This is not uncommon. Higher quality goods in a variety of areas have an initially higher purchase price, but last longer, resulting in lower "per use" costs.

c. If you were Libbey, which product alternative would you select? Explain your answer.

   Answer: Libbey's best purchase choice, in this scenario, is the "middle" quality product that has an attractively lower (than the highest quality item) initial purchase price, as well as the lowest per use cost.

9. The cost of maintaining a website is increasingly considered to be an expense that can be justified by many foodservice operations. Name some specific "other expense" costs that could be reduced through the use of an operation's website if it were properly designed and utilized.

   Answers:

   Student answers will vary, however, two important areas of potential cost savings resulting from a well designed web site are those related to communication costs and labor.

   Communication costs can be reduced, for example, when information that had previously been printed for distribution can now be posted on the website. Examples include items such as employee manuals, recipes, and standard operating procedures (SOPs). Especially cost-effective is communication that targets customers, for example, promotional flyers, weekly or daily specials, announcements, and other customer-oriented information.

   Labor costs can be reduced when employee time previously devoted to guest services can be eliminated, streamlined, or enhanced via the use of an effective website. Examples include providing directions to the operation, taking reservations, or accepting "to-go" orders.

Exam Questions

Multiple Choice
Choose the letter of the best answer to the questions listed below.

1. Increasing and decreasing expenses for cocktail napkins varies with the number of customers. This relationship is an example of a:
   a. Mixed expense
   b. Variable expense
   c. Fixed expense
   d. Noncontrollable expense
   Correct answer is b (See: Fixed, Variable, and Mixed Other Expenses)

2. _____ is working with food manufacturers and wholesalers to reduce product packaging waste. This practice can reduce cost.
   a. Source reduction
   b. SOP
   c. Controllable systems
   d. Other expenses
   Correct answer is a (See: Managing Other Expenses)

3. What does the acronym SOP stand for?

   a. Service of people
   b. Standard operating procedure
   c. Sales of productivity
   d. None of the above
   Correct answer is b (See: Managing Other Expenses)

4. All the following are direct operating expenses except:
   a. Uniforms
   b. Linen rental
   c. China and glassware
   d. Musicians
   Correct answer is d (See: Costs Related to Food and Beverage Operations)

5. All of the following are controllable expenses except:
   a. Charitable donations
   b. Electricity
   c. Cleaning supplies
   d. Interest on long-term debt
   Correct answer is d (See: Controllable and Noncontrollable Other Expenses)

6. Which is not a part of occupancy costs?
   a. Rent
   b. Real estate taxes
   c. Building insurance
   d. Employee benefits
   Correct answer is d (See: Occupancy Costs)

7. A _____ expense is one that remains constant despite increases or decreases in sales volume and a _____ expense is one that generally increases as sales volume increases, and decreases as sales volume decreases.
   a. Fixed and variable
   b. Variable and fixed
   c. Mixed and fixed
   d. Variable and mixed
   Correct answer is a (See: Fixed, Variable, and Mixed Other Expenses)

8. A _____ expense is one that the foodservice manager can neither increase nor decrease and a _____ expense is one in which decisions made by the foodservice manager can have an effect of either increasing or reducing the expense.
   a. Controllable and controllable
   b. Controllable and noncontrollable
   c. Noncontrollable and controllable
   d. Noncontrollable and noncontrollable
   Correct answer is c (See: Controllable and Noncontrollable Other Expenses)

Stephanie has kept records of the costs and sales volume of the last four bands she has booked at Stephanie's Bar. Calculate the Cost % and Cost per Guest Served for the bands, and answer Questions 9 and 10 below.

Unit Name: **Stephanie's Bar**

Date	Band	Band Expense	Lounge Sales	Cost %	# of Guests Served	Cost Per Guest Served
1/1	The Pierced Ears	$3,200	$26,000		2,167	
2/1	Geeks and Guys	3,800	24,500		2,042	
3/1	Pear Shaped Bodies	4,000	27,000		2,250	
4/1	Claws and Fangs	4,200	21,000		1,750	

9. Based on the information above, which band should Stephanie choose based on Cost %?
   a. The Pierced Ears
   b. Geeks and Guys
   c. Pear Shaped Bodies
   d. Claws and Fangs
   Correct answer is b (See: Monitoring Other Expenses)

10. Based on the information above, which band should Stephanie choose based on Cost Per Guest Served?
    a. The Pierced Ears
    b. Geeks and Guys
    c. Pear Shaped Bodies
    d. Claws and Fangs
    Correct answer is a (See: Monitoring Other Expenses)

11. Which of the following software/hardware applications can assist in controlling other expenses?
   a. Reducing beverage costs
   b. Menu and promotional materials printing
   c. Tracking food costs
   d. Monitoring scheduling of employees
   Correct answer is b (See: Technology Tools)

12. Calculate the other expense cost % using the following information: other expenses $5,500; number of guests served 10,000; total sales $75,000.
   a. 4.7%
   b. 7.3%
   c. 4.5%
   d. 5.8%
   Correct answer is b (See: Monitoring Other Expenses)

True/False
Choose the letter of the best answer to the questions listed below.

13. There is no demand to control other expenses since they are an insignificant financial expenditure.

   a. True
   b. False
   Correct answer is b (See: Managing Other Expenses)

14. Proper care of mechanical equipment prolongs its life but also increases its operational costs.

   a. True
   b. False
   Correct answer is b (See: Reducing Costs Related to Facility Maintenance)

15. An example of controlling other expenses can be seen with the current reduction in product packaging.

   a. True
   b. False
   Correct answer is a (See: Managing Other Expenses)

16. Other expenses are generally the same for all operations.

   a. True
   b. False
   Correct answer is b (See: Managing Other Expenses)

17. Fixed expenses decline as volume declines.

    a. True
    b. False
    Correct answer is b (See: Fixed, Variable, and Mixed Other Expenses)

18. A fixed expense, expressed as a percentage of sales, will decrease as sales increases.

    a. True
    b. False
    Correct answer is a (See: Fixed, Variable, and Mixed Other Expenses)

19. Variable expenses change as volume changes.

    a. True
    b. False
    Correct answer is a (See: Fixed, Variable, and Mixed Other Expenses)

20. Increasing variable costs is never desirable.

    a. True
    b. False
    Correct answer is b (See: Fixed, Variable, and Mixed Other Expenses)

21. A noncontrollable expense is one that the foodservice manager can neither increase nor decrease.

    a. True
    b. False
    Correct answer is a (See: Controllable and Noncontrollable Other Expenses)

22. The cost per guest formula is of value when a sales figure is not available.

    a. True
    b. False
    Correct answer is a (See: Monitoring Other Expenses)

23. To attempt to reduce employee benefits and retain a well qualified workforce is management at its best.

    a. True
    b. False
    Correct answer is b (See: Reducing Costs Related to Labor)

24. At the minimum, most independent operators should computerize their records related to taxes at all levels to ensure accuracy, safekeeping, and timeliness of required filings.

    a. True
    b. False
    Correct answer is a (See: Technology Tools)

25. Trayless operations experience a 30-50% reduction in food and beverage waste. Diners take less food because they only want to carry what they know they will eat.

    a. True
    b. False
    Correct answer is a (See: Green and Growing)

Chapter 9

Analyzing Results Using the Income Statement

Learning Outcomes

At the conclusion of this chapter, you will be able to:

- Prepare an income (profit and loss) statement.
- Analyze sales and expenses using the P&L statement.
- Evaluate a facility's profitability using the P&L statement.

Lecture Outline

1. Introduction to Financial Analysis

- Foodservice managers, more often than not, find themselves awash in numbers! This information, in an appropriate form, is necessary not only to effectively operate your business, but also to serve many interest groups that are directly or indirectly involved with the financial operation of your facility.
- Documenting and analyzing sales, expenses, and profits is sometimes called **cost accounting,** but more appropriately is known as **managerial accounting** to reflect the importance managers place on this process.
- It is important for you to be aware of the difference between bookkeeping, the process of simply recording and summarizing financial data, and the actual analysis of that data.
- Bookkeeping is essentially the summarizing and recording of data. Managerial accounting involves the summarizing, recording, and most importantly, the analysis of those data.
- The United States Congress, in 2002, passed the **Sarbanes-Oxley Act (SOX).** Technically known as the Public Company Accounting Reform and Investor Protection Act, the law provides criminal penalties for those found to have committed accounting fraud.

2. Uniform Systems of Accounts

- Financial reports related to the operation of a foodservice facility are of interest to management, stockholders, owners, creditors, governmental agencies, and, often, the general public.

- To ensure that this financial information is presented in a way that is both useful and consistent, **uniform systems of accounts** have been established for many areas of the hospitality industry.
- The National Restaurant Association has developed *the Uniform System of Accounts for Restaurants* (USAR). The USAR seeks to provide a consistent and clear manner in which managers can record sales, expenses, and the overall financial condition.
- The uniform systems of accounts are guidelines, not a mandated methodology.

3. Income Statement (USAR)

- The **income statement** referred to as the profit and loss (P&L) statement, is a summary report that describes the sales achieved, the money spent on expenses and the resulting profit generated by a business in a specific time period.
- A purpose of the **profit and loss statement** is to identify net income, or the profit generated after all appropriate expenses of the business have been paid.
- Each operation's P&L statement will look slightly different.
- **Net income** is the profit generated after all appropriate expenses of the business have been paid.
- **Fiscal year** is the year established for accounting purposes.
- The USAR can best be understood by dividing it into three sections: gross profit, operating expenses, and nonoperating expenses.
- These three sections are arranged on the income statement *from most controllable to least controllable* by the foodservice manager.
- The **gross profit section** consists of food and beverage sales and those food and beverage related costs that can and should be controlled by the manager on a daily basis.

The **operating expenses section** is also under the control of the manager but more so on a weekly or monthly basis (with the exception of wages which you can control daily).

- **Nonoperating expenses section** is the least controllable by the foodservice manager. For example, interest paid to creditors as part of short-term or long-term debt repayment is due regardless of the ability of the manager to control day-to-day operating costs.
- The income statement is an **aggregate statement**. This means that all details associated with the sales, cost, and profits of the foodservice establishment are *summarized* on the P&L statement. Although this summary gives the manager a one-shot look at the performance of the operation, the details are not included directly on the statement.
- These details can be found in **supporting schedules**. Each line item on the income statement should be accompanied by a schedule that outlines all of the information that you, as a manager, need to know to operate your business successfully.

- It is in the schedules that you collect the information you need to break down sales or costs and determine problem areas and potential opportunities for improving each item on the income statement.
- Each revenue and expense category on the income statement can be represented both in terms of its whole dollar amount, and its percentage of total sales. All ratios can be calculated as a percentage of *total sales* except the following:

  Food Costs are divided by food sales.
  Beverage Costs are divided by beverage sales.
  Food Gross Profit is divided by food sales.
  Beverage Gross Profit is divided by beverage sales.

- Food and beverage items use their respective food and beverage sales as the denominator so that these items can be evaluated separately from total sales.
- Since food costs and beverage costs are the most controllable items on the income statement, sales and costs need to be separated out of the aggregate and evaluated more carefully.
- The P&L statement is one of several documents that can help evaluate profitability.

4. Analysis of Sales/Volume

- Foodservice operators can measure sales in terms of either dollars or number of guests served. A sales increase or decrease must, however, be analyzed carefully if you are to truly understand the revenue direction of your business.
- Overall sales increases or decreases can be computed using the following steps:

  1. Determine sales for this accounting period.
  2. Calculate the following: this period's sales minus last period's sales.
  3. Divide the difference in #2 above by last period's sales to determine percentage variance.

- There are several ways a foodservice operation experiences total sales volume increases. These are:

  1. Serve the same number of guests at a higher check average.
  2. Serve more guests at the same check average.
  3. Serve more guests at a higher check average.
  4. Serve *fewer* guests at a *much* higher check average.

- The procedure to adjust sales variance to include known menu price increases is as follows:

  Step 1. Increase prior period sales (last year) by amount of the price increase.
  Step 2. Subtract the result in Step 1 from this period's sales.
  Step 3. Divide the difference in Step 2 by the value of Step 1.

- Every critical factor must be considered when evaluating sales revenue including the number of operating meal periods or days; changes in menu prices, guest counts, and check averages; and special events.

5. Analysis of Food Expense

- For the effective foodservice manager, the analysis of food expense is a matter of major concern.
- It is important to remember that the numerator of the food cost % equation is cost of food sold while the denominator is total food sales, rather than total food and beverage sales.
- A food cost percentage can be computed for each food subcategory. For instance, the cost percentage for the category Meats and Seafood would be computed as follows:

$$\frac{\text{Meats and Seafood Cost}}{\text{Total Food Sales}} = \text{Meats and Seafood Cost \%}$$

- **Inventory turnover** refers to the number of times the total value of inventory has been purchased and replaced in an accounting period.
- The formula used to compute inventory turnover is as follows:

$$\frac{\text{Cost of Food Consumed}}{\text{Average Inventory Value}} = \text{Food Inventory Turnover}$$

- Note that it is cost of food consumed rather than cost of food sold that is used as the numerator in this ratio. This is because all food inventories should be tracked so that you can better determine what is sold, wasted, spoiled, pilfered, or provided to employees as employee meals.
- Be sure that a high inventory turnover is caused by increased sales and not by increased food waste, food spoilage, or employee theft.
- The average inventory value is computed by adding beginning inventory for this period to the ending inventory from this period and dividing by 2 as follows:

$$\frac{\text{Beginning Inventory Value} + \text{Ending Inventory Value}}{2} = \text{Average Inventory Value}$$

6. Analysis of Beverage Expense

- Beverage inventory turnover is computed using the following formula:

$$\frac{\text{Cost of Beverages Consumed}}{\text{Average Beverage Inventory Value}} = \text{Beverage Inventory Turnover}$$

- If an operation carries a large number of rare and expensive wines, it will find that its beverage inventory turnover rate is relatively low. Conversely, those beverage operations that sell their products primarily by the glass are likely to experience inventory turnover rates that are quite high.
- Similar to the method for adjusting sales, the method for adjusting expense categories for known cost increases is as follows:

  Step 1. Increase prior-period expense by amount of cost increase.
  Step 2. Determine appropriate sales data, remembering to adjust prior-period sales, if applicable.
  Step 3. Divide costs determined in Step 1 above by sales determined in Step 2 above.

- All food and beverage expense categories must be adjusted both in terms of costs and selling price if effective comparisons are to be made over time.
- As product costs increase or decrease, and as menu prices change, so too will food and beverage expense percentages change.

7. Analysis of Labor Expense

- When total dollar sales volume increases, fixed labor cost percentages will decline.
- Variable labor costs will increase along with sales volume increases, but the percentage of revenue they consume should stay constant.
- When you combine a declining percentage (fixed labor cost) with a constant one (variable labor cost), you should achieve a reduced overall percentage, although your total labor dollars expended can be higher.
- Declining costs of labor may be the result of significant reductions in the number of guests served.
- Salaries and wages expense percentage is computed as follows:

$$\frac{\text{Salaries and Wages Expense}}{\text{Total Sales}} = \text{Salaries and Wages Expense \%}$$

- Just as adjustments must be made for changes in food and beverage expenses before valid expense comparisons can be made, so too must adjustments be made for changes, if any, in the price an operator pays for labor such as a **COLA** (cost of living adjustment), or raise.
- Adjust both sales and cost of labor using the same steps as those employed for adjusting food or beverage cost percentage and compute a new labor cost as follows:

Step 1. Determine sales adjustment.
Step 2. Determine total labor cost adjustment.
Step 3. Compute adjusted labor cost percentage.

- This year's projected labor cost is computed as follows:

> **This Year's Sales** x **Last Year's Adjusted Labor Cost %**
> **= This Year's Projected Labor Cost**

- Increases in payroll taxes, benefit programs, and employee turnover all can affect labor cost percentage.
- One of the fastest increasing labor-related costs for foodservice managers today is cost of health insurance benefit programs.

8. Analysis of Other Expense

- For comparison purposes, managers are able to use industry trade publications to get national averages on other expense categories. One helpful source is an annual publication, the *Restaurant Industry Operations Report* published by the National Restaurant Association and prepared by Deloitte & Touche (can be ordered through www.restaurant.org).
- For operations that are a part of a corporate chain, unit managers can receive comparison data from district and regional managers who can chart performance against those of other operators in the city, region, state, and nation.

9. Analysis of Profits

- Profit percentage using the profit margin formula is as follows:

> **Net Income**
> **Total Sales = Profit Margin**

- **Profit margin** is also known as **return on sales**, or **ROS**. For the foodservice manager perhaps no number is more important than ROS. This percentage is the most telling indicator of a manager's overall effectiveness at generating revenues and controlling costs in line with forecasted results.
- While it is not possible to state what a "good" ROS figures should be for all restaurants, industry averages, depending on the specific segment, range from 1% to over 20%.
- Some operators prefer to use operating income (see Figure 9.1) as the numerator for profit margin instead of net income. This is because interest and income taxes are considered nonoperating expenses and thus, not truly reflective of a manger's ability to generate a profit.

- % variance for the year can be measured by the following formula:

$$\frac{\text{Net Income This Period} - \text{Net Income Last Period}}{\text{Net Income Last Period}} = \%\text{Variance}$$

- Monitoring selling price, guest counts, sales per guest, operating days, special events, and actual operating costs is necessary for accurate profit comparisons. Without knowledge of each of these areas, the effective analysis of profits becomes a risky proposition.
- Perceptive foodservice operators now clearly recognize that profits, planet, and people all benefit from an operation's green commitment.
- "Planet friendly" management yields many positive financial outcomes for businesses, as well as for the health of the local communities these businesses count on to support them.
- Buying local (to minimize transportation costs and environmental impact) creates relationships with those who produce food and keeps money flowing through a local economy, resulting in a healthier community and reduced health care costs.

10. Technology Tools

- This chapter introduced the concept of management analysis as it relates to sales, expenses, and profits. In this area, software is quite advanced and the choice of tools available to help you with your own analyses is many. The best of the programs on the market will:

1. Analyze operating trends (sales and costs) over management-established time periods.
2. Analyze food and beverage costs.
3. Analyze labor costs.
4. Analyze other expenses.
5. Analyze profits.
6. Compare operating results of multiple profit centers within one location or across several locations.
7. Interface with an operation's point of sales (POS) system or even incorporate it completely.
8. Red flag" areas of potential management concern.
9. Evaluate the financial productivity of individual servers, day parts, or other specific time periods established by management.
10. Compare actual to budgeted results and compute variance percentages as well as suggest revisions to future budget periods based on current operating results.

Consider The Cost

"Wow, I can't believe the size of the electricity bill this month," said Wendy. She was talking to Matt, the Assistant Manager of the Aussie Steakhouse in Phoenix Arizona where Wendy served as General Manager.

"Is it higher than last month?" asked Matt.

"It's a lot higher," replied Wendy. "I guess I thought it would be a little higher because it was really hot last month."

"So our usage was up?" asked Matt.

"Yes," said Wendy, "and the rate per kilowatt hour we pay is up from last year too. It seems like that rate goes up a little more every year."

"Is the bill so high it will affect our monthly bonus?" asked Matt. "I hope not," he continued, "because we had a great month last month and I was really counting on the extra money in my next check."

"I don't know," said Wendy. "Let me get the calculator and we'll see."

1. What would be the likely affect on both the dollar amount and the percent of sales reported on the monthly P&L of the Aussie Steakhouse if there were:
    a. An increase in the amount of electricity used in the restaurant?
    b. An increase in the cost per unit (kilowatt hour) of the electricity consumed?
    c. An increase in the number of guests served by the restaurant?

2. In this scenario, it appears that if the cost of "other expenses" in this restaurant is too high, its managers may not achieve their monthly bonus. Do you believe the cost of electricity is a controllable or noncontrollable operating expense?

3. Regardless of your answer to question 2, what are at least three specific actions Wendy and Matt could take to minimize the future impact on their P&Ls of rising electricity costs?

Answers:

This case was developed to do three things. First, it examines the impact of energy usage on an operation's P&L. Second, it seeks to focus students' attention on the issue of controllable vs. noncontrollable costs. Finally, it seeks to stimulate discussion about the concrete actions managers can take to reduce the impact on a P&L of energy consumption.

a. An increase in the amount of electricity used in the restaurant will, in most cases, cause an increase in the dollar amount of this expense shown on the P&L, as well as an increase in Utility Services costs as a percent of sales.

b. An increase in the cost per unit (kilowatt hour) of electricity consumed will, in most cases, cause an increase in the dollar amount of this expense shown on the P&L, as well as an increase in Utility Services costs as a percent of sales.

c. If the number of guests served is significantly increased during a month and the result is increased revenues, increased electricity usage will still result in an increase in the dollar amount of this expense shown on the P&L. However, Utility Services cost as a percent of sales may show a decrease (due to the fixed cost portion of some Utility Services expenses).

2. Electricity, like many foodservice expenses, consists of both fixed and variable components. Likewise, some aspects of utility usage are controllable while others are not. For example, the cost required to light a parking lot at night is fixed and clearly beyond management's direct control. Similarly, external factors such as outdoor temperatures and the resulting energy usage required to cool or heat interior spaces are not under the control of management. In most cases, the price paid per unit of energy consumed is also not controllable.

Managers can still positively impact their operations' profitability, however, by continually increasing sales (revenues) at a rate higher than the increase in their utility (as well as all other) noncontrollable costs. The greatest impact managers can have on utility costs, however, relate to energy conservation. This concept is addressed in this case's final question.

3. Student answers will vary, however, three specific actions that could be addressed include:

a. Consider adjusting interior temperatures during times of extreme weather to conserve energy (e.g., allowing dining rooms to be somewhat warmer during times of excessively high outdoor temperatures and cooler during times of extremely low outside temperatures.)

b. Conduct an energy audit to ensure all electrical equipment is operating at maximum efficiency.

c. Emphasize customer service to increase sales, and as a result, ultimately serve more guests. This would provide a "per guest served" utility cost that is lower than the one that would be achieved when serving fewer guests.

Apply What You Have Learned

Terri Settles is a registered dietitian (R.D.). She supervises five hospitals for Maramark Dining Services, the company the hospitals have selected to operate their foodservices. Her company produces a monthly and annual income statement for each hospital.

1. Discuss five ways in which income statements can help Terri do her job better.

   Answer: By utilizing income statements, Terri can:
   1. Identify and analyze each of her five hospitals' sales, expenses, and net income.
   2. Make comparisons of the performance of her five hospitals' operations.
   3. Make comparisons between her hospitals' performance last month and this month and last year and this year.
   4. Develop future plans and budgets.
   5. Present and clarify her budgets to management.

2. What would a hospital do with "profits" or surpluses made in the foodservice area?

   Answer: With surpluses made in the foodservice area, a hospital could provide its employees incentives such as awards and prizes, additional training, and enhanced health insurance coverage. Surpluses could also be used to upgrade kitchen equipment and provide better furniture in the dining areas.

3. What effect will "profit" or "loss" have on the ability of Terri's company to continue to manage the foodservices for these hospitals?

   Answer: If Terri's company's performance results in a "profit", the hospital will probably continue to employ her company in the future. If not, the hospital will probably reconsider its contract with Terri's company. However, if a loss does occur, Terri should analyze her income statements and provide reasons for the "loss", as well as report to the hospital how to solve the problems and plan for profit in the future.

Test Your Skills

1. Lucir manages a German restaurant in a large western city. The owner wants to know how well Lucir did this year at generating sales, controlling costs, and providing a profit. The owner promised Lucir that he would give her a raise if she increased return on sales (profit margin) by at least 1%. Complete Lucir's P&L below. Should she receive a raise?

Lucir's P&L

	Last Year	%	This Year	%
SALES:				
Food	$2,647,415	84.2%	$2,675,889	73.5%
Beverage	498,119	15.8%	965,660	26.5%
Total Sales	3,145,534	100.0%	3,641,549	100.0%
COST OF SALES:				
Food	855,104	32.3%	1,074,420	40.2%
Beverage	104,005	20.9%	115,879	12.0%
Total Cost of Sales	959,109	30.5%	1,190,299	32.7%
GROSS PROFIT:				
Food	1,792,311	67.7%	1,601,469	59.8%
Beverage	394,114	79.1%	849,781	88.0%
Total Gross Profit	2,186,425	69.5%	2,451,250	67.3%
OPERATING EXPENSES:				
Salaries and Wages	769,319	24.5%	785,487	21.6%
Employee Benefits	118,996	3.8%	122,994	3.4%
Direct Operating Expense	146,669	4.7%	145,357	4.0%
Music and Entertainment	2,767	0.1%	8,386	0.2%
Marketing	52,579	1.7%	69,883	1.9%
Utility Services	88,555	2.8%	97,836	2.7%
Repairs and Maintenance	41,510	1.3%	39,135	1.1%
Administrative and General	80,252	2.6%	78,269	2.1%
Occupancy	144,000	4.6%	132,000	3.6%
Depreciation	49,812	1.6%	61,498	1.7%
Total Operating Expenses	1,494,459	47.5%	1,540,845	42.3%
Operating Income	691,966	22.0%	910,405	25.0%
Interest	104,100	3.3%	93,378	2.6%
Income Before Income Taxes	587,866	18.7%	817,027	22.4%
Income Taxes	235,146	7.5%	343,150	9.4%
Net Income	352,720	11.2%	473,877	13.0%

Answer: Lucir should receive a raise because she increased her return on sales by more than 1%.

2. Faye manages Faye's Tea Room in a small suburban town. She sells gourmet food and a variety of teas. This year, Faye increased her selling prices by 5%, and she increased her wages by 10%. Faye's condensed P&L follows. Help her calculate her variance and variance % from last year to this year. Use her adjusted sales and labor cost to provide a more accurate picture of her performance this year.

Faye's Condensed P & L

	Last Year	Adjusted Sales and Labor (for Last Year)	This Year	Variance	Variance %
Sales	$1,865,000	$1,958,250	$2,315,000	$356,750	18.22%
Cost of food	615,450		717,650	102,200	16.61%
Cost of labor	540,850	594,935	671,350	76,415	12.84%
Other expenses	428,950		486,150	57,200	13.33%
Total Expenses	1,585,250		1,875,150	289,900	18.29%
Profit	279,750		439,850	160,100	57.23%

3. (a) Rudolfo owns Rudolfo's Italian Restaurante in the Little Italy section of New York City. He wants to compare last year's costs to this year's costs on his food expense schedule to see how he performed in each food category. Help Rudolfo complete his schedule.

Rudolfo's Food Expense Schedule

	Last Year	% of Food Sales	This Year	% of Food Sales
Food Sales	$2,836,517	100.0%	$3,087,564	100.0%
Cost of Food Sold				
Meats and Seafood	$386,734	13.6%	$445,982	14.4%
Fruits and Vegetables	122,915	4.3%	165,178	5.3%
Dairy	71,951	2.5%	52,858	1.7%
Baked Goods	20,985	0.7%	29,731	1.0%
Other	323,778	11.4%	303,927	9.8%
Total Cost of Food Sold	926,363	32.7%	997,676	32.3%

3. (b) In addition to calculating the food cost % for each of his food categories, Rudolfo wishes to calculate his inventory turnover for the year. Rudolfo's inventory turnover target for this year was 32 times. Did he meet his target? If not, what may have caused this? (Assume cost of food sold, part a, and cost of food consumed, part b, are the same for Rudolfo's.)

Rudolfo's Food Inventory Turnover

Inventory Category	This Year Beginning Inventory	This Year Ending Inventory	Average Inventory Value	Cost of Food Consumed	Inventory Turnover
Meats and Seafood	$21,476	$17,489	$19,483	$445,982	22.9
Fruits and Vegetables	$1,708	$1,015	1,362	165,178	121.3
Dairy	$772	$372	572	52,858	92.4
Baked Goods	$160	$131	146	29,731	204.3
Other	$10,538	$11,035	10,787	303,927	28.2
Total	$34,654	$30,042	32,348	997,676	30.8

Answer: Rudolfo did not meet his target of 32 times. His inventory turnover was 30.8 times. Since his sales were higher this year, the slower inventory turnover would not be caused by lower sales. He must have made some bulk purchases in order to receive volume discounts. With more inventory sitting in his storeroom, his inventory would turn more slowly.

4. Jaymal is Director of Club Operations for five military bases in Florida. He has just received year-end income statements for each. Information from the revenue and labor portion of those statements is shown below. Jaymal wants to use the current year's data to create next year's budget. Assume that Jaymal is happy with his labor productivity in each unit and that both wages and revenue in each will increase 2% next year. How much should Jaymal budget for revenue and labor in each unit? What will Jaymal's labor cost % be for each unit if he meets his budget?

	This Year's Results		Next Year's Budget		
Location	This Year's Cost of Labor	This Year's Revenue	Projected Cost of Labor	Projected Revenue	Projected Labor Cost %
Pensacola	$285,000	$980,500	$290,700	$1,000,110	29.1%
Daytona	$197,250	$720,000	$201,195	$734,400	27.4%
Fort Myers	$235,500	$850,250	$240,210	$867,255	27.7%
Tampa	$279,750	$921,750	$285,345	$940,185	30.3%
Miami	$1,190,250	$3,720,000	$1,214,055	$3,794,400	32.0%

5. Ron MacGruder is Senior Vice President of Acquisitions for Yummy Foods. Yummy is a large multinational food service company. It owns over 2,000 restaurants. Among its famous brands are a chain of pizza parlors, a Mexican carryout group, a chain of fried chicken stores and a large group of fried fish stores. Ron is constantly on the lookout for growing food service concepts that could be purchased at a fair price and added to the Yummy group. One such concept that is currently available for sale is a small but expanding group of upscale Thai restaurants called "Bow Thais." The current owners wish to sell the 17-unit chain and retire to Florida. They proudly point to the fact that both their sales and profits have increased in each of the last three years. Revenue has more than doubled this year compared to two years ago. Profits have risen from just $600,000 two years ago to over $1,000,000 this year. The summary P&Ls they have supplied to Ron indicate the following:

Two Years Ago

Revenue	$ 6,500,000
Profit	$ 600,000

Last Year

Revenue	$ 9,900,000
Profit	$ 800,000

This Year

Revenue	$ 13,500,000
Profit	$ 1,010,000

Assume that two years ago, the Bow Thais chain consisted of 6 units. One year ago it consisted of 12 units, and this year it consists of 17 units. Develop a summary P&L for each of Bow Thais' last three years showing revenue, expense, and profit. Next compute a "per unit" revenue, expense, profit, and profit margin level for each of the three years for which you have data. Would you advise Ron to buy the company? Why or why not?

	Revenue	Expense	Profit	# of Units	Revenue per Unit	Expense per Unit	Profit per Unit	Profit Margin %
2 Years Ago	$6,500,000	$5,900,000	$600,000	6	$1,083,333	$983,333	$100,000	9.2%
Last Year	9,900,000	9,100,000	800,000	12	825,000	758,333	66,667	8.1%
This Year	13,500,000	12,490,000	1,010,000	17	794,118	734,706	59,412	7.5%

Answer: I would advise Ron to not buy the company. Total revenues and profit have increased over the past 3 years primarily due to the addition of units. However, **per unit** profits and profit margins have declined over the past three years. This indicates that there may be some problems with revenues, expenses, or both.

6. Basil Bakal is the newly appointed Food and Beverage Director at Telco Industries. Telco creates and markets software programs developed for use with iPods. The company has 500 employees and operates its own cafeteria and Executive Dining Room where it daily offers free lunches to all employees. Basil's cafeteria serves between 375 and 425 lunches per day. Approximately 50 more meals per day are served in the Executive Dining Room. Basil has created his own modified version of a P&L for use in his operation. Calculate the percentages of meals served in the cafeteria and Executive Dining Room and the costs per meal served, and then answer the questions that follow.

Telco Industries Food Services Department

	Meals Served Last Year	% of Total Meals Served
NUMBER OF MEALS SERVED:		
Cafeteria	104,250	89.6%
Executive Dining Room	12,150	10.4%
Total Served	116,400	100.0%

	Total Cost $	Per Meal Cost $
COST OF SALES:		
Cafeteria	$248,750	$2.39
Executive Dining Room	48,450	$3.99
Total Cost of Sales	$297,200	$2.55
OPERATING EXPENSES:		
Salaries and Wages	244,440	$2.10
Employee Benefits	61,110	$0.53
401(k) Match	25,350	$0.22
Administrative and General Expense	46,669	$0.40
China/ Glass Replacement	12,767	$0.11
Paper Products	52,579	$0.45
Other Direct Operating Expenses	46,669	$0.40
Utilities	96,000	$0.82
Repairs and Maintenance	21,510	$0.18
Equipment Rental	1,500	$0.01
Total Operating Expenses	$608,594	$5.23

a. How much more did it cost (cost of sales) Basil to serve a meal in the Executive Dining Room than it did in the employee cafeteria? Why do you think that would be so?

Answer: It cost $1.60 more to serve a meal in the Executive Dining Room than in the employee cafeteria. Even in commercial operations, the cost of providing meals at various quality and service levels will differ as they do in this scenario and in most business's Executive Dining Rooms.

b. Basil's modified P&L combines all wage and salary-related costs when calculating cost per meal served. Why do you think he elected to not allocate labor costs between the two serving areas? How could he do so?

Answer: While it is easy to count the number of meals served in various foodservice outlets, it is more difficult to prorate labor and salary-related costs among them. It can be done, however, based upon the proportion of meals served in each area. In this example, 10.4% of the meals are served in the Executive Dining room, thus 10.4% of labor-related costs could be allocated to that area. Another alternative is to allocate labor-related cost based on the number of units operated. In this example, two units are operated, thus 50% of the labor costs could be assigned to each unit. The point is that the P&L should be designed to provide the specific information needed to assist the managers using it.

c. Assume you were on the Board of Directors of Telco. How would you decide how much more money you should allocate to Basil's area next year to account for rising food prices? Who would you expect to provide you with the information you need to make an informed decision about the appropriate size of the increase?

Answer: Clearly, "Basil" is the answer to both of these questions. Only Basil will know his food costs per meal and the future likelihood of price increases in the items he buys most well enough to advise the board. This is commonly the case in noncommercial foodservice operations where the main function of the organization being served is something other than food preparation and service. In such cases, the Food and Beverage Manager will often be called upon to provide critical information to those upper-level decision makers in the organization who must have it.

7. In this chapter you learned that a P&L statement is used to report revenue, expense and profit. In many cases, noncommercial foodservice operators such as those responsible for schools, colleges and universities, health care facilities including retirement complexes and nursing homes, as well as hospitals are severely restricted in their ability to increase their revenues. This is so because the operating budgets of many such facilities are fixed annually based upon the number of meals estimated to be served. Also, such facilities do not seek to earn a "profit" in the traditional sense of the word. In these noncommercial operations, however, the preparation and

thoughtful analysis of monthly P&Ls is considered essential. Why do you believe this is so?

Answers:

Effective noncommercial foodservice operators are keenly interested in their operating results as shown on monthly P&Ls. This is so because, for noncommercial operators, the P&L's three major reporting sections reveal critical operating information.

1. Revenue-related information: All foodservice operators must maintain records of the number of dollars they earn, guests served or meals prepared. In the case of noncommercial operations, the revenue section of a P&L may not consist of dollars, but it will always identify the number of meals prepared or served and/or guests served. This information is critical for calculating such important noncommercial foodservice efficiency measures such as cost per meal produced or per person served.

2. Expense-related information: For noncommercial operations, the costs reported on the expense portion of a P&L are equally or even more important to assess than is the information on the expense portion of a commercial operator's P&L. This is so because, when selling prices cannot be easily increased nor can the number of guests served be varied significantly, management control of operational expenses becomes the single key to operating within pre-established budgets.

3. Profit-related information: While non-profit entities by their very definition do not seek to make a profit, all foodservice operators have need for revenue that exceeds expense. If this were not so, repairs and replacement of production equipment as it wears out would not be possible. Dishes and glassware could not be replaced as they break, nor could employees receive raises for a job well done. In addition, careful examination of a P&L reveals that the calculation for "profit" is the same as that for staying within budget, that is:

   Budgeted Revenue – Budgeted Expense = Amount Over/Under Budget

   Thus, while making a "profit" may not be a primary objective, analysis of the P&L allows operators the ability to assess their own effectiveness in staying within budget.

For all of these reasons, noncommercial foodservice operators now and in the future will continue to be keenly interested in the operating results of their facilities as shown on their monthly and annual P&L statements.

Exam Questions

Multiple Choice
Choose the letter of the best answer to the questions listed below.

1. The textbook discussed several ways a restaurant could have experienced total sales volume increases in the current year. Which of the following best describes these ways?
   a. Serve the same number of guests at a higher check average.
   b. Serve more guests at the same check average.
   c. Serve more guests at a higher check average.
   d. All of the above
   e. Only a. and b. above
   Correct answer is d (See: Analysis of Sales/Volume)

2. Identify the section of the income statement that is least controllable by the foodservice manager.
   a. Operating Expenses section
   b. Gross Profit section
   c. Nonoperating expenses section
   d. All of the above
   Correct answer is c (See: The Income Statement USAR)

3. Calculate the sales variance in dollars and as a percentage given the following information: last year's sales $3,000,000; this year's sales $3,300,000.
   a. $300,000 and 10%
   b. $300,000 and 9.1%
   c. $6,300,000 and 4.8%
   d. None of the above
   Correct answer is a (See: Analysis of Sales/Volume)

4. When evaluating sales revenue which critical factor must be considered?
   a. Number of operating meal periods or days
   b. Changes in menu prices, guest counts, and check averages
   c. Special events
   d. All of the above
   e. Only a. and b. above
   Correct answer is d (See: Other Factors Influencing Sales Analysis)

5. _____ refers to the number of times the total value of inventory has been purchased and replaced in an accounting period.
   a. Inventory turnover
   b. Return on sales
   c. COLA
   d. Cost accounting
   Correct answer is a (See: Food Inventory Turnover)

6. Calculate the beverage inventory turnover given the following information: cost of beverages consumed $100,000; beginning inventory $9,000; ending beverage inventory $11,000; beverage sales $500,000.
   a. 5 times
   b. 10 times
   c. 20%
   d. 22%
   e. Cannot be determined from the information given
   Correct answer is b (See: Analysis of Beverage Expense)

7. What is the correct formula for food inventory turnover?
   a. Cost of food consumed/average inventory value
   b. Cost/sales
   c. Beginning inventory + ending inventory / 2
   d. Cost of beverage consumed/average inventory value
   Correct answer is a (See: Food Inventory Turnover)

8. Calculate the average inventory given the following information: Revenues $685,000; ending inventory $250,000; and beginning inventory $450,000.
   a. $300,000
   b. $295,000
   c. $350,000
   d. $425,000
   Correct answer is b (See: Analysis of Food Expense)

9. Which of the following software functions will help with performing management analyses?
   a. Analyze labor costs
   b. Analyze other expenses
   c. Analyze food and beverage costs
   d. Analyze profits
   e. All of the above
   Correct answer is e (See: Technology Tools)

10. Calculate the average inventory given the following information: Revenues $75,000; ending inventory $13,000; and beginning inventory $48,000
   a. $27,000
   b. $30,500
   c. $61,000
   d. $62,000
   Correct answer is b (See: Analysis of Food Expense)

True/False
Choose the letter of the best answer to the questions listed below.

11. Gross profit is the profit generated after all appropriate taxes of the business have been paid.
    a. True
    b. False
    Correct answer is b (See: Income Statement USAR)

12. For the foodservice manager, perhaps no figure is more important than the ROS.
    a. True
    b. False
    Correct answer is a (See: Analysis of Profits)

13. High beverage inventory turnover accompanied by frequent product outages may indicate inventory levels are too low.
    a. True
    b. False
    Correct answer is a (See: Analysis of Beverage Expense)

14. Low inventory turnover rates and many slow moving inventory items may indicate the need to increase inventory levels.
    a. True
    b. False
    Correct answer is b (See: Food Inventory Turnover)

15. Managerial accounting is documenting and analyzing sales, expenses, and profits.
    a. True
    b. False
    Correct answer is a (See: Introduction to Financial Analysis)

16. The operating expenses section of the income statement consists of food and beverage sales and costs that can and should be controlled by the manager on a daily basis.
    a. True
    b. False
    Correct answer is b (See: Income Statement USAR)

17. Each line item on the income statement should be accompanied by a schedule that outlines all of the information that you, as a manger, need to know to operate your business successfully.
    a. True
    b. False
    Correct answer is a (See: Income Statement USAR)

18. The three sections of the USAR are arranged on the income statement from most controllable to least controllable.
    a. True
    b. False
    Correct answer is a (See: Income Statement USAR)

19. Technology can be used to help managers evaluate the financial productivity of individual servers or day parts.
    a. True
    b. False
    Correct answer is a (See: Technology Tools)

20. Buying local (to minimize transportation costs and environmental impact) creates relationships with those who produce food and keeps money flowing through a local economy, resulting in a healthier community.
    a. True
    b. False
    Correct answer is a (See: Green and Growing)

Chapter 10

Planning for Profit

Learning Outcomes

At the conclusion of this chapter, you will be able to:

- Analyze a menu for profitability.
- Prepare a cost/volume/profit (break-even) analysis.
- Establish a budget and monitor performance to the budget.

Lecture Outline

1. Financial Analysis and Profit Planning

- In addition to analyzing the P&L statement, you should also undertake a thorough study of three areas that will assist you in planning for profit. These three areas of analysis are menu analysis, cost/volume/profit (CVP) analysis, and budgeting.
- Whereas menu analysis concerns itself with the profitability of the menu items you sell, CVP analysis deals with the sales dollars and volume required by your foodservice unit to avoid an operating loss and to make a profit. The process of budgeting allows you to plan your next year's operating results by projecting sales, expenses, and profits to develop a budgeted P&L statement.

2. Menu Analysis

- Menu analysis involves marketing, sociology, psychology, and emotions. Remember that guests respond best not to weighty financial analyses, but rather to menu item descriptions, the placement of items on the menu, their price, and their current popularity.
- Many components of the menu such as pricing, layout, design, and copy play an important role in the overall success of a foodservice operation.
- Three of the most popular systems of menu analysis are food cost %, contribution margin, and goal value analysis. (See figure 10.1)

The **matrix analysis** provides a method for comparisons between menu items.

- A matrix allows menu items to be placed into categories based on whether they are above or below menu item averages for factors such as food cost %, popularity, and contribution margin.

- When analyzing a menu using the food cost percentage method, you are seeking menu items that have the effect of minimizing your overall food cost percentage.
- The characteristics of the menu items that fall into each of the four matrix squares are unique and thus should be marketed differently. (See figure 10.3)
- When analyzing a menu using the contribution margin approach, the operator seeks to produce a menu that maximizes the overall contribution margin.
- **Contribution margin per menu item** is defined as the amount that remains after the product cost of the menu item is subtracted from the item's selling price.
- Contribution margin per menu item would be computed as follows:

Selling Price – Product Cost = Contribution Margin per Menu Item

- To determine the total contribution margin for the menu, the following formula is used:

Total Sales – Total Product Costs = Total Contribution Margin

- You can determine the average contribution margin per item, using the following formula:

$$\frac{\text{Total Contribution Margin}}{\text{Number of Items Sold}} = \text{Average Contribution Margin per Item}$$

- Contribution margin is the amount that you will have available to pay for your labor and other expenses and to keep for your profit.
- When contribution margin is the driving factor in analyzing a menu, the two variables used for the analysis are contribution margin and item popularity.
- Each of the menu items that fall in the squares requires a special marketing strategy, depending on its square location. (See figure 10.4)
- A frequent and legitimate criticism of the contribution margin approach to menu analysis is that it tends to favor high-priced menu items over low-priced ones, since higher priced menu items, in general, tend to have the highest contribution margins.
- The selection of either food cost percentage or contribution margin as a menu analysis technique is really an attempt by the foodservice operator to answer the following questions:

1. Are my menu items priced correctly?
2. Are the individual menu items selling well enough to warrant keeping them on the menu?
3. Is the overall profit margin on my menu items satisfactory?

- Some users of the contribution margin method of menu analysis refer to it as **menu engineering** and classify the squares used in the analysis with colorful names. The most common of these are "Plow horses" (square 1), "Stars" (square 2), "Dogs" (square 3), and "Puzzles" or sometimes "Challenges" (square 4).
- Goal value analysis uses the power of an algebraic formula to replace less sophisticated menu averaging techniques.
- The advantages of goal value analysis are many, including ease of use, accuracy, and the ability to simultaneously consider more variables than is possible with two-dimensional matrix analysis.
- **Goal value analysis** does evaluate each menu item's food cost percentage, contribution margin, and popularity and, unlike the two previous analysis methods introduced, however, it includes the analysis of the menu item's nonfood variable costs as well as its selling price.
- Menu items that achieve goal values higher than that of the menu's overall goal value will contribute greater than average profit percentages. As the goal value for an item increases, so too, does its profitability percentage.
- The goal value formula is as follows:

$$A \: x \: B \: x \: C \: x \: D = \textbf{Goal Value}$$

where
A = 1.00 - Food Cost %
B = Item Popularity
C = Selling Price
D = 1.00 - (Variable Cost % + Food Cost %)

- The computed goal value carries no unit designation; that is, it is neither a percentage nor a dollar figure because it is really a numerical target or score.
- Every menu will have items that are more or less profitable than others.
- A **loss leader** is a menu item that is priced very low, sometimes even below total costs, for the purpose of drawing large numbers of guests to the operation.
- Items that do not achieve the targeted goal value tend to be deficient in one or more of the key areas of food cost percentage, popularity, selling price, or variable cost percentage.
- In theory, all menu items have the potential of reaching the goal value. Management may, however, determine that some menu items can best serve the operation as loss leaders, an approach illustrated by the continued use of "value" menu items by leading chains in the **Quick Service Restaurant (QSR)** segment.
- Goal value analysis will allow you to make better decisions more quickly. Goal value analysis is also powerful because it is not, as is matrix analysis, dependent on past performance to establish profitability but can be used by management to establish future menu targets.
- A purely quantitative approach to menu analysis is neither practical nor desirable. Menu analysis and pricing decisions are always a matter of experience, skill, insight and educated predicting.

3. Cost/Volume/Profit Analysis

- Each foodservice operator knows that some accounting periods are more profitable than others. Often, this is because sales volume is higher or costs are lower during certain periods. Profitability, then, can be viewed as existing on a graph similar to the following:

Cost/Volume/Profit Graph

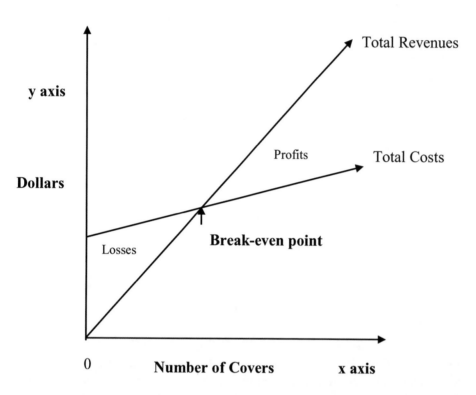

- At the **break-even point**, operational expenses are exactly equal to sales revenue; below the break-even point, costs are higher than revenues, so losses occur; above the break-even point, revenues exceed costs, so profits are made.

- A **cost/volume/profit (CVP) analysis** helps predict the sales dollars and volume required to achieve desired *profit* (or break-even) based on your known costs.

- CVP calculations can be done on either; 1.) the dollar sales volume required to break even or achieve the desired profit, or 2.) the number of guests (covers) required that must be served to break even.

- A **contribution margin income statement** simply shows P&L items in terms of sales, variable costs, contribution margin, fixed costs, and profit. (See figure 10.9)

- **Contribution margin for the overall operation** is defined as the dollar amount that *contributes* to covering fixed costs and providing for a profit.
- Contribution margin is calculated as follows:

$$\text{Total Sales} - \text{Variable Costs} = \text{Contribution Margin}$$

- To determine the dollar sales required to break even, use the following formula:

$$\frac{\text{Fixed Costs}}{\text{Contribution Margin \%}} = \text{Break-Even Point in Sales}$$

- In terms of the number of guests that must be served in order to break even, use the following formula:

$$\frac{\text{Fixed Costs}}{\text{Contribution Margin per Unit (Guest)}} = \text{Break-Even Point in Guests Served}$$

- To determine sales dollars and covers to achieve the after tax profit goal, use the following formula:

$$\frac{\text{Fixed Costs} + \text{Before-Tax Profit}}{\text{Contribution Margin \%}} = \text{Sales Dollars to Achieve Desired After-Tax Profit}$$

- To convert after-tax profit to before-tax profit, compute the following:

$$\frac{\text{After Tax Profit}}{1 - \text{Tax Rate}} = \text{Before-Tax Profit}$$

- In terms of calculating the number of guests that must be served in order to make the desired after-tax profit, use the following formula:

$$\frac{\text{Fixed Costs} + \text{Before-Tax Profit}}{\text{Contribution Margin per Unit (Guest)}} = \begin{array}{c}\text{Guests to Be Served to}\\ \text{Achieve Desired After-Tax Profit}\end{array}$$

- When calculating sales and covers to achieve break-even and desired after-tax profits, you can easily remember which formulas to use if you know the following:

    1. Contribution Margin *%* is used to calculate sales *dollars*.
    2. Contribution Margin per *unit* is used to calculate sales volume in *units* (guests).

- Once you fully understand the CVP analysis concepts, you can predict any sales level for break-even or after-tax profits based on your selling price, fixed costs, variable costs, and contribution margin.

- Cost/volume/profit analysis is used to establish targets for the entire operation, whereas, goal value analysis evaluates individual menu items against those operational targets. Therefore, the two analyses can be strategically linked.

Cost/Volume/Profit Analysis	Goal Value Analysis
Food cost % from contribution margin income statement	Food cost % goal
Guests served to achieve desired after-tax profit	Total average number of covers per menu item goal
Selling price	Selling price goal
Labor and other variable cost % from contribution margin income statement	Variable cost % goal

- By looking at these two analyses, you can learn how the overall goals of the operation affect menu item profitability. Conversely, you can see how changes you make to menu items affect the overall profitability of the operation.
- **Minimum Sales Point (MSP)** is the sales volume required to justify staying open for a given period of time.
- The information needed to calculate a MSP is:
    1. Food cost %
    2. Minimum payroll cost needed for the time period
    3. Variable cost %

- Fixed costs are eliminated from the calculation because even if volume of sales equals zero, fixed costs still exist and must be paid.
- In calculating MSP, food cost % + variable cost % is called the **minimum operating cost**.
- The MSP formula is shown as follows:

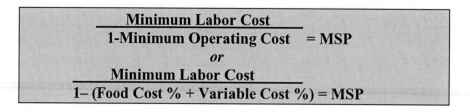

$$\frac{\text{Minimum Labor Cost}}{1-\text{Minimum Operating Cost}} = \text{MSP}$$

or

$$\frac{\text{Minimum Labor Cost}}{1- (\text{Food Cost \%} + \text{Variable Cost \%})} = \text{MSP}$$

- Corporate policy, contractual hours, promotion of a new unit, competition, and other factors must all be taken into account before the decision is made to modify operational hours.

4. The Budget

- The **budget**, or financial plan, will detail the operational direction of your unit and your expected financial results.
- The budget should not be a static document. It should be modified and fine-tuned as managerial accounting presents data about sales and costs that affect the direction of the overall operation.
- Just as the P&L tells you about your past performance, the budget is developed to help you achieve your future goals.

Budgeted Revenue – Budgeted Expense = Budgeted Profit

- To prepare the budget and stay within it assures you predetermined results.
- The effective foodservice operator builds his or her budget, monitors it closely, modifies it when necessary, and achieves the desired results.
- Budgeting is best done by the entire management team, for it is only through participation in the process that the whole organization will feel compelled to support the budget.
- Foodservice budgets can be considered as one of three main types: long-range budget, annual budget, and achievement budget.
- The **long-range budget** is typically prepared for a period of three to five years.
- The **annual budget** is for a one-year period or, in some cases, one season. An annual budget need not follow a calendar year. An annual budget need not consist of 12, one-month periods. While many operators prefer one-month budgets, some prefer budgets consisting of 13, 28-day periods, while others use quarterly (three-month) or even weekly budgets to plan for revenues and costs throughout the budget year.
- The **achievement budget** is always of a shorter range, perhaps a month or a week. It provides current operating information and thus assists in making current operational decisions.

5. Developing the Budget

- To establish any type of budget, you need to have the following information available:

  1. Prior-period operating results
  2. Assumptions of next-period operations
  3. Goals
  4. Monitoring policies

- To determine a food budget, compute the estimated food cost as follows:

> 1. **Last Year's Food Cost per Meal = Last Year's Cost of Food / Total Meals Served**
>
> 2. **Last Year's Food Cost per Meal + % Estimated Increase in Food Cost = This Year's Food Cost per Meal**
>
> 3. **This Year's Food Cost Per Meal x Number of Meals to Be Served This Year = Estimated Cost of Food This Year**

- To determine a labor budget, compute the estimated labor cost as follows:

> 1. **Last Year's Labor Cost per Meal = Last Year's Cost of Labor / Total Meals Served**
>
> 2. **Last Year's Labor Cost per Meal + % Estimated Increase in Labor Cost = This Year's Labor Cost per Meal**
>
> 3. **This Year's Labor Cost per Meal x Number of Meals to Be Served This Year = Estimated Cost of Labor This Year**

- Budgeting for utility costs is one a foodservice operator's biggest challenges. This is due to both the instability of energy prices and the impact of the weather on usage.
- Strategies for reducing energy usage should include:

    1. Investigating the instillation of smart lighting systems that automatically turn off lights when storage areas are vacant.
    2. Replacement of all incandescent lighting with an appropriate type of electric discharge lamp (such as fluorescent, mercury vapor, metal halide or sodium) wherever possible.
    3. The use of dual-flush, low-flow or waterless toilets to reduce water waste.
    4. Installing low-flow faucet aerators on all sinks to cut water usage by as much as 40%; from a standard 4 gallons per minute to a cost-saving 2.5 gallons a minute.
    5. Implementation of an effective preventive maintenance program for all cooking equipment including frequent and accurate temperature recalibrations.
    6. Reducing waste disposal costs by implementing effective source reduction plans as well as pre and post-production recycling efforts.

6. Monitoring the Budget

- In general, the budget should be monitored in each of the following three areas:

    1. Revenue
    2. Expense
    3. Profit

- Some foodservice operators relate revenue to the number of seats they have available in their operation. The formula for the computation of sales per seat is as follows:

$$\frac{\text{Total Sales}}{\text{Available Seats}} = \text{Sales per Seat}$$

- Some commercial foodservice operators relate revenue to the number of square feet their operations occupy. These operators budget revenues based on a **sales per square foot** basis. The formula of sales per square foot is as follows:

$$\frac{\text{Total Sales}}{\text{Total Square Footage Occupied}} = \text{Sales per Square Foot}$$

- Effective managers compare their actual revenue to that which they have projected on a regular basis.
- If revenue should fall below projected levels, the impact on profit can be substantial.
- Effective foodservice managers are careful to monitor operational expense because costs that are too high or too low may be cause for concern.
- Some operators elect to utilize the **yardstick method** of calculating expense standards so determinations can be made as to whether variations in expenses are due to changes in sales volume, or other reasons such as waste or theft.
- Developing Yardstick Standards for Food

Step 1. Divide total inventory into management-designated sub-groups, for example, meats, produce, dairy, and groceries.

Step 2. Establish dollar value of subgroup purchases for prior accounting period.

Step 3. Establish sales volume for the prior accounting period.

Step 4. Determine percentage of purchasing dollar spent for each food category.

Step 5. Determine percentage of revenue dollar spent for each food category.

Step 6. Develop weekly sales volume and associated expense projection. Compute % cost to sales for each food grouping and sales estimate.

Step 7. Compare weekly revenue and expense to projection. Correct if necessary.

- Developing Yardstick Standards for Labor

  Step 1. Divide total labor cost into management-designated sub-groups, for example, cooks, warewashers, and bartenders.
  Step 2. Establish dollar value spent for each subgroup during the prior accounting period.
  Step 3. Establish sales volume for the prior accounting period.
  Step 4. Determine percentage of labor dollar spent for each subgroup.
  Step 5. Determine percentage of revenue dollar spent for each labor category.
  Step 6. Develop weekly sales volume and associated expense projection. Compute % cost to sales for each labor category and sales estimate.
  Step 7. Compare weekly revenue and expense to projection. Correct if necessary.

- As business conditions change, changes in the budget are to be expected. This is because budgets are based on a specific set of assumptions, and if these assumptions change, so too will the budgets.
- Budgeted profit levels must be realized if an operation is to provide adequate returns for owner and investor risk.
- The primary purpose of management is to generate the profits needed to continue the business. Budgeting for these profits is a fundamental step in the process.

7. Technology Tools

- While menu analysis software is often packaged as part of a larger program and is somewhat limited, the software required to do an overall break-even analysis is readily available, as well as that required for budgeting. Specialized software in this area is available to help you:

  1. Evaluate item profitability.
  2. Conduct menu matrix analysis.
  3. Perform break-even analysis.
  4. Budget revenue and expense levels.
  5. Budget profit levels.
  6. Assemble budgets based on days, weeks, months, years, or other identifiable accounting periods.
  7. Conduct performance to budget analysis.
  8. Maintain performance to budget histories.
  9. Blend budgets from multiple profit centers (or multiple units).
  10. Perform budgeted cash flow analysis.

- For commercial operators, it is simply not wise to attempt to operate an effective foodservice unit without a properly priced menu and an accurate budget that reflects estimated sales and expense levels.

Consider The Cost

Sophia Lancaster is the registered dietitian (R.D.) responsible for all dietary services at Parker Memorial Hospital. Her operation consists of two departments. The first, and largest, is patient feeding. It consists of the tray line staff and the majority of her food production staff. The second department is the public cafeteria, which includes special dining areas for hospital staff and a large dining area for patient visitors. Each year, she submits to her supervisor an annual labor expense budget broken down by month for each department.

In June, and after four months of consideration and planning, Sophia and her staff were excited to implement a new cafeteria menu. The response from the public was excellent. The dining room staff reported that there were many positive comments about the food selected for the new menu, and the production staff reported a 25% increase in the amount of food prepared for cafeteria service.

On July 7, when Sophia's assistant, Jason, brought her the financial reports for the month of June, he was concerned. "I think we are in big trouble Boss," he said. "As I read the reports, we were over our labor budget by more than $3,000 last month! How could that happen?"

Sophia reviewed the labor portion of the budget and found the following:

	August Budget	August Actual
Patient Line Labor:	$ 33,750	$ 33,824
Cafeteria Labor:	$ 26,500	$ 29,850

1. What do you think is the cause of Sophia's labor budget overage? How would you determine if you are correct?

2. What other operational data do you think Sophia should include in this month's report to the administration?

Answers:

This case was created to demonstrate to students that variations in expense budgets can occur for a variety of reasons, some of which are very "good!" In this case, Sophia's success in improving her operation has resulted in increased labor costs required to serve the additional guests her innovative menu has attracted. That is good news for her, her hospital, and the guests who eat in her cafeteria.

1. It is the most likely case that Sophia's labor budget has increased due to the 25% increase in food being served in the cafeteria. It is reasonable to assume that the increase in the amount of food served means an estimated 25% increase in guests served. With that level of increase in guest count, the number of line servers, dining room attendants, cashiers, and other staff positions required would likely be increased to service these guests.

   Sophia would want to check her guest counts, check average, and her preferred labor productivity measure to confirm that this is indeed the case.

2.

	June Budget	June Actual	$ Variance	% Variance
Patient Line Labor	$ 33,750	$ 33,824	$ 74	0.2 %
Cafeteria Labor	$ 26,500	$ 29,850	$ 3,350	12.6 %
Total	$ 60,250	$ 63,674	$ 3,424	5.7 %

Sophia should include in her monthly report the number of additional guests she has served, as well as the incremental revenue generated by those guests. Sophia will very likely find that the amount of revenue she budgeted for June is too low. If she was efficient with her labor scheduling (perhaps measured in "Guests served per labor hour used"), the additional revenue she generated should easily be enough to pay for the extra labor costs she has incurred and still contribute a significant number of additional dollars to her department P&L's "bottom line" (profit).

In summary, Sophia's innovation caused an overage in her labor expense budget…but it also very likely created an overage in her profit budget! Good job Sophia!!

Apply What You Have Learned

Ananda Fields is the CEO of a company that operates a very large number of quick service restaurants. Recently, competitors have been increasing sales at their restaurants at a faster rate than at Ananda's. Joseph Smith, Vice President of Operations is encouraging Ananda to introduce a new line of higher priced, higher quality, and higher contribution margin items to increase sales and improve profits. Sonya Miller, her V.P. for Marketing, is recommending that Ananda introduce a "value" line of products that would be priced very low, but significantly increases traffic to the stores.

1. Do you think more customers would be attracted using the recommendation suggested by Joseph or by Sonya?

   Answer: It would depend on her customer base and what her competition is offering. If her competitors are increasing sales because they are offering higher priced, higher quality items, then Ananda should probably take the advice of Joseph. However, if customers are demanding lower priced items and her competitors are generating more sales with lower prices, Ananda should probably take Sonya's advice. If I were Ananda, I would probably take Sonya's advice, assuming Sonya came to her recommendation based on market research.

2. What factors would cause Ananda to choose one V.P.'s menu recommendation over the other?

Answer: The primary factor would be the recommendation that is more likely to bring additional profit to her bottom line. She could conduct a cost/volume/profit analysis to determine how different prices and different costs would affect her ability achieve her desired overall profit. She could also conduct a goal value analysis to see the potential affects both higher and lower prices have on her menu items based on her goals.

3. What impact will Ananda's menu decision have on the image projected by her stores? What can she do to influence this image?

Answer: By offering higher priced, higher quality items, Ananda's fast-food restaurants will have a higher "quality" image. This may impact her business negatively or positively. The impact would be negative if most of her customer base demands lower prices. It would be positive if there is a niche market she could fill with "gourmet" fast food. The reverse could occur if she offers lower priced items. Her customers may perceive that lower prices mean lower quality, thus negatively impacting her business. On the other hand, lower prices may be just what her customers want. Either way the image of her company will be impacted. In order to influence the image that she wants, she needs to have Sonya prepare a carefully constructed advertising campaign that will shape the company's image and bring customers to her restaurants.

Test Your Skills

1. Boniso operates Boniso's Mexican Restaurant in an urban city in the South. He has worked hard at setting up cost control systems, and he is generally happy with his *overall* results. However, he is not sure if all of his menu items are providing profitability for his restaurant. He decides to use food cost matrix and contribution margin matrix analyses to study each of his menu items.

   a. Complete his menu analysis worksheet.

Menu Analysis Worksheet

Menu Item	# Sold	Selling Price	Total Sales	Item Cost	Total Cost	Item CM	Total CM	Food Cost %
Fajita Plate	147	$12.95	$1,903.65	$4.92	$723.24	$8.03	$1,180.41	38%
Enchilada Dinner	200	$9.95	$1,990.00	$3.48	$696.00	$6.47	$1,294.00	35%
Menudo	82	$6.95	$569.90	$1.74	$142.68	$5.21	$427.22	25%
Mexican Salad	117	$7.95	$930.15	$2.39	$279.63	$5.56	$650.52	30%
Chalupa Dinner	125	$8.95	$1,118.75	$2.51	$313.75	$6.44	$805.00	28%
Burrito Dinner	168	$9.95	$1,671.60	$3.25	$546.00	$6.70	$1,125.60	33%
Taco Dinner	225	$5.95	$1,338.75	$1.55	$348.75	$4.40	$990.00	26%
Total	1,064		$9,522.80		$3,050.05		$6,472.75	
Weighted Average	152	$8.95	$1,360.40	$2.87	$435.72	$6.08	$924.68	32%

b. Using the results of Boniso's menu analysis worksheet (in part a), fill in the appropriate average food cost, popularity, and contribution margin in the blanks below. Then, type in the menu items in the appropriate squares in the matrices.

Food Cost Matrix

High Food Cost %
(Above 32 %)

Low Food Cost %
(Below 32%)

Fajita plate	Enchilada Dinner, Burrito Dinner
Menudo, Mexican Salad, Chalupa Dinner	Taco Dinner

Low Popularity	**High Popularity**
(Below 152 sales)	**(Above 152 sales)**

Contribution Margin Matrix

High Contribution Margin
(Above $ 6.08)

Low Contribution Margin
(Below $ 6.08)

Fajita Plate, Chalupa Dinner	Enchilada Dinner, Burrito Dinner
Menudo, Mexican Salad	Taco Dinner

Low Popularity	**High Popularity**
(Below 152 sales)	**(Above 152 sales)**

2. Garikai is a manager at Boniso's Mexican Restaurant (from previous question), and he believes that goal value analysis, rather than Boniso's matrix analysis, is a better way to study the profitability of his menu items.

a. Using the following goal value analysis data, help Garikai analyze the restaurant's menu items.

Goal Value Analysis Data

	Food Cost % (in decimal form)	Number Sold	Selling Price	Variable Cost % (in decimal form)
Fajita Plate	0.38	147	$12.95	0.28
Enchilada Dinner	0.35	200	9.95	0.28
Menudo	0.25	82	6.95	0.28
Mexican Salad	0.30	117	7.95	0.28
Chalupa Dinner	0.28	125	8.95	0.28
Burrito Dinner	0.33	168	9.95	0.28
Taco Dinner	0.26	225	5.95	0.28
Overall Menu (Goal Value)	0.32	152	8.95	0.28

After computing the following goal values, sort (in descending rank order) by goal value. Be sure to include the *overall menu* in the appropriate rank order.

Goal Value Analysis Results

Item	Food Cost % (in decimal form)	Number Sold	Selling Price	Variable Cost % (in decimal form)	Goal Value
Enchilada Dinner	0.35	200	9.95	0.28	478.6
Taco Dinner	0.26	225	5.95	0.28	455.7
Burrito Dinner	0.33	168	9.95	0.28	436.8
Fajita Plate	0.38	147	12.95	0.28	401.3
Overall Menu (Goal Value)	*0.32*	*152*	*8.95*	*0.28*	*370.0*
Chalupa Dinner	0.28	125	8.95	0.28	354.4
Mexican Salad	0.30	117	7.95	0.28	273.5
Menudo	0.25	82	6.95	0.28	200.9

b. After analyzing his menu items, Garikai believes he can improve the chalupa dinner by lowering the selling price to $8.55. He believes that this lower price will increase number of chalupa dinners sold to 150. However, the change in price will increase both his food cost % and variable cost % to 29% for the chalupa dinner. If he makes these changes, will the chalupa dinner meet or exceed the overall menu goal value? Should Garikai make these changes?

Results of Changes Made to Chalupa Dinner

Item	Food Cost % (in decimal form)	Number Sold	Selling Price	Variable Cost % (in decimal form)	Goal Value
Chalupa Dinner	0.29	150	8.55	0.29	382.4

Answer: The changes will cause the chalupa dinner to exceed the goal value; therefore, he should make the changes.

3. Eunice manages a Thai restaurant in a primarily Asian section of a major West Coast city. She is interested in determining dollar sales and number of guests needed to break even and to generate her desired profits. Her check average (selling price) is $16.00, her variable cost per unit (guest) is $5.60, and her fixed costs are $170,000.

a. Complete the following grid, and determine her before-tax profit.

	Per Unit (Guest)	Percentage
SP	$16.00	100%
VC	5.60	35%
CM	10.40	65%

Fixed costs	$170,000.00
Desired after-tax profit	$24,000.00
Tax rate	40%
Before-tax profit	$40,000.00

b. Using the information from part a, calculate the following. (Spreadsheet hint: Use the ROUNDUP function for "Rounded up - Break-even point in guest served" and "Rounded up – Guests served to achieve desired after-tax profit.")

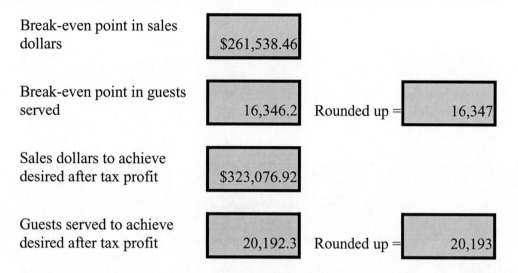

Break-even point in sales dollars $261,538.46

Break-even point in guests served   16,346.2   Rounded up =   16,347

Sales dollars to achieve desired after tax profit $323,076.92

Guests served to achieve desired after tax profit   20,192.3   Rounded up =   20,193

c. Based on her calculations, Eunice doesn't think that she can attract as many guests as she needs to achieve her desired after-tax profit. Therefore, she has decided to make some changes to improve her situation. Due to these changes, she has been able to reduce her selling price by $1.00, decrease her variable cost % by 5%, and lower her fixed costs by $5,000. After these changes, what are Eunice's sales dollars and guests served to achieve her after-tax profit? Complete the following grid and the calculations. (Spreadsheet hint: Use the ROUNDUP function for "Rounded up – Guests served to achieve desired after-tax profit.")

	Per Unit (Guest)	Percentage
SP	$15.00	100%
VC	4.50	30%
CM	10.50	70%

Fixed Costs $165,000.00

Sales dollars to achieve desired After Tax Profit $292,857.14

Guests served to achieve desired After Tax Profit   19,523.8   Rounded up =   19,524

4. Sinqobile runs a restaurant in an East Coast city that specializes in African-American cuisine. She has compiled her sales and cost data from last year, and she wants to develop a budget for this year. She has projected the following increases for this year:

Projected Increases

Meals served	3%
Selling price per meal	2%
Cost of food	5%
Cost of labor	10%
Other expenses	2%

Using this information, help Sinqobile complete her budget.

	Last Year	Budget
Meals Served	122,000	125,660
Selling Price per Meal	$12.50	$12.75

Last year's food cost per meal:	$5.00
Last year's food cost per meal + estimated increase:	$5.25
Estimated cost of food this year:	$659,715.00

Last year's labor cost per meal:	$4.00
Last year's labor cost per meal + estimated increase:	$4.40
Estimated cost of labor this year:	$552,904.00

	Last Year $	Last Year %	Budget $	Budget %
Revenue	$1,525,000.00	100.0%	$1,602,165.00	100.0%
Cost of Food	610,000.00	40.0%	$659,715.00	41.2%
Cost of Labor	488,000.00	32.0%	$552,904.00	34.5%
Other Expenses	245,760.00	16.1%	$250,675.20	15.6%
Total Expenses	1,343,760.00	88.1%	$1,463,294.20	91.3%
Profit	181,240.00	11.9%	$138,870.80	8.7%

The owner of the restaurant has requested that Sinqobile make at least a 10% profit for this year. Based on her budget figures, is she likely to meet this goal? If not, what can she do to achieve a 10% profit?

Answer: Based on her budget figures, Sinqobile will not be likely to meet her 10% profit goal. She will have to plan on either increasing revenue and/or reducing costs to meet her goal. She must adjust her budget to incorporate these changes.

5. Sitabiso manages an executive dining room in an office building of a major food manufacturing company. Her sales, on average, run between $17,000 and $21,000 per week. She has decided to use yardstick standards for labor to predict labor costs for varying sales levels. With these data, she can determine if variations in her expenses are due to changes in sales volume or other reasons such as waste or theft. She has compiled information from last year to help her predict her weekly labor costs. Using this information, help Sitabiso complete her yardstick standards for labor. (Spreadsheet hint: Use the ROUND function for "% to Total Cost" and "% Cost to Total Sales" columns. Also, round to 3 decimal places, e.g., .123 or 12.3%)

Yardstick Standards for Labor

Total Sales: $900,000   Average Sales per Month: $75,000

Labor Costs:

Management	$84,000
Food Production	143,000
Service	27,600
Sanitation	34,200
Total	288,800

	% Cost to Total Cost	% Cost to Total Sales	Weekly Sales Estimate				
Category			$17,000	$18,000	$19,000	$20,000	$21,000
Management	29.1%	9.3%	$1,581	$1,674	$1,767	$1,860	$1,953
Food Production	49.5%	15.9%	$2,703	$2,862	$3,021	$3,180	$3,339
Service	9.6%	3.1%	$527	$558	$589	$620	$651
Sanitation	11.8%	3.8%	$646	$684	$722	$760	$798
Total	100.0%	32.1%	$5,457	$5,778	$6,099	$6,420	$6,741

6. Toni Lamazza is developing next year's foodservice budget for the Springdale school system, consisting of 17 different schools in a two-county area. Toni knows the revenue she will get from the School Board, but is not sure how much the Board will give her to pay for anticipated increases in employee benefits. Complete the chart below to help Toni determine the amount employee benefits can increase and still allow her to show a budget surplus.

At what level of employee benefit cost increase will Toni have a "break-even" budget? How much would her surplus/deficit be if benefits increase by 20%?

	Current Budget	Budget with Employee Benefits Increases			
		5% Increase	**10% Increase**	**15% Increase**	**20% Increase**
Revenue	$7,000,000	$7,000,000	$7,000,000	$7,000,000	$7,000,000
Cost of Food	$2,095,000	$2,095,000	$2,095,000	$2,095,000	$2,095,000
Cost of Payroll	$3,700,000	$3,700,000	$3,700,000	$3,700,000	$3,700,000
Cost of Employee Benefits	$ 700,000	$ 735,000	$ 770,000	$ 805,000	$ 840,000
Other Expenses	$ 400,000	$ 400,000	$ 400,000	$ 400,000	$ 400,000
Total Costs	$6,895,000	$6,930,000	$6,965,000	$7,000,000	$7,035,000
Budget Surplus/ Deficit	$ 105,000	$ 70,000	$ 35,000	$ --	$ (35,000)

Answer: Toni will have a "break-even" budget at a 15% increase in employee benefits. If benefits increase by 20%, Toni will have a deficit of $35,000.

7. J.D. McAllister is really happy. He has just succeeded in securing a $2,000,000 bank loan with a variable percentage interest rate to build his dream restaurant. JD's loan is for 25 years, and it carries an interest rate that is set at 7% for the first year (this year). Thus, his first year's monthly interest payments will be $14,136. An experienced restaurateur, JD has prepared the following annual budget for this year.

Annual Budget for This Year

Total Sales	$2,046,000.00
Variable Costs	
Food	429,660.00
Beverage	257,796.00
Labor	572,880.00
Other Variable Costs	171,864.00
Total Variable Costs	1,432,200.00
Fixed Costs (excluding loan repayment)	239,568.00
Loan Repayment (7% interest)	169,632.00
Total Fixed Costs	409,200.00
Before Tax Profit	204,600.00
Taxes (40%)	81,840.00
After Tax Profit	122,760.00

JD's interest rate will likely vary over the life of the loan because it is tied to the "prime" interest rate established by the Federal Reserve Board (part of the federal government). Assume the "Fed" increases interest rates next year by ½%, and thus JD's interest rate moves to 7.5%. As a result, his new monthly loan repayment will be $14,780.

Also assume that his total variable cost % and fixed costs (excluding loan repayment) will be the same next year, and his check average (selling price) will be $20 per cover. What sales dollars and guests served will JD need to achieve next year to maintain the same number of after tax profit dollars as he budgeted for this year?

	Per Unit (Guest)	Percentage
SP	$20.00	100%
VC	14.00	70%
CM	6.00	30%

Fixed Costs (excluding loan repayment)	$239,568.00
Loan Repayment (7.5% interest)	$177,360.00
Total Fixed Costs	$416,928.00
Desired after tax profit	$122,760.00
Tax rate	40%
Before tax profit	$204,600.00

Sales dollars to achieve desired after tax profit	$2,071,760.00
Guests served to achieve desired after tax profit	103,588

8. The Wheatfield Valley golf course has been owned by the Miley family for two generations. Currently it is managed by Cyrus Miley, a graduate of State University where he majored in hospitality management. Last year was a good one for the golf course. Now Cyrus is preparing next year's operating budget. He has gathered a great deal of information to help him prepare the best budget possible. After carefully analyzing that information, Cyrus predicts that next year the course will experience:

- A 5% increase in food sales
- A 3% increase in beverage sales
- No change in food or beverage product cost percentage
- Salaries and wages that will increase 4.5%
- Benefits that will increase 10%
- An increase of 2.5% in each Other Expense category except for Occupancy Cost and Depreciation. His accountant states those to categories will be unchanged.
- Interest payments of $1,000 per month
- Tax payments that are estimated to be 25% of income before income taxes

Calculate this year's operating percentages for the food and beverage department on the budget worksheet provided, and then using his assumptions about next year, create Cyrus' new operating budget in dollars and percentages.

The Wheatfield Valley Golf Course
F&B Department
Budget Worksheet for Next Year

	This Year Actual $	%	Next Year Budget $	%
SALES:				
Food	173,250.00	75.33%	181,912.50	75.68%
Beverage	56,750.00	24.67%	58,452.50	24.32%
Total Sales	**230,000.00**	100.00%	**240,365.00**	100.0%
COST OF SALES:				
Food	58,250.00	33.62%	61,162.50	33.62%
Beverage	9,375.00	16.52%	9,656.25	16.52%
Total Cost of Sales	**67,625.00**	29.40%	**70,818.75**	29.46%
GROSS PROFIT:				
Food	115,000.00	66.38%	120,750.00	66.38%
Beverage	47,375.00	83.48%	48,796.25	83.48%
Total Gross Profit	**162,375.00**	70.60%	**169,546.25**	70.54%
OPERATING EXPENSES:				
Salaries and Wages	36,250.00	15.76%	37,881.25	15.76%
Employee Benefits	6,200.00	2.70%	6,820.00	2.84%
Direct Operating Expenses	8,275.00	3.60%	8,481.88	3.53%
Outing Rentals	1,600.00	0.70%	1,640.00	0.68%
Beer Cart Expense	3,325.00	1.45%	3,408.13	1.42%
Utility Allocation	5,975.00	2.60%	6,124.38	2.55%
Kitchen Repair and Maintenance	1,750.00	0.76%	1,793.75	0.75%
Administrative and General	6,375.00	2.77%	6,534.38	2.72%
Occupancy	15,000.00	6.52%	15,000.00	6.24%
Depreciation	4,200.00	1.83%	4,200.00	1.75%
Total Operating Expenses	**88,950.00**	38.67%	**91,883.75**	38.23%
Operating Income	**73,425.00**	31.92%	**77,662.50**	32.31%
Interest	12,000.00	5.22%	12,000.00	4.99%
Income Before Income Taxes	**61,425.00**	26.71%	**65,662.50**	27.32%
Income Taxes	15,356.25	6.68%	16,415.63	6.83%
Net Income	**46,068.75**	20.03%	**49,246.88**	20.49%

9. Menu analysis is typically associated with commercial foodservice operators who charge individual selling prices for their menu items. In many cases, however, noncommercial foodservice operators receive a fixed amount of money per guest served regardless of the menu items selected by the guest. Those managers in charge of foodservice in a college dormitory cafeteria are one such example. Despite the differences in how they charge for the items they serve, managers in both commercial and noncommercial operations are concerned about guest acceptance of the menu items they offer. Identify and then compare or contrast at least two other areas of concern shared by menu planners in the commercial and noncommercial segments of the foodservice industry.

Answers:
There are several areas in which commercial and noncommercial foodservice menu planners share concerns. These include:

Financial concerns. In a commercial operation, the goal of menu planners is to maximize contribution margin (profit); the financial goal of college and university menu planners is usually to minimize (or to stay within a specified budget related to) food costs.

Recipe selection concerns. Commercial menu planners most often choose menu items based on their ability to generate profit; college and university menu planners select recipes based on their resulting food costs.

Sales (popularity) related concerns. Popularity concerns in commercial operations require that menu planners search for high popularity, high contribution margin items. Menu planners in college and university foodservice are especially interested in adding low cost and popular items because offering more of these items allows them to, on occasion, offer higher cost, but less popular items that lead to wider menu variety and improved student reaction to the overall menu.

Service. The commercial operator's concern focuses on service because it impacts profits. Service and adequate nutrition are usually the primary focus of a college and university foodservices department, as well as that of many other noncommercial operators.

Volume of production. In commercial operations, there is typically more customized demand. Orders are placed one at a time and the menu items are often cooked-to-order, or made in very small batches. College and university menu planners must choose menu items based in part upon the equipment and labor needed to produce large volumes with minimized cost and maximized quality.

Menu mix. Commercial menu planners are concerned about offering items that may have different individual contribution margins, but that work together to maximize profits. By contrast, noncommercial menu planners are very cost sensitive; they are more concerned about minimizing the costs to produce all the menu items offered.

Exam Questions

Multiple Choice
Choose the letter of the best answer to the questions listed below.

1. A _____ is a menu item that is priced very low, sometimes even below total costs, for the purpose of drawing large numbers of guests to the operation.
    a. Loss leader
    b. Yardstick
    c. Goal value
    d. Achievement budget
    e. All of the above
    Correct answer is a (See: Goal Value Analysis)

2. A restaurant has a check average of $12 and has variable costs per cover of $4.80. If its fixed costs are $36,000 for the month, the number of covers that must be sold to reach the monthly break-even point is:
    a. 3,750 covers
    b. 4,500 covers
    c. 5,000 covers
    d. 1,500 covers
    Correct answer is c (See: Cost/Volume/Profit Analysis)

3. Which of the following statements regarding goal value analysis is correct?
    a. As the goal value for an item increases, so does its profitability percentage.
    b. The computed goal value is a numerical target. It is not a percent or dollar figure.
    c. Goal Value = A x B x C x D (A = 1 - food cost %), (B = item popularity), (C= selling price) and D = 1 - (variable cost % + food cost %)
    d. All of the above
    e. Only a. and b. above
    Correct answer is d (See: Goal Value Analysis)

4. Calculate the goal value for the following Italian pasta plate: food cost % 35%, number sold 150, selling price $12.50, variable cost % 30%.
    a. 196.88
    b. 426.56
    c. 534.82
    d. 233.76
    e. Cannot be determined
    Correct answer is b (See: Goal Value Analysis)

5. Given the following information, calculate the desired before-tax profit: tax rate 25%, desired after-tax profit $12,000, contribution margin % 50%.
   a. $6,000
   b. $8,000
   c. $12,000
   d. $16,000
   Correct answer is d (See: Cost/Volume/Profit Analysis)

6. Given the following information, calculate the sales dollars needed to achieve the desired after-tax profit of $12,000: tax rate 40%, fixed costs $30,000, variable cost % 50%.
   a. $84,000
   b. $60,000
   c. $100,000
   d. $150,000
   e. Cannot be determined
   Correct answer is c (See: Cost/Volume/Profit Analysis)

7. Which of the following items do you need to have available to develop a budget?
   a. Prior period operating results
   b. Assumptions of next period operations
   c. Goals
   d. Monitoring policies
   e. All of the above
   Correct answer is e (See: Developing the Budget)

8. Given the information shown below, what are the costs for the labor category, production, for the weekly sales estimate level of $20,000?
   a. $2,000
   b. $3,000
   c. $6,600
   d. $10,000
   e. None of the above
   Correct answer is b (See: Developing Yardstick Standards for Labor)

Labor Category	%Cost to Total Costs	%Cost to Total Sales	Weekly Sales Estimate		
			$19,000	$20,000	$21,000
Management	30.0%	10.0%			
Production	50.0%	15.0%			
Service	10.0%	3.0%			
Sanitation	10.0%	3.0%			
Total	100.0%	31.0%			

9. Items that do not achieve the targeted goal value tend to be deficient in one or more key areas. What are these key areas?
   a. Food cost percentage
   b. Popularity
   c. Selling price and/or variable cost percentage
   d. All of the above
   e. Only a. and b. above
   Correct answer is d (See: Goal Value Analysis)

10. When the contribution margin matrix is used and the menu item has a low contribution margin and high popularity, which of the following may be part of the marketing strategy?
    a. Promote well.
    b. Reduce prominence on the menu.
    c. Consider reducing selling price.
    d. All of the above
    e. Only a. and b. above
    Correct answer is b (See: Figure 10.4 Analysis of Contribution Margin Matrix Results)

11. How do you calculate the break-even point in sales?
    a. Fixed costs / contribution margin %
    b. Contribution margin / fixed costs
    c. Profit / variable costs
    d. Fixed costs / total sales
    e. None of the above
    Correct answer is a (See: Cost/Volume/Profit Analysis)

12. The matrix analysis:
    a. Allows menu items to be placed into categories based on whether they are above or below menu item averages.
    b. Compares menu items to a goal value.
    c. Analyzes food cost % and contribution margin.
    d. All of the above
    e. Only a. and c. above
    Correct answer is e (See: Menu Analysis)

13. Total sales – total product costs equals:
    a. Food cost
    b. Total profit
    c. Total contribution margin
    d. None of the above
    Correct answer is c (See: Cost/Volume/Profit Analysis)

Brian owns Brian's Bakery and he wants to analyze how well he has done this year based on his budget. Complete the Revenue Budget Summary below and answer questions 14 and 15.

Brian's Bakery Revenue Budget Summary			

Meal Period	Budget	Actual	% of Budget
A.M.	$500,000	$355,000	71%
P.M.		$111,000	44%
Total	$750,000		

14. Assuming Brian's Bakery has 750 available seats, compute the actual sales per seat for the A.M. meal period.
   a. $473.33
   b. $666.67
   c. $193.33
   d. $185.33
   Correct answer is a (See: Monitoring the Budget)

15. What overall % of budget did Brian's Bakery reach?
   a. 115%
   b. 57.5%
   c. 62%
   d. 27%
   Correct answer is c (See: Monitoring the Budget)

16. Which of the following software programs can help a manager plan for profit?
   a. Budget profit levels
   b. Conduct menu matrix analysis
   c. Perform budgeted cash flow analysis
   d. All of the above
   e. Only a. and c. above
   Correct answer is d (See: Technology Tools)

17. Calculate the goal value for the following chicken parmesan plate: food cost % 40%, number sold 250, selling price $11.95, variable cost % 25%.
   a. 435.98
   b. 590.34
   c. 543.23
   d. 627.38
   e. Cannot be determined
   Correct answer is d (See: Goal Value Analysis)

True/False

Choose the letter of the best answer to the questions listed below.

18. A criticism of using the food cost percentage method of menu analysis is that items that have a lower food cost percentage may be sacrificed in favor of higher per item profits.
    a. True
    b. False
    Correct answer is b (See: Food Cost Percentage)

19. If an item on the food cost matrix has a low food cost % and high popularity management should not waste money or time marketing it; the item obviously sells itself.
    a. True
    b. False
    Correct answer is b (See: Figure 10.3 Analysis of Food Cost Matrix Results)

20. A criticism of using the contribution margin method of menu analysis is that it tends to favor high priced menu items over low priced menu items.
    a. True
    b. False
    Correct answer is a (See: Contribution Margin)

21. A goal value for a menu item carries no unit designation; instead it is simply a numerical target or score.
    a. True
    b. False
    Correct answer is a (See: Goal Value Analysis)

22. Budgeting is best done by upper management.
    a. True
    b. False
    Correct answer is b (See: The Budget)

23. Long range and achievement budgets are synonymous.
    a. True
    b. False
    Correct answer is b (See: The Budget)

24. In general, budgets should be monitored in terms of revenue, expense, and profit.
    a. True
    b. False
    Correct answer is a (See: Monitoring the Budget)

25. In the foodservice industry, budgets are static documents.
    a. True
    b. False
    Correct answer is b (See: The Budget)

26. The financial summary known as a budget or plan, tells management where they are, and how they got there.
    a. True
    b. False
    Correct answer is b (See: The Budget)

27. It is simply not wise to attempt to operate an effective foodservice unit without a properly priced menu and an accurate budget that reflects estimated sales and expense levels.
    a. True
    b. False
    Correct answer is a (See: Technology Tools)

28. Installing low-flow faucet aerators on all sinks cuts water usage by as much as 40%.
    a. True
    b. False
    Correct answer is a (See: Green and Growing)

29. Implementation of an effective preventive maintenance program for all cooking equipment including frequent and accurate temperature recalibrations can reduce energy usage.
    a. True
    b. False
    Correct answer is a (See: Green and Growing)

Chapter 11

Maintaining and Improving the Revenue Control System

Learning Outcomes

At the conclusion of this chapter, you will be able to:

- Identify internal and external threats to revenue.
- Create effective countermeasures to combat internal and external theft.
- Establish and monitor a complete and effective revenue security system.

Lecture Outline

1. Revenue Security

- Errors in revenue collection can come from simple employee mistakes or, in some cases, outright theft by either guests or employees.
- In its simplest form, revenue control and security is a matter of matching products sold with funds received. Thus, an effective revenue security system ensures that the following five formulas reflect what really happens in your foodservice operation:

    1. Documented Product Requests = Product Issues
    2. Product Issues (by the kitchen)= Guest Charges
    3. Total Charges = Sales Receipts
    4. Sales Receipts = Sales (bank) Deposits
    5. Sales Deposits = Funds Available to Pay *Legitimate* Expenses (called Accounts Payable)

- The potential for guest or employee theft or fraud exists in all of these areas.

2. External Threats to Revenue Security

- A guest is said to have **walked**, or **skipped** a check when he or she has consumed a product but has left the foodservice operation without paying the bill.
  (See Figure 11.2 Steps to Reduce Guest "Walks" or "Skips.")

- A second form of guest theft that you must guard against is that of fraudulent payment. This includes passing counterfeit money, bad checks, or most commonly, the use of invalid credit or debit cards.
- A **credit card** is simply a system by which banks loan money to consumers as the consumer makes purchases.
- **Travel and entertainment (T&E) cards** are a payment system by which the card issuer collects full payment from the card users on a monthly basis.
- A **debit card** is an extremely popular form of guest payment. In this system, the funds needed to cover the user's purchase are automatically transferred from the user's bank account to the entity issuing the debit card.
- If restaurant managers are to ensure that they collect all of the money they are due from payment card companies, they must effectively manage the **interface** (electronic connection) between the various payment card issuers and their restaurant.
- **Merchant service provider (MSP)** plays an important role as the restaurant's coordinator/manager of payment card acceptance and funds collection.
- A restaurant accepting payment cards does not actually "receive" immediate cash from its card sales but, rather, it will be credited via **electronic funds transfer (EFT)** the money it is due after all fees have been paid.
- If you agree to accept checks, you will likely experience some loss.
- In addition to skipping a bill and fraudulent payment attempts, the last method of guest theft you must be aware of is that used by the **quick-change artist**. A quick-change artist is a guest who, having practiced the routine many times, attempts to confuse the cashier; in his or her confusion, the cashier gives the guest too much change.

3. Internal Threats to Revenue Security

- Service personnel can use a variety of techniques to cheat an operation of a small amount at a time.
- One of the most common server theft techniques involves the omission of recording the guest's order.
- Complete revenue control is a matter of developing the checks and balances necessary to ensure that the value of products sold and the amount of revenue received equal each other.
- Servers can misrepresent the amount they charged guests.
- Food operations should require a written **guest check** recording each sale. A guest check is simply a written record of what the guest purchased and how much the guest was charged for the item(s).
- Paper guest checks should be recorded by number and then safely stored or destroyed, as management policy dictates.
- Another method of service personnel fraud is one in which the server gives the proper guest check to the guest, collects payment, and destroys the guest check but keeps the money.

- For this reason, many operators implement a **precheck/postcheck system** for guest checks.
- A **user workstation,** that is, a terminal records the items ordered and then displays the order in the production area. In some systems, the order may even be printed in the production area.
- Not all service personnel are dishonest, of course, but POS systems are especially designed to prevent dishonest employees from committing theft and fraud.
- It is important to remember, however, that even sophisticated POS systems hold the potential for employee fraud.
- If a cashier is responsible for the collection of money, several areas of potential fraud can exist. The cashier may collect payment from a guest but destroy the guest check that recorded the sale. Another method of cashier theft involves failing to finalize a sale recorded on the precheck, while pocketing the money.
- **Open checks** are those that have been used to authorize product issues from the kitchen or bar, but that have not been added to the operation's sales total.
- In addition to theft of your own business financial assets, the hospitality industry affords some employees the opportunity to defraud guests as well. Some techniques include:

1. Charging guests for items not purchased, then keeping the overcharge.
2. Changing the totals on credit card charges after the guest has left, or entering additional credit card charges and pocketing the cash difference.
3. Misadding legitimate charges to create a higher than appropriate total, with the intent of keeping the overcharge.
4. Purposely shortchanging guests when giving back change with the intent of keeping the extra change.
5. Charging higher than authorized prices for products or services, recording the proper price, and then keeping the overcharge.

- Cashiers rarely steal large sums directly from the cash drawer because such theft is easily detected.
- Management can compare the sales recorded by the cash register with the money actually contained in the cash register. If it contains less than sales recorded, it is said to be **short,** if it contains more than sales recorded, it is said to be **over.**
- Consistent cash shortages may be an indication of employee theft or carelessness.
- If the POS system has a void key, a dishonest cashier could enter a sales amount, collect for it, and then void, or erase, the sale after the guest has departed.
- Another method of cashier theft involves the manipulation of complimentary meals or meal coupons.
- It is important to remember that even good revenue control systems present the opportunity for theft if management is not vigilant or if two or more employees conspire to defraud the operation.
- **Bonding** is simply a matter of management purchasing an insurance policy against the possibility that an employee will steal.

- If an employee has been bonded and an operation can determine that he or she was indeed involved in the theft of a specific amount of money, the operation will be reimbursed for the loss by the bonding company.

4. Developing the Revenue Security System

- An effective revenue security system will help you accomplish the following important tasks: verification of product issues, verification of guest charges, verification of sales receipts, verification of sales deposits and verification of account payable.
- In an ideal world, a product would be sold, its sale recorded, its selling price collected, the funds deposited in the foodservice operation's bank account, and the cost of providing the product would be paid for, all in a single step. Rapid advances in the area of computers and "smart" cards are making this a reality for more foodservice operators each day.

- The five-step process of revenue security is as follows:

> **Product Issues = Guest Charges = Sales Receipts = Sales Deposits = Funds Available for Accounts Payable**

- The key to verification of product issues in the revenue security system is to follow one basic rule: *No product should be issued from the kitchen or bar unless a permanent record of the issue is made.*

> **Documented Product Requests = Product Issues**

- When the production staff is required to distribute products only in response to a documented request, it is critical that those documented requests result in charges to the guest. *Product issues must equal guest charges.*
- Each guest check must be accounted for, and employees must know that they will be held responsible for each check they are issued.

> **Product Issues = Guest Charges**

- Sales receipts refer to actual revenue received by the cashier or other designated personnel, in payment for products served. *Both the cashier and a member of management must verify sales receipts.*

> **Total Charges = Sales Receipts**

- Sales receipts refer to all forms of revenue, such as cash, checks (if accepted), and bank (credit or debit) cards.

- In general, there are five basic payment arrangements in use in typical foodservice operations. They are as follows:

    1. Guest pays cashier.
    2. Guest pays at the table.
    3. Guest pays service personnel, who pay cashier.
    4. Guest pays service personnel, who have already paid cashier.
    5. Guest is direct billed.

- **Accounts receivable** is the term used to refer to guest charges that have been billed to the guest but not yet collected.
- In some cases, variations on the five payment systems presented can be put in place, such as the drink ticket, or coupon sold or issued in hotel reception areas for use at cocktail receptions.
- The deposit slip may be completed by a cashier or other clerical assistant, but management alone should bear the responsibility for monitoring the actual deposit of sales. This concept can be summarized as follows: *Management must personally verify all bank deposits.* This involves the actual verification of the contents of the deposit and the process of matching bank deposits with actual sales.
- **Embezzlement** is the term used to describe employee theft where the embezzler takes company funds he or she was entrusted to keep and diverts them to personal use.
- Falsification of bank deposits is a common method of embezzlement. To prevent this activity, you should take the following steps to protect your deposits:

    1. Make bank deposits of cash and checks daily if possible.
    2. Ensure that the person preparing the deposit is not the one making the deposit-unless you or the manager does both tasks. Also, ensure that the individual making the daily deposit is bonded.
    3. Establish written policies for completing **bank reconciliations**, the regularly scheduled comparison of the business's deposit records with the bank's acceptance records. Payment card funds transfers to a business's bank account should be reconciled each time they occur. Increasingly, cash and payment card reconciliations can be accomplished on a daily basis via the use of online banking features.
    4. Review and approve written bank statement reconciliations at least once each month.
    5. Change combinations on safes periodically and share the combinations with the fewest employees possible.
    6. Require that all cash handling employees take regular and uninterrupted vacations on a regular basis so that another employee can assume and uncover any improper practices.
    7. Employ an outside auditor to examine the accuracy of deposits on an annual basis.

- If verification of sales deposits is done correctly and no embezzlement is occurring, the following formula should hold true:

> **Sales Receipts = Sales Deposits**

- **Accounts payable,** as defined in this step, refers to the legitimate amount owed to a vendor for the purchase of products or services. The basic principle to be followed when verifying accounts payable is: *The individual authorizing the purchase should verify the legitimacy of the vendor's invoice before it is paid.*
- In a revenue system that is working properly, the following formula should be in effect:

> **Sales Deposits = Funds Available for Accounts Payable**

- You can protect your revenue from vendors who would attempt to defraud you. Here are steps you can take:

  1. Know your rights.
  2. Assign designated buyers and utilize purchase orders at all times.
  3. Check the documentation before paying bills.
  4. Train your staff.

- The five key principles of a revenue security system are as follows:

  1. No product shall be issued from the kitchen or bar unless a permanent record of the issue is made.
  2. Product issues must equal guest charges.
  3. Both the cashier and a supervisor must verify sales receipts.
  4. Management must personally verify all bank deposits.
  5. The individual authorizing the purchase should verify the legitimacy of the vendor's invoice before it is paid.

- It is possible to develop and maintain a completely manual revenue control system.
- When properly selected and understood, technology-enhanced systems can be a powerful ally in the cost control/revenue security system.
- When considering a POS system, that means choosing energy efficient systems designed for upgradability, expandability and long life. By using energy efficient POS equipment for longer periods of time, operating costs are reduced and landfill waste lessened.
- Some recently introduced POS solutions consume less energy than a standard 100-watt light bulb! Efficiency advancements such as these help operators save money from high energy costs, while also helping to relieve the stress of excess energy consumption on the environment.

5. Technology Tools

- Protecting sales revenue from external and internal threats of theft requires diligence and attention to detail.
- Software and specialized hardware now on the market that can help in this area includes those that:

  1. Maintain daily cash balances from all sources, including those of multiunit and international operations.
  2. Reconcile inventory reductions with product issues from kitchen.
  3. Reconcile product issues from kitchen with guest check totals.
  4. Reconcile guest check totals with revenue totals.
  5. Create over and short computations by server, shift, and day.
  6. Balance daily bank deposits with daily sales revenue and identify variances.
  7. Maintain database of returned checks.
  8. Maintain accounts receivable records.
  9. Maintain accounts payable records.
  10. Maintain records related to the sale and redemption of gift cards.
  11. Interface back office accounting systems with data compiled by the operation's POS system.
  12. Interface budgeting software with revenue generation software.
  13. Create income statements, statements of cash flows, and balance sheets.

- It is important to note that interfacing (connecting) the various software programs you select is very helpful.

Consider The Cost

"The beauty of our system," said Phil Larson, "is that you can monitor the actions of all your employees and all your managers."

Phil was talking to Gene Monteagudo, Chief Operating Officer for Fazziano's Fast Italian Kitchens, a chain of 150 casual dining and carry-out Italian food restaurants. Gene had called POS-Video Security, the company Phil represented, because, for the second time this year, one of Gene's regional managers had discovered a case of employee/manager collusion. Working together, the employee and manager stole revenue from their restaurant by manipulation of their unit's POS system.

"I'm pretty sure I see how your company's product would have detected our most recent theft problem, but go over it one more time," said Gene.

"O.K. Gene, I'd be glad to," said Phil. "Essentially, our new system goes beyond traditional surveillance methods by synchronizing the video with the data mined from your POS system to create detailed, customized video reports. Potentially fraudulent activity such as manager overrides, coupons or comps, or even a cash drawer being open for too long is tracked, and the corresponding video surveillance can be searched by transaction number. Data reports and streaming video, both real-time and stored, can be accessed securely on a PC or handheld device via a web browser."

"So, for example," replied Gene, "when a sales void occurs, your system identifies the portion of video tape that was recording at the time of the void and would then allow my regional managers to view just that portion of the video. So, they could see what was going on in the store at the precise time of that transaction."

"Exactly," said Phil.

1. What types of employee fraud do you think could be uncovered utilizing the technology offered by POS-Video Security's new product?

2. Do you think that the behavior of most dishonest cashiers and managers would be changed if they knew their actions were being video recorded?

3. What issues should Gene consider as he evaluates the potential benefits to be gained from the purchase of an advanced technology control system such as the one offered by Phil's company?

Answers:

This case study was designed to reinforce to students the difficulty of detecting and preventing employee theft, as well as the importance of utilizing modern technology to do so. Products similar to Phil's really do exist. They are expensive, however, and as a result students should be aware that they, like Gene, must carefully weigh the cost/benefits of purchasing them.

1. Most POS systems are designed to minimize the potential for employee (not manager) fraud. Thus, many POS features are designed to restrict actions (such as voids or refunds) to managers only. Unfortunately, mangers can sometimes collude with employees to steal company assets including sales revenues. Such theft can be difficult to detect. Phil's new system seems to address this collusion issue well because the actions of both employee and manager are monitored.

2. It has been said that control systems are designed more to help keep honest people honest than to catch thieves. It is likely true that knowing they were on video tape would serve to make most honest people even more honest. Some thieves would undoubtedly be caught by the implementation of this new system. Realistically, however, Gene must recognize that some of his very dishonest employees (and managers) would immediately begin trying to devise methods of theft designed to outwit the new control system.

3. When considering the implementation of any control device or system, managers such as Gene must weigh the costs incurred versus the benefits to be gained. It makes little sense, for example, to spend thousands of dollars carefully controlling potential revenue or product losses that would be measured in pennies.

   Control system-related costs typically include those required for purchase of the new system as well as any labor-related costs. In a large company such as Gene's, the product offered by Phil's company may well be worth the initial investment in equipment and the on-going investment in staff time that would be required monitor the system's continual data output.

Apply What You Have Learned

Donald Wright worked for 15 years as a snack bar cashier for the Sports Arena managed by Stanley Harper's company. Donald had twice won the company's "Employee of the Year" award, and Stanley considered Donald a valued and trusted employee who had, on many occasions, performed above and beyond the call of duty.

Stanley was surprised when newly installed video surveillance equipment confirmed that Donald, despite rules against it, had, on several occasions, given free food and beverages to friends of his who had visited the arena.

On the advice of the company's Human Resources representative, Stanley is documenting, in writing, his decision on handling the situation.

1. Assuming you are Stanley, draft a letter to Donald indicating the consequences of his actions.

   Answer:
   Dear Donald Wright,

   With newly installed video surveillance equipment in our snack bar, it is confirmed that you have given free food and beverages to your friends on several occasions. As stated in the company's policies, employees are *not* allowed to give free food and beverages to friends or other people without management's consent. All actions by employees that are against company policies will result in disciplinary action and possibly termination.

   I am extremely concerned about this situation as you have been an exemplary employee for 15 years. I would hate for your recent actions to jeopardize your position with the company. Any further violations to company policies will result in negative consequences.

   I have discussed your case with Human Resources. This letter, along with any future documentation will go in your personnel file. Please see to it that this problem stops immediately, or further disciplinary action and/or termination may be necessary.

   Sincerely,
   Stanley Harper

2. Do you believe an employee caught defrauding his/her employer should ever be given a second chance? If so, under what circumstances?

    Answer: Giving an employee a second chance depends on the violation. The more serious the violation, the less likely the employee will be given a second chance. For example, if an employee steals a case of hamburger patties from the freezer, he or she should be written up and reprimanded. If it happens again, he or she may be suspended or terminated. However, if an employee steals $5,000 over a period of time, he or she should not be given a second chance.

3. What impact will Stanley's decision in this case have if, in the future, other employees are caught stealing?

    Answer: If Stanley's decision in this case were terminating Donald Wright, this would definitely affect other employees. Employees who want to keep their jobs would be less likely to defraud or do anything against the company's rules. On the other hand, if Stanley's decision were to give Donald Wright a second chance, this would affect other employees in a different way. They would expect to also get a second chance if they stole from the company.

Test Your Skills

1. Trisha Sangus manages a large hotel. Recently, her hotel controller identified a problem in one of the hotel dining rooms. Essentially, one of the evening cashiers was voiding product sales after they had been rung up on the POS, then removing an equal amount of money from the cash drawer so that the drawer balanced at the end of the shift. What procedures would you recommend to Trisha to prevent a further occurrence of this type incident? Assume a pre-check/post-check guest check system is in place.

    Answer: To prevent further theft, Trisha should implement a rule that requires all cash register voids to be performed by a supervisor or be authorized by management on an individual basis. Management should also closely monitor the time and amount of voids performed. A print out of all voids should be kept as well. Another method to prevent internal theft is with the use of video cameras that would be installed near the cash register area in the hotel dining rooms. Also, Trisha should use management-issued guest checks, and multicopy guest checks.

2. Counterfeit money is a problem for all U.S. businesses including those in the hospitality industry. The U.S. Department of Treasury has developed educational aids to assist managers who must train those who handle cash. To do so, they have compiled information that is critical in the detection of imitation currency and coins.

Fun on the Web!

Go to this United States Secret Services site to learn about how to detect counterfeit money: www.treas.gov/usss. Click on "Know Your Money", then click on "How to Detect Counterfeit Money" to see what discrepancies to look for on counterfeit bills.

Prepare a training session appropriate for cashiers who may routinely be responsible for the detection of counterfeit money. Include a memo to your cashiers detailing what they should do if they suspect a bill is counterfeit.

Answer: In the training session for cashiers who routinely handle cash, tell them step by step the certain characteristics of what is on a bill and what to look for when inspecting money. In addition, if one of the employees comes across money that he or she suspects of being counterfeit, he or she should never give the money back to the guest. The employee should immediately notify a manager who then will notify the proper authorities.

MEMORANDUM

TO:	Cashiers
FROM:	Management
DATE:	February 1
SUBJECT:	Detection of Counterfeit Money

If a guest hands you money that you suspect of being counterfeit, here are some hints from the U.S. Department of Treasury (www.treas.gov/usss) that will allow you to detect counterfeit money:

- *Portrait* – The genuine portrait appears lifelike and stands out distinctly from the background. The counterfeit portrait is usually lifeless and flat. Details merge into the background, which is often too dark or mottled.
- *Federal Reserve and Treasury Seals* – On a genuine bill, the saw-tooth points of the Federal Reserve and Treasury seals are clear, distinct, and sharp. The counterfeit seals may have uneven, blunt, or broken saw-tooth points.
- *Border* – The fine lines in the border of a genuine bill are clear and unbroken. On the counterfeit, the lines in the outer margin and scrollwork may be blurred and indistinct.
- *Serial Numbers* – Genuine serial numbers have a distinctive style and are evenly spaced. The serial numbers are printed in the same ink color as the Treasury Seal. On a counterfeit, the serial number may differ in color or shade of ink from the Treasury seal. The numbers may not be uniformly spaced or aligned.
- *Paper* – Genuine currency paper has tiny red and blue fibers embedded throughout. Often counterfeiters try to simulate these fibers by printing tiny red and blue lines on their paper. Close inspection reveals, however, that on the counterfeit note the lines are printed on the surface, not embedded in the paper. It is illegal to reproduce the distinctive paper used in the manufacturing of United State currency.

3. Mary Margaret and Blue are the owners/operators of an extremely upscale bakery goods boutique, and they are interested in a complete asset control system that includes protection of both products and revenue. Identify two control devices/procedures that they could implement to help them control revenue security in the following areas, and explain your reason for choosing each.
   a. Product issues
   b. Guest charges
   c. Sales receipts
   d. Sales deposits
   e. Accounts payable

Answers:
a. Product issues
   1. No product shall be issued from the kitchen or bar unless a permanent record of issue is made. It is used to prevent a server from stealing either food or beverages out of the kitchen or bar area.
   2. Use a POS system to match products issued with sales receipts.

b. Guest charges
   1. Product issues must equal guest charges. It is used to prevent employees from destroying checks after they have received payment.
   2. Do not allow servers to void orders; all voids must be done by management to prevent employee fraud.

c. Sales receipts
   1. Sales receipts must be verified by both the cashier and a supervisor to reduce the possibilities of theft.
   2. Have management periodically check and investigate "overs" or "shorts", reducing chances of cashier theft.

d. Sales deposits
   1. Management must personally verify all bank deposits.
   2. Management must review and approve the bank statement reconciliation each month.

e. Accounts payable
   1. The authorized purchaser must verify the legitimacy of accounts payable to be paid out of sales deposits.
   2. Management must verify legitimate expenses that result from a purchase that can be verified by *authorized* personnel within the hospitality operation. Also, to help reduce revenue loss due to unscrupulous suppliers and unwitting employees, management should buy only from vendors they know and trust.

4. Each of the following payment methods allows for potential employee and/or guest theft. Assume that Debbie operates a semi-private country club where club members and the general public may purchase products in a variety of settings. Specify at least two potential methods of theft for each of the following, as well as a description of the specific procedures Debbie should implement to prevent such theft.
   a. Guest pays cashier.
   b. Guest pays at table.
   c. Guest pays service personnel, who have already paid cashier.
   d. Guest is direct billed.

Which system would you favor using?

Answers:
   a. Guest pays cashier.
   1. Cashiers could shortchange or overcharge guests and pocket the difference. They could ring the item in, collect the cash, and then void the item. This can be avoided by involving the manager in all voids, and having a video camera monitoring the cashier station.
   2. Stolen credit cards. To avoid this, train the cashier to ask for another form of identification to verify identity, and check signatures with the signature on the back of the credit card.

   b. Guest pays at table.
   1. The service personnel could pocket the money, and say the guest walked. This can be prevented by having service staff monitor the doors in case of guests exiting without payment.
   2. The service personnel could use the same check twice and pocket the difference. Have a POS system that sends all orders to the kitchen electronically. No orders will be issued unless they come through the POS system.

   c. Guest pays service personnel, who have already paid cashier.
   1. Servers could charge guests for items not purchased, then keep the difference.
   2. The service personnel could say that the guest walked check. To prevent these possible thefts, managers should keep a close eye on employees and make them personally responsible for walked checks. Also, management should use the POS system to tabulate check amounts instead of manually adding check amounts. In addition, management should make sure that product issues are equal to guest charges as well as sales receipts.

   d. Guest is direct billed.
   1. Guests can be over billed, and the additional money is pocketed.
   2. Guests refuse to pay.
      Management needs to make sure that guest charges equal sales receipts and have all charges verified by the guest before check out. Also, management needs to ensure that the guests who are direct billed are creditworthy.

The system that many managers favor using is when the guest pays at the table. Although there is always the opportunity for theft, this system provides a POS-generated bill which the guest reviews at the table. The receipts at the end of the shift can then be verified against the POS record.

5. Denise Cronin operates a quick service sandwich restaurant in a busy section of a major downtown area. Last week, the POS system in Denise's operation reported the following guest charges, and Denise, upon verifying cash on hand at the end of each day, generated the following sales receipts. Determine Denise's daily and weekly overage and shortage amounts.

Day	Sales Receipts	Guest Charges	Over/(Short)
Monday	$3,587.74	$3,585.28	$2.46
Tuesday	$3,682.22	$3,693.35	($11.13)
Wednesday	$3,120.35	$3,110.54	$9.81
Thursday	$2,985.01	$3,006.27	($21.26)
Friday	$4,978.80	$4,981.50	($2.70)
Saturday	$6,587.03	$6,588.82	($1.79)
Sunday	$1,733.57	$1,737.93	($4.36)
Total	$26,674.72	$26,703.69	($28.97)

Does Denise have a cash control problem? How often in a day do you believe Denise should balance her sales receipts with her guest charges? Why?

Answer: Denise definitely has a cash control problem since each day shows a variance. Over time, these variances will cost her quite a bit of money. In order to gain control of her problem, Denise should balance her sales receipts with her guest charges at the end of each shift. This would help her determine which cashiers and/or servers are causing the problems. She can either train them, or discipline them, if necessary. If she starts having her cashiers or servers pay for shortages, they will probably be less likely to be careless or steal in the future.

6. Allison Holmes has just been promoted to the job of Regional Beverage Manager at Appleboy's Restaurants. Her district includes six successful units. In one unit, Allison suspects that Ron, the restaurant manager and Tony, the bar manager, have collaborated to defraud their restaurant by serving cash paying guests at the bar, not ringing up the sales, and then splitting the revenue collected from those guests.

Since the unit's cash drawers are always in balance, no one has previously investigated the possibility of employee theft in this unit. What are some indications of such fraudulent activity that would lend support to Allison's suspicions? How would you suggest Allison find out if she is actually correct?

Answer: If Allison's bar has an automated dispensing system, inventory deducted can be compared to cash sales. If a discrepancy exists, then Allison would have an indication that fraudulent activity is occurring. If no automated dispensing system exists, then Allison could, over time, compare physical inventory with sales receipts. However, fraudulent actions of her restaurant manager and bar manager would be very difficult to detect in this situation.

The best advice to Allison is simply to be vigilant. She should watch the bar area carefully, or enlist the aid of a spotter, a professional who, for a fee, will observe the bar operation with an eye toward reporting any unusual or inappropriate behavior by the bar manager and the restaurant manager.

7. Kathy, the general manager, was shocked to discover that the thief in her successful seafood restaurant was Dan, her own dining room supervisor. Dan used his detailed knowledge of weaknesses in the POS data monitoring system Kathy had designed to void legitimate sales after the fact and thus defraud the restaurant out of an average of $800.00 in revenue per day, every day, for the past six months. When finally confronted, Dan confessed to the thefts, citing a gambling problem as the reason for his actions.

The information below details Kathy's reported revenue, food cost, labor cost, other costs, and profit for the past 180 days. Calculate the potential financial performance in dollars and percentages her restaurant would have achieved had it not been for Dan's actions. (Spreadsheet hint: Food Cost, Labor Cost, and Other Costs will be the same for Actual $ and Potential $.)

Kathy's Restaurant Performance

Revenue Stolen	144,000

	Actual %	Actual $	Potential $	Potential %
Revenue	100.0%	1,566,000	$1,710,000	100.0%
Food Cost	37.0%	579,420	$579,420	33.9%
Labor Cost	29.0%	454,140	$454,140	26.6%
Other Costs	26.5%	414,990	$414,990	24.3%
Profit	7.5%	117,450	$261,450	15.3%

a. How much profit in dollars did Kathy lose because of Dan's fraudulent activities (difference between potential and actual)?

Answer:
$261,450 - $117,450 = $144,000

b. How much profit percent did Kathy lose because of Dan's fraudulent activities (difference between potential and actual)?

Answer:
15.3% - 7.5% = 7.8%

c. List three things that Kathy could have done to minimize the effect of Dan's theft.

Answer:
Do not allow employees to share POS passwords, develop a system of checks and balances, and bond employees (insurance policy against employee theft).

8. Sometimes it can be difficult to determine whether errors made in the payment of an operation's bills, when they are uncovered by an audit, represent intentional fraud or simply are mistakes resulting from an employee's poor training or lack of knowledge. Assume an audit uncovered duplicate invoice payments made to three different food vendors. The payments were made to them by the individual in your operation who is responsible for accounts payable. What specific action would you take to determine whether the individual's mistakes were intentional or simply exposed other weaknesses in your accounts payable system?

Answers:
Duplicate payments made to vendors can indeed be an indication of fraud on the part of the individual paying an operation's bills. As a manager, the first thing to do is contact the vendor's managers (not their accounts receivable clerk) to inform them that duplicate payments have been made. If such payments were credited to the account of the operation paying the bills, fraud on the part of the bill payer is unlikely. What is more likely in that case is that the system used for recording the payment of bills must be strengthened because duplicate payments are being made. If, however, the duplicate payments were not credited to the operation's account, collusion between the vendor and the individual paying the operation's bills is highly likely. In this case, kickbacks from the vendor to the individual paying the operation's bills are probable.

If duplicate payments to vendors are made but no collusion is evident (i.e. the operation's payment funds are accounted for with the double-paid vendor, but they have simply been misapplied), then modifications of the operation's bill payment system are in order. In this scenario, the missing control ingredient may be the stamping of "Paid" on each invoice for which a payment check is processed. This will prevent double payment of the same invoice.

If the operation is properly using a "Paid" stamp, then the likely error (if the operation's employees are not committing fraud) is double payment resulting from 1) the vendor sending a second (follow-up invoice) or 2) the listing of previously billed, legitimately owed, but previously paid amounts on newly arrived invoices.

For these reasons, payment checks should always indicate the specific vendor invoices (by identifying invoice number) that are to be paid by the check. Utilizing one of today's modern and computerized payment systems (for example, Peachtree or Microsoft Books) can also help eliminate duplicate payment of invoices because these payment systems are specifically designed (programmed) to guard against unintentional double payments of these types.

Exam Questions

Multiple Choice
Choose the letter of the best answer to the questions listed below.

1. Which of the following is not an external threat to revenue security?
   a. A "walk" or "skip" check
   b. A quick-change artist
   c. A credit card
   d. Bonding
   Correct answer is d (See: External Threats to Revenue Security)

2. Which of the following is not a way to reduce guest walks or skips?
   a. Have a cashier available and visible at all times in a central location in the dining area.
   b. If an employee sees a guest leave without paying the bill, management should be notified immediately.
   c. The manager should publicly embarrass the guest who tries to leave without paying the bill so that this situation will not happen again.
   d. Train employees to be observant of exit doors near restrooms or other areas of facility so that the guest will not leave without paying the bill.
   e. All of the above
   Correct answer is c (See: External Threats to Revenue Security)

3. Which of the following is not a payment arrangement in a foodservice operation?
   a. Guest is direct billed.
   b. Guest pays service personnel, who pay cashier.
   c. Guest pays management, who have already paid cashier.
   d. Guest pays cashier.
   e. All of the above
   Correct answer is c (See: Developing the Revenue Security System)

4. An effective revenue security system will help you accomplish the following important tasks:
   a. Verification of product issues
   b. Verification of guest charges
   c. Verification of sales receipts
   d. Verification of sales deposits
   e. All of the above
   Correct answer is e (See: Developing the Revenue Security System)

5. The purchase of an insurance policy against the possibility that an employee will steal is called what?
   a. Bonding
   b. Precheck system
   c. Embezzlement
   d. Accounts receivable
   Correct answer is a (See: Internal Threats to Revenue Security)

6. _____ is the term used to refer to guest charges that have been billed to the guest but not yet collected.
   a. Direct bill
   b. Accounts receivable
   c. Walk out
   d. None of the above
   Correct answer is b (See: Developing the Revenue Security System)

7. All of the following are external threats except:
   a. Walk
   b. Skip
   c. Guest who forgot to pay
   d. Employee theft
   Correct answer is d (See: External Threats to Revenue Security)

8. To prevent embezzlement what can you do to protect your operation against it?
   a. Make bank deposit daily.
   b. Ensure that the individual that makes daily deposits is bonded.
   c. Review and approve bank statement reconciliations each month.
   d. All of the above
   e. Only a. and b. above
   Correct answer is d (See: Developing the Revenue Security System)

9. When a guest refuses to pay what should the manager note in the report?
   a. Number of guests involved
   b. Time and date of the incident
   c. Amount of the bill
   d. All of the above
   Correct answer is d (See: External Threats to Revenue Security)

10. Which of the following software can help protect sales revenue from external and internal threats of theft?
    a. Reconcile inventory reductions with product issues from kitchen.
    b. Reconcile product issues from kitchen with guest check totals.
    c. Create over and short computations by server, shift, and day.
    d. All of the above
    e. Only a. and b. above
    Correct answer is d (See: Technology Tools)

11. When considering a POS system, that means choosing energy efficient systems designed for:
    a. Upgradability
    b. Expandability
    c. Long life
    d. All of the above
    Correct answer is d (See: The Complete Revenue Security System)

True/False
Choose the letter of the best answer to the questions listed below.

12. Errors in revenue collection can come from employee mistakes, or in some cases, theft by customers or employees.
    a. True
    b. False
    Correct answer is a (See: Revenue Security)

13. In its simplest form, revenue security is a matter of matching cash to register receipts.
    a. True
    b. False
    Correct answer is b (See: Revenue Security)

14. A customer is said to have "walked" a check when he or she has consumed a product, but leaves the operation without paying.
    a. True
    b. False
    Correct answer is a (See: External Threats to Revenue Security)

15. Some foodservice operators have found that the cost of accepting credit cards exceeds the amount of additional revenue they generate.
    a. True
    b. False
    Correct answer is a (See: External Threats to Revenue Security)

16. All sales must be recorded if management is to develop a system that matches products sold to revenue received.
    a. True
    b. False
    Correct answer is a (See: Internal Threats to Revenue Security)

17. If an operation is small, such as a snack bar, it does not need to record its sales.
    a. True
    b. False
    Correct answer is b (See: Internal Threats to Revenue Security)

18. Management should insist that all POS voids be performed by a waitperson, to prevent dishonesty on the part of the cashier.
    a. True
    b. False
    Correct answer is b (See: Internal Threats to Revenue Security)

19. A good revenue control system will not prevent all types of theft.
    a. True
    b. False
    Correct answer is a (See: Internal Threats to Revenue Security)

20. If an employee is bonded and steals, the operation will be reimbursed by the employee's insurance policy.
    a. True
    b. False
    Correct answer is a (See: Internal Threats to Revenue Security)

21. No product should be issued from the kitchen or bar unless a written record of issue is made.
    a. True
    b. False
    Correct answer is a (See: Developing the Revenue Security System)

22. Management must personally verify all bank deposits.
    a. True
    b. False
    Correct answer is a (See: Developing the Revenue Security System)

23. A quick-change artist is when a guest consumes a product but has left the foodservice operation without paying the bill.
    a. True
    b. False
    Correct answer is b (See: External Threats to Revenue Security)

24. If a guest attempts to "skip" a check, the server should make every attempt to follow and catch the guest, and hold the guest in custody until the police arrive.
    a. True
    b. False
    Correct answer is b (See: External Threats to Revenue Security)

25. Software programs that compare sales recorded on the POS with daily bank deposits is preferable to one that does not connect these two independent but correlated functions.
    a. True
    b. False
    Correct answer is a (See: Technology Tools)

26. When considering a POS system, that means choosing energy efficient systems designed for upgradability, expandability, and long life.
    a. True
    b. False
    Correct answer is a (See: The Complete Revenue Security System)

Chapter 12

Global Dimensions of Cost Control

Learning Outcomes

At the conclusion of this chapter, you will be able to:

- Recognize the increasingly important role international expansion plays on the growth of foodservice companies.
- Identify important challenges faced by all foodservice professionals who are responsible for managing their company's international business operations.
- Determine how operational, cultural, financial, and technological challenges can affect the cost control-related activities of international foodservice managers.

Lecture Outline

1. Multinational Foodservice Operations

- The global expansion of the restaurant industry really should come as no surprise to anybody working in this industry. This is so because travel, tourism, and the sampling of international cuisines have historically been integral parts of the hospitality industry.
- While Coca-Cola and McDonald's are among the best known, many other food service companies now operate in the international market and the number doing so increases each year.
- Burger King, Wendy's, Hilton, Dave and Busters, Hooters, T.G.I. Friday's, Mrs. Fields, Dunkin Donuts, Baskin Robbins, Pizza Hut, Marriott, Taco Bell, Aramark, TCBY, and Rainforest Cafe are just a few examples of the increasingly large number of U.S.-based restaurant companies expanding internationally.

2. Managing in a Global Economy

- Most companies want to exercise a specific level of control over their international operations. The control may be quite significant or it may be advisory in nature only.

- As a professional in the hospitality industry, there are a variety of reasons why you might be assigned the responsibility of controlling and monitoring costs in one or more of your company's international operations.
  - Your education and past work history give you the experience you need to succeed in the job.
  - No local staff (in the foreign country) is currently qualified to assume the responsibility.
  - Your responsibilities include the training of local staff.
  - Local persons are being trained for positions that will ultimately replace the need for your assistance, but they are not yet qualified to assume 100% responsibility.
  - Your employer wants to instill a global perspective in you (and other) managers.
  - It is in the company's best long-term interest to improve the cultural understanding between managers and employees in the company's various international components.
  - An international assignment is considered an integral part of your professional development process.
  - There is an interest in obtaining tighter administrative control over a foreign division or addressing and correcting a significant problem.
  - There are property start-up, operating, or other issues that require long-term on-site management direction to properly address the issues.
- Experienced **expatriate** (a citizen of one country who is working in another country) managers and those whose offices are located in their home country but who travel extensively to their foreign assignments report that they sometimes confront issues in one or more of the following areas:

  - **Language**
    - While English is widely spoken in many parts of the world, in many cases it will not be the primary language of the restaurant's employees, and thus expatriate managers must be sensitive to the variety of issues language barriers and the direct translation of languages may present.
  - **Local Governmental Entities**
    - Routine items such as operating permits and permissions to do business may be slower in coming than in the United States. As well, local customs may dictate that money, paid directly or indirectly to governmental officials, may accompany the granting of these permissions.
  - **Facilities**
    - Foodservice operators will find it more difficult to build, service, and maintain their physical facilities in foreign countries. This is especially true if the company has not identified a dependable, cost-effective, and local service representative for the building they occupy or the major equipment they utilize.

- **Employees**
  - The local labor force that is available to international managers can vary greatly from one area of the world to another. In addition, employee attitudes toward gender equality, appropriate dress, work ethic, religious tolerance, and the rights of minorities are all areas that may present significant challenges to you as an international food service manager.
- **Suppliers**
  - The actual operation of an international food service unit can be challenging for a variety of reasons. Among these challenges is the potential unreliability of the unit/s food **supply chain**. If a restaurant is dependent upon a unique product that is prepared in another location, frozen, and then shipped to the unit, a dependable refrigerated storage and delivery company will likely be of critical importance if a high level of food quality is to be maintained.

3. Cost Control Challenges in Global Operations

- One convenient way to view international cost control–related challenges is by categorizing them as one of the following types:
  - Operational challenges
  - Cultural challenges
  - Financial challenges
  - Technological challenges
- **Operational Challenges**
  - The cost control issues encountered by expatriate hospitality managers can be related to what is done, when things are done, and exactly how they are done.
  - U.S. companies are accustomed to the **day parts** that have traditionally been defined as the breakfast, lunch, and dinner periods; in other countries the names for, and the times of, these day parts may vary significantly.
  - For those managers who have learned food production techniques using the **British Imperial** (U.S. Standard) **measurement system** of ounces, pounds, gallons, and tablespoons, converting recipes and purchasing standards to the metric system can often seem challenging.
  - Other important areas that can be greatly affected include:
    - Marketing
    - Menu Planning
    - Pricing
    - Safety standards
    - Purchasing
    - Receiving
    - Beverage production and service
    - Equipment selection and maintenance
    - Utility (natural resource) management

- According to Pacific Gas and Electric's Food Service Technology Center, 80% of the $10 billion annual energy bill for the commercial food service sector is expended by inefficient food cooking, holding, and storage equipment.
- Energystar, the US government operated web site devoted to energy efficiency, reports that the average food service operator who invests strategically can cut his or her utility costs 10 to 30% without sacrificing service, quality, style, or comfort.
- On its website, Energystar also points out that "the money you save on operating costs adds to what you get to keep, so saving 20% on energy operating costs can increase your profit as much as one-third."
- **Cultural Challenges**
    - **Culture** can be defined as the customary beliefs, social norms, and characteristic traits of a racial, religious, or social group.
    - As a manager, it will be your responsibility to ensure the smooth operation of your facilities by fairly addressing issues that may arise.
    - Expatriate managers who succeed best do so by demonstrating the real respect and understanding for local culture that is most often missing in less successful international managers.
    - Utilizing the following guidelines can help you effectively meet cultural challenges.
        - Foster an environment that encourages open discussion.
        - Encourage interaction.
        - Celebrate diversity.
        - Foster a healthy understanding of group identity.
        - Model appropriate behavior.
- **Financial Challenges**
    - It is a fundamental principle of accounting that the financial results of a business should be reported in an identifiable monetary unit.
    - A **monetary unit** is simply defined as a specific and recognized currency denomination. The reporting of cash sales may be complex in international companies because of a potential variety of monetary units being used.
    - Credit, debit, and bank card sales (which constitute a large portion of many restaurants' total sales) create further complications because the company's merchant service provider must apply an **exchange rate** (to convert the value of one currency to another) before the funds can be credited.
- **Technological Challenges**
    - Carefully consider the following essential elements before selecting and purchasing any technological enhancement to your existing cost control efforts.
    - **Cost**
        - When it is possible to demonstrate that the technology-related purchase will pay for itself (such as in reduced labor or product cost) relatively quickly, the decision to buy can be an easy one. If the cost of the tool exceeds its value to your operations, it likely should not be purchased.

- **Complexity**
  - Some technology systems are so advanced that their implementation and routine operation requires very high levels of skills. Difficulties can be reduced or eliminated through the implementation of thorough training programs.

System Warranty/Maintenance

- Because technology items are machines, they need routine maintenance and can break down. Items of particular importance to you will be:
  - A listing of precisely which items are covered under the terms of the warranty
  - The length of the warranty
  - The allowable charges for repair service for non-warranty-covered items
  - Expected response time of the service/repair technicians
- **Upgradability**
  - While it is difficult to predict what new technological developments may occur in the future, it is true that advancements that are compatible with your current system will likely prove to be less expensive than those that require completely new software, hardware, or communication devices.
- **Reliability**
  - There are two areas of importance which are: reliability of the product or service, and reliability of the vendor. A variety of factors can influence vendor reliability including location, experience, quality of service staff, response time, and reputation.
- It is simply not possible to know about every technological advance that could directly affect your international business. You can, however, stay abreast of the commercial application of these advances.
- Choices for continuing education in this area are varied but most foodservice managers can choose from one or more of the following methods:
  - **Trade Shows/Professional Associations**
    These associations typically serve the certification, educational, social, and legislative goals of their members. Trade shows are an extremely efficient way to see the product offerings of a large number of vendors in a very short time.
  - **Publications**
    Technology and its application have become such a large part of the editorial interest of these publications that a special technology editor is employed to monitor technological changes that could be of interest to the publication's readers.

- **Current Vendors**

  Your current technology suppliers should be a valuable source of no-cost information. An added advantage of working with your current technology suppliers is the fact that the new systems they develop are likely to be compatible with those systems you already have and maintain.

- **Competitive Vendors**

  Identifying your current vendor's strongest and best competitors is a good way to monitor advances in technology. Competitor visits can help you quickly identify improvements in procedures and features that your own vendor may have overlooked or dismissed.

- **Your Own Organization**

  Often, large international companies will produce newsletters, conduct in-service training, or hold regularly scheduled conventions that can be a source of information on changing technology.

Consider The Cost

"We open our two new plants in Reynosa next year," said Bill Richardson, V.P. of Operations for Tech-Mar Manufacturing. "We love the work you do for us here in our US operations and feel our partnership will be just as successful in Mexico."

Bill was talking to Ellen Luros, President of Luros Associates, a foodservice management company that had, for the past five years, been providing in-plant food services for Tech-Mar, an auto parts supplier whose client list included General Motors and Ford.

Bill had just laid out for Ellen the size and operational hours envisioned for the two new Tech-Mar manufacturing facilities to be located in Reynosa, Mexico, a city of 500,000 residents located just across the border from McAllen, Texas.

"I'm sure we will do a good job for you," replied Ellen.

"We're excited about the new manufacturing facilities we have built, and we recognize the importance to our success of a well-run and cost-effective employee meal program. It's good to have an experienced partner like you ready to help us ramp up!" said Bill.

1. Assume this is Luros Associates' first contract to operate foodservice outside the US. What challenges will Ellen likely face as she selects the foodservice managers currently in her company who will help operate the new Mexican facilities? What challenges will she face choosing new managers?

2. What menu development and food production-related challenges do you think Ellen may encounter as her company begins operations in Reynosa? How will these affect her managers' cost control efforts?

3. Do you think Ellen and any other managers currently employed by her will encounter culture-related operational challenges in the new plants? Where would you advise her to go to learn more about how she and her managers might best address those challenges?

Answers:

The purpose of this case is to introduce students to the practical issues they will face if they are the person charged with leading international expansion in their own foodservice organizations. Increasingly, US foodservice companies operate internationally. Similarly, increasing numbers of international foodservice companies have established operations in the US. This same exchange process is occurring in countries world-wide. The questions associated with this case challenge students to consider the cost control-related operational implications of international expansion as well as their own attitudes toward it.

1. Ellen will, no doubt, face operational challenges as she seeks to put together the management and hourly work teams required to fully staff the new plants. Important initial decisions to be made include determining whether she will employ expatriate managers chosen from the US and assigned to Mexico, or whether she will seek to hire qualified Mexican nationals as the new plants' foodservice managers. In either case, Ellen's new managers will likely face challenges. These will result from, in the case of US managers, the new operational and life-style realities they will encounter in Mexico. If Ellen chooses to employ Mexican managers, those individuals too may experience a significant and challenging learning curve as they adjust to the specific manner in which Ellen's US-based organization operates.

2. Mexico operates under the metric measurement system. While Reynosa is directly across the border from Texas, Ellen should assume that most foodservice production workers in that city will require some level of re-training if Ellen elects to keep her recipes and cost control programs based in the Imperial measurement system. If she converts her recipes to metric, some level of work will also be involved to change the recipes initially and to blend the monthly or annual operating results from the new Mexican operations with those of her US operations. Either decision will directly affect how her managers will approach establishing and implementing their initial cost management and reporting systems.

3. There is no doubt that Ellen and any US managers she assigns to Mexico will encounter culture-related operational challenges. Understanding that this is to be expected is essential to Ellen and her company's quick development of an effective work force in the new plants. Assistance is available. Area chambers of commerce such as the one operating in Reynosa can be a good source of local cultural and business information. National governments in the host country (Mexico in this case) can supply additional information. The US Chamber of Commerce can be of assistance, as can Ellen's professional foodservice association; especially if the association has international members from the host country. Perhaps most importantly, Ellen and one or more of her company's principal leaders should travel to the new plant locations to see for themselves the cultural environment in which they will now operate.

Apply What You Have Learned

Beyonce Powers is Director of North American operations for ARADEXO, a US-based food service management company that has just secured the contract to provide food services for the 2014 Winter Olympic Games to be held in Sochi, Russia. As the leading foodservice provider at the games, ARADEXO will serve more than 3.5 million meals over a two-month period (which includes not only the Olympics but also the Paralympic Games) in the Olympic Village. At the peak, the company will serve over 100,000 meals a day. Beyonce has been placed in charge of coordinating her company's Olympic efforts. A big challenge will be finding enough skilled workers to do all the cooking as ARADEXO will need 6,000 kitchen staff members to prepare all the different types of foods it will be required to serve.

Bess Haley, Beyonce's boss, and the CEO of ARADEXO has instructed Beyonce to ensure that the company makes the most of this important opportunity. As Bess put it, "I want the world to see how well we can perform…but at the same time I want to make sure we make this a profitable venture. I know you can do both!"

1. Of the management issues in a global economy presented in this chapter, which do you feel will be experienced by Beyonce as she leads her company's Olympic feeding efforts?

   Beyonce will most likely experience all the management issues presented in this chapter including:
   - Language
   - Local Governmental Entities
   - Facilities
   - Employees
   - Suppliers

   She will likely experience these issues as they relate to operating in Russia, as there are probably major differences from operating in the US. As stated in the case, her biggest challenge will most likely be finding 6,000 qualified employees to prepare the food. These employees most likely will be accustomed to different languages, equipment, cooking techniques, and facilities. It will be a challenge to get them all working efficiently with common procedures and standards.

2. Of the four cost control-related challenges presented in this chapter which do you feel will be most critical challenge Beyonce will face? Why?

   The four cost control-related challenges presented in this chapter include:
   - Operational challenges
   - Cultural challenges
   - Financial challenges
   - Technological challenges

   Of these four, probably cultural challenges will be the most critical. Beyonce will not only have to understand the cultural differences of operating in Russia, but she will also have to understand the unique cultural differences of her customers, the Olympians.

3. Assume you were Beyonce. How important would it be for you to physically attend the 2014 Olympic Games? Explain your answer.

   It will be critical for Beyonce to attend the 2014 Olympic Games. Because of the management issues and cost control-related challenges she will likely face in preparing for the Olympics, she will need to be at the games to oversee operations. She will not be able to prepare for every eventuality, and she will be needed to make decisions that will affect the overall success of the operation.

Test Your Skills

1. Assume that you were an expatriate Food and Beverage manager for an international hotel company that had operated a 5-Star resort in a nation with a very modest standard of living. How would you respond to the criticism that your company was creating more damage to the area's environment than it was contributing to the local economy?

   Answer: As an expatriate Food and Beverage manager, I would respond as follows:

   There are certainly those who believe that the expansion of U.S. companies to foreign countries has a negative effect on the local environment of the areas in which they are located. Others just as firmly believe that the impact of international expansion and development, in terms of economic benefit to the local area, job creation and the expansion of entrepreneurship among local citizens, is extremely positive.

   International companies may or may not have done all they should have done in the past to ensure that the impact of their operations was positive. All would agree that these companies, through managers can, however, shape the future through the positive activities they can undertake to improve their own profitability as well as the quality of life in the communities in which they have come to work.

2. One of the most significant changes in the American hospitality industry in the past two decades has been the introduction of the drive-thru window in the quick-service restaurant (QSR) segment. Analyze this development in terms of its dependence on the automobile. Do you think the drive-thru feature will be important in all countries in which these QSRs operate? Defend your answer.

   Answer: Technological advances such as drive-thrus typically occur because of both the availability of technology and a societal need. In countries in which either automobiles are too expensive for the average consumer or the population density is such that most people ride public transportation or bicycles, drive-thrus may not be feasible or profitable. In these countries, a walk-up kiosk may be more reasonable and popular than a drive-thru.

3. Increasingly, American companies are using advances in technology such as monitors and surveillance cameras to both observe and reduce employee theft and to help ensure the safety and security of their assets. Placement of these devices in food and beverage storage, production, and, in some cases, service areas has become commonplace. Assume that in your company you are responsible for maintaining such surveillance systems in all of your US and international operations. How would you respond to a European guest who protested to you that he or she resented being videotaped while dining?

   Answer:

   The manager should explain that the videotapes are not intended to intrude on the guest's dining experience. They are in place to prevent theft and keep customers safe. More important, they allow managers to see where they can improve to better serve the guests.

4. Advances in technology are often associated with improvements in production-related cost control issues such as food and beverage preparation, purchasing, storage, and inventory. Technological advances, however, also influence human resource management. Identify three ways you believe technology advancements will influence how individuals across the globe will seek jobs and how employers will find them.

   Answer:

   Three ways technological advances will influence job seekers and employers:
   - Employers will be able to use technology, specifically the Internet, to search for appropriate candidates to fill particular positions. Conversely, job seekers will have more opportunities to apply online for job openings that are located worldwide.
   - Employers can eliminate hours of interview time by having potential candidates fill out their profiles online before they are interviewed.
   - Interviews can take place across the globe through Internet conferencing technologies, thus reducing expensive travel costs.

5. As a foodservice professional, what do you feel are your responsibilities to ensure the operations you manage minimize their carbon footprints in all of its international operations? Would your feelings change if you operated in a country in which yours was the only company committed to Green initiatives? Explain your position.

   Answer: The global responsibilities of minimizing carbon footprints are paramount. It would be difficult to operate in a country in which yours was the only company committed to Green initiatives, because measures you make would likely be negated by the rest of the country. For example, if yours is the only company committed to recycling in a major city, then it will be difficult, if not impossible, to actually get your materials recycled. In this situation, your Green initiatives will have to be primarily internal and have an initial impact that can then be used as an example for the rest of the country. Good luck!

6. The restaurant industry is fortunate to have an additional resource for professional development that exists in only a few other industries. It is called the National Restaurant Association Educational Foundation, and it offers a variety of continuing education opportunities. It products and services can be accessed at www.nraef.org. Visit the site, and then identify at least five programs they offer that could help international foodservice operators better control their costs and increase their profitability.

   Answer:

   Six programs from www.nraef.org that are related to controlling costs and increasing profitability are:

   1. ServSafe Alcohol® Responsible Alcohol Training Program
   2. **ProStart® High School Program**
   3. ServSafe® Food Safety Training Program
   4. Manage First® Program
   5. Leadership & Management Program
   6. Foodservice Management Professional® (FMP®) Program

7. Many organizations implement green initiatives because of the potential for increased profitability that will ultimately be measured on their P&L statements. Would you implement a worthwhile green initiative that you knew would *not* increase profits, but rather would unquestionably reduce them? What specific factors would influence your decision to undertake initiatives of this type?

   Answer: Some green initiatives, like solar energy produced by solar panels, can cost a great deal of money in up-front costs. Initiatives which require significant modifications to a foodservice operation would most definitely decrease profits in the short term due to business interruptions or closing of operations. However, the benefits of these types of energy-saving initiatives would result in long-term cost reduction, and thus, increased profits.

8. In some countries, the culture will be very different from that of an expatriate manager's home culture. The impact of such differences can vary among managers. For example, assume you were offered a food service cost control-related position in a country whose culture reflected very significant differences in the rights afforded to women and men. How would you personally determine if such an assignment were right for you?

   Answer: Students will have to make their own determination how to answer this question based on what they feel is right for them. Depending on students' beliefs, they may find it very difficult working in a country whose culture treats men and women differently with regard to issues such as basic human rights, working conditions/privileges, dress code, job position (rank), gender hierarchy, and respect. The main point is for students to understand that they must research the culture of a country before they agree to work there, so they can determine if they, personally, will be able to thrive in the new environment. This question may be good to discuss in class so that several points of view may be heard.

Exam Questions

Multiple Choice
Choose the letter of the best answer to the questions listed below.

1. A currency is converted from one country to another at a(n):
   a. Exchange rate
   b. Dollar rate
   c. Money rate
   d. Coin rate
   Correct answer is a (See: Cost Control Challenges in Global Operations)

2. In order to effectively meet cultural challenges, a manager should:
   a. Keep people from interacting too much to avoid arguments
   b. Minimize the obvious differences in people
   c. Foster an understanding of cultural group identity
   d. Discourage open discussion of differences
   Correct answer is c (See: Cost Control Challenges in Global Operations)

3. The British Imperial measurement system includes all of the following *except*:
   a. Ounces
   b. Gallons
   c. Tablespoons
   d. Grams
   Correct answer is d (See: Cost Control Challenges in Global Operations)

4. For international managers seeking to electronically interface their individual units with their corporate office, which of the following considerations would be *most* important?
   a. Vendor stock price
   b. Vendor attitude
   c. Vendor service reliability
   d. Vendor pricing
   Correct answer is c (See: Cost Control Challenges in Global Operations)

5. A specific currency denomination is known as a(n):
   a. Monetary unit
   b. Exchange rate
   c. Conversion factor
   d. Paper money
   Correct answer is a (See: Cost Control Challenges in Global Operations)

6. Your technology purchase will include a warranty and items of particular importance to you including:
   a. A listing of precisely which items are covered under the terms of the warranty
   b. The length of the warranty
   c. Expected response time of the service/repair technicians
   d. All of the above
   e. Only a. and b. above
   Correct answer is d (See: Cost Control Challenges in Global Operations)

7. Trade shows and professional associations typically serve which of the following goals of its members?
   a. Certification
   b. Educational
   c. Social
   d. All of the above
   e. Only a. and b. above
   Correct answer is d (See: Cost Control Challenges in Global Operations)

8. Operators seeking to use technology to enhance their cost control system are interested in the following, except:
   a. New information
   b. More accurate information collection
   c. Improved analysis of information
   d. More complex and time-consuming data analysis
   Correct answer is d (See: Cost Control Challenges in Global Operations)

9. How does a manager monitor the industry advances in cost control technology?
   a. Word of mouth
   b. Trade shows
   c. Conduct surveys
   d. Go with the lowest price
   Correct answer is b (See: Cost Control Challenges in Global Operations)

10. Day parts in the US are defined as
    a. Morning, afternoon, and evening
    b. Dawn, midday, and dusk
    c. Mid-morning, late afternoon, and late evening
    d. Breakfast, lunch, and dinner
    Correct answer is d (See: Cost Control Challenges in Global Operations)

11. Managers working abroad report that they sometimes confront problems in the following area(s):
    a. Language
    b. Local government entities
    c. Facilities
    d. All of the above
    e. Only a. and b. above
    Correct answer is d (See: Managing in a Global Economy)

12. If a technology product is purchased for international implementation the warranty for the product must be carefully reviewed. Items of particular importance to you will be:
    a. A listing of precisely which items are covered under the terms of the warranty
    b. The length of the warranty
    c. The allowable charges for repair service for non-warrantee items
    d. All of the above
    Correct answer is d (See: Cost Control Challenges in Global Operations)

True/False
Choose the letter of the best answer to the questions listed below.

13. Your technology vendor should be more than will to help you secure training programs at little or no cost to you.
    a. True
    b. False
    Correct answer is a (See: Cost Control Challenges in Global Operations)

14. Advancements that are compatible with your current system will likely prove to be less expensive than those that require completely new software or hardware.
    a. True
    b. False
    Correct answer is a (See: Cost Control Challenges in Global Operations)

15. It is best to get a service person who works as an independent contractor or for a company not directly related to the one from which you are buying technology.
    a. True
    b. False
    Correct answer is b (See: Cost Control Challenges in Global Operations)

16. A 24-hour response time to service technology-related problems is adequate for the hospitality industry.
    a. True
    b. False
    Correct answer is b (See: Cost Control Challenges in Global Operations)

17. When working as an expatriate, it is important to break up the local group identity so that employees conform to the American way of doing things.
    a. True
    b. False
    Correct answer is b (See: Cost Control Challenges in Global Operations)

18. As a manager, you may be assigned to international operations because there is interest in obtaining tighter administrative control over a foreign division.
    a. True
    b. False
    Correct answer is a (See: Managing in a Global Economy)

19. An expatriate is a person who is no longer patriotic for his/her country of origin.
    a. True
    b. False
    Correct answer is b (See: Managing in a Global Economy)

20. In a foreign country, local customs may dictate that money, paid directly or indirectly to government officials, may accompany the granting of permissions to do business.
    a. True
    b. False
    Correct answer is a (See: Managing in a Global Economy)

21. As a general rule, an expatriate from the United States can depend on a reliable food supply chain in a foreign country.
    a. True
    b. False
    Correct answer is b (See: Managing in a Global Economy)

22. As a general rule, an expatriate from the United States can expect that foreign employee attitudes will be the same as US attitudes regarding gender equality, appropriate dress, and work ethic.
    a. True
    b. False
    Correct answer is b (See: Managing in a Global Economy)

23. Culture can be defined as the customary beliefs, social norms, and characteristic traits of a racial, religious, or social group.
    a. True
    b. False
    Correct answer is a (See: Cost Control Challenges in Global Operations)

24. When monitoring developments in cost control technology, your current vendor's competitors will not be good sources of information since they will most likely try to convince you that your current vendor is incompetent.
    a. True
    b. False
    Correct answer is b (See: Cost Control Challenges in Global Operations)

25. When introducing new technology to a foodservice operation, managers will find that it almost always provides a positive psychological impact on their employees and customers.
    a. True
    b. False
    Correct answer is b (See: Cost Control Challenges in Global Operations)

26. Energystar, the US government operated website devoted to energy efficiency, reports that the average food service operator who invests strategically can cut his or her utility costs 10 to 30% without sacrificing service, quality, style, or comfort.
    a. True
    b. False
    Correct answer is a (See: Cost Control Challenges in Global Operations)